AF737397

The Moral Psychology of Anxiety

Moral Psychology of the Emotions

Series Editor

Mark Alfano, Macquarie University

How do our emotions influence our other mental states (perceptions, beliefs, motivations, intentions) and our behavior? How are they influenced by our other mental states, our environments, and our cultures? What is the moral value of a particular emotion in a particular context? This series explores the causes, consequences, and value of the emotions from an interdisciplinary perspective. Emotions are diverse, with components at various levels (biological, neural, psychological, social), so each book in this series is devoted to a distinct emotion. This focus allows the author and reader to delve into a specific mental state, rather than trying to sum up emotions en masse. Authors approach a particular emotion from their own disciplinary angle (e.g., conceptual analysis, feminist philosophy, critical race theory, phenomenology, social psychology, personality psychology, neuroscience) while connecting with other fields. In so doing, they build a mosaic for each emotion, evaluating both its nature and its moral properties.

Recent titles in the series

The Moral Psychology of Anxiety, edited by David Rondel and Samir Chopra
The Moral Psychology of Trust, edited by David Collins, Iris Vidmar Jovanović, and Mark Alfano
The Moral Psychology of Shame, edited by Alessandra Fussi and Raffaele Rodogno
The Moral Psychology of Envy, edited by Sara Protasi
The Moral Psychology of Love, edited by Arina Pismenny and Berit Brogaard
The Moral Psychology of Hate, edited by Noell Birondo
The Moral Psychology of Boredom, edited by Andreas Elpidorou
The Moral Psychology of Amusement, edited by Brian Robinson
The Moral Psychology of Hope, edited by Claudia Blöser and Titus Stahl
The Moral Psychology of Regret, edited by Anna Gotlib
The Moral Psychology of Guilt, edited by Bradford Cokelet and Corey J. Maley
The Moral Psychology of Admiration, edited by Alfred Archer and André Grahle
The Moral Psychology of Gratitude, edited by Robert Roberts and Daniel Telech

The Moral Psychology of Anxiety

Edited by David Rondel and Samir Chopra

LEXINGTON BOOKS
Lanham • Boulder • New York • London

Published by Lexington Books
An imprint of The Rowman & Littlefield Publishing Group, Inc.
4501 Forbes Boulevard, Suite 200, Lanham, Maryland 20706
www.rowman.com

86-90 Paul Street, London EC2A 4NE

Copyright © 2024 by The Rowman & Littlefield Publishing Group, Inc.

All rights reserved. No part of this book may be reproduced in any form or by any electronic or mechanical means, including information storage and retrieval systems, without written permission from the publisher, except by a reviewer who may quote passages in a review.

British Library Cataloguing in Publication Information Available

Library of Congress Cataloging-in-Publication Data

Names: Rondel, David, 1978- editor. | Chopra, Samir, editor.
Title: The moral psychology of anxiety / edited by David Rondel and Samir Chopra.
Description: Lanham : Lexington Books, [2024] | Series: Moral psychology of the emotions | Includes bibliographical references and index.
Identifiers: LCCN 2023051300 (print) | LCCN 2023051301 (ebook) | ISBN 9781666928402 (cloth) | ISBN 9781666928419 (ebook)
Subjects: LCSH: Anxiety.
Classification: LCC BF575.A6 M655 2023 (print) | LCC BF575.A6 (ebook) | DDC 152.4/6--dc23/eng/20231130
LC record available at https://lccn.loc.gov/2023051300
LC ebook record available at https://lccn.loc.gov/2023051301

Contents

Acknowledgments

We are grateful to Mark Alfano, editor of Lexington's wonderful series of books on the moral psychology of the emotions, for his initial belief in this project and for many helpful suggestions along the way. Thanks are also due to Deanna Biondi, Jana Hodges-Kluck, and Emilia Rivera at Lexington for their amazing patience, professionalism, and publishing expertise. We also want to express our gratitude to Edward Alfano for permission to reprint the artwork on the book's cover. Samir Chopra would like to thank "his coeditor, David Rondel, without whose hard work and vision this project would not have gotten off the ground or across the line. Clichés aside, thanks very much, David, for your generosity of spirit and action." David Rondel would like to return the favor and thank "his coeditor, Samir Chopra, whose wisdom, experience, and sound judgment made this volume much better than it would have been otherwise. Thank you, Samir. It was a pleasure working with you."

This project was hatched during the worst days of the COVID 19 pandemic. Understandably, it took a lot longer to complete than it might have under different conditions. We're grateful to everyone involved for their patience and good cheer. We hope the final product was worth the wait.

David Rondel and Samir Chopra

Introduction

David Rondel and Samir Chopra

The Moral Psychology of Anxiety is a volume of ten new essays, written by philosophers, cognitive scientists, and historians, that explores the causes, the consequences, and the value of anxiety. The volume is organized into two equal halves. The first is more historical. It features five essays that explore the meaning of anxiety in different philosophical traditions and historical periods. The second half features another five essays that focus on a cluster of questions having to do with anxiety's nature and significance: Is anxiety something biological or cultural, or perhaps both? What is at the root of anxiety? Why should human beings suffer in this way? What is the experience of anxiety like, and what, if anything, are the benefits associated with it? Does anxiety have the potential to make us more virtuous or improve the quality of our inquiry?[1]

There are obviously numerous perspectives from which to tackle a subject as vast and consequential as anxiety. Choosing the optimal perspective will depend, as always, on what one is trying to find out, on the specific task or inquiry one has in mind. A physician prescribing medicine; a metaphysician trying to figure out whether "anxiety" picks out a natural or unified kind; an evolutionary biologist investigating the nature of the human "alarm response"; a philosopher trying to understand what Søren Kierkegaard famously dubbed "the dizziness of freedom"; and an historian exploring different cultural attitudes about anxiety and mental illness, will all approach the topic of anxiety from different angles. Correctly so.

As a field of academic research, moral psychology happily makes room for these different perspectives. At its best, moral psychology is typified by a commitment to *inter* and *multi*disciplinarity—zigzagging across traditional disciplinary boundaries and drawing on research and knowledge from numerous academic fields. As Manuel Vargas and John Doris point out in the introduction to their gigantic volume, *The Oxford Handbook of Moral Psychology*, one important reason for moral psychology's growth and ascendancy as a locus of research is its "collaborative ethos manifested in a degree of interdisciplinarity rivaled by few fields in the academy" (Vargas and Doris 2022, 2). That ethos, we believe, is very much on display in the current volume. Straddling philosophy, psychology, clinical medicine, history, and other disciplines, the essays in this volume explore anxiety from an impressively wide range of perspectives: from ancient Chinese Confucianism to twentieth-century European existentialism, from the Roman Stoics to the current edition of the *DSM*, from the evolutionary origins of anxiety to the positive role that anxiety plays in human inquiry and moral decision-making.

One obvious and immediate difficulty is that the word "anxiety" is regularly used in a variety of different ways. As a result, it can be extremely difficult to say what exactly anxiety is.[2] As Scott Stossel asks,

> Is . . . anxiety a medical illness, as Hippocrates and Aristotle and modern pharmacologists would have it? Or is it a philosophical problem, as Plato and Spinoza and the cognitive-behavioral therapists would have it? Is it a psychological problem, a product of childhood trauma and sexual inhibition, as Freud and his acolytes would have it? Or is it a spiritual condition, as Søren Kierkegaard and his existentialist descendants claimed? Or, finally, is it—as W.H. Auden and David Reisman and Erich Fromm and Albert Camus and scores of modern commentators have declared—a cultural condition, a function of the times we live in and the structure of our society? (Stossel 2013, 14).

Sometimes, the term "anxiety" is used to name an ordinary, commonly felt human emotion. So it is that Jason Freeman and Daniel Freeman tell their readers in their "very short introduction" to the subject that anxiety is "one of the fundamental emotions, as central a part of what it means to be human as happiness, sadness, or anger" (Freeman and Freeman 2015, xiii). Anxiety in this "ordinary" or "normal" sense is an important evolutionary legacy. Emotions like anxiety are plausibly understood as evolved responses, adaptive mechanisms that helped our hominid ancestors survive and thrive. Anxiety helped our human ancestors stay alert to the dangers of predators, poisonous substances, carriers of disease, or behaviors that could lead to social ostracization. But sometimes there is a mismatch between an evolved response and life in the modern world; a response that is advantageous in one context turns out to be dysfunctional in another. As Jesse Prinz quips: "When you put a cave man in a glass skyscraper, something may go awry." "Anxiety," he continues,

> is fear about future outcomes, and fear is clearly adaptive. Fear warns us about dangers and helps us prepare for them. Anxiety is plausibly an evolved response,

> and abnormalities in normal functioning can be regarded as dysfunctions. . . . This is even more obvious in the case of phobias. Many of the classic phobias, such as acrophobia, arachnophobia and social phobias, concern things that could have been sources of serious danger in our ancestral past: heights, spiders and other people. But these evolved mechanisms may be dysfunctional for some people in the modern world. . . . Dysfunctions arise when there is a mismatch between an intact mechanism and the environment. Fear of heights is dysfunctional when you are staring out of the window in your office building, because there is no risk of falling. Fear of spiders is dysfunctional when your hometown has few venomous species and several top-notch hospitals. Fear of people is dysfunctional when you are not a hunter-gatherer competing with violent neighbours for precious resources.[3] (Prinz 2012, 275)

Not all instances of anxiety are dysfunctional inheritances from our remote hominid ancestors, of course. Anxiety, when properly placed and not so severe so as to be debilitating, can serve as a useful signal that something important requires our attention or action. The emotion of anxiety evolved in human beings for good reason, and there are advantages associated with being anxious (more about that in a moment).

These days, the term "anxiety" is most frequently deployed to refer to a widespread mental health disorder. (According to the most recent 5th edition of the *Diagnostic and Statistical Manual of Mental Disorders* there are eleven different diagnoses that fall within anxiety's larger diagnostic ambit.) As Michael S. Brady and Ian Dowbiggin independently point out in their respective contributions to this volume, anxiety is the most prevalent mental health diagnosis in the United States today, affecting an estimated 40 million adults per year. Globally, the Institute for Health Metrics and Evaluation estimates that 284 million people had an anxiety disorder as of 2017, making anxiety by far the most diagnosed mental disorder in the world.

It can sometimes be unclear in scholarly work on anxiety when anxiety is being considered in the first sense (viz., the ordinary human emotion), or in the second one (viz., the mental health disorder). So, for instance, when David Barlow says in his magisterial work on the subject that anxiety is a "*future oriented* mood state in which one is ready or prepared to attempt cope with upcoming negative events" (Barlow 2001, 64), or when Charlie Kurth argues that anxiety is "a negatively valenced affective state" and an "aversive emotional response to problematic uncertainty" (Kurth 2018, 7), it can be difficult to determine which sense of "anxiety" (the regular emotion or the mental health disorder) these characterizations apply to.

We take no firm view here about what it takes for anxiety (understood as an everyday human emotion) to ascend to the level of a mental health disorder. On the distinction between "everyday" and "pathological" anxiety, we agree with psychologist Lucy Foulkes when she says that,

> everything exists on a spectrum. Along each spectrum, every psychological problem shifts gradually from being mild and controllable to something that can entirely take over your life. There is no sudden change, no distinct shift on any graph that indicates mental illness has begun. In addition, the processes that make a person susceptible to mental illness in the first place—genetic vulnerabilities, stressful life events, coping styles—are the very same ones that make a person susceptible to experiencing non-pathological distress as well. (Foulkes 2021, 164)

On this view, there is no "natural dividing line" to which we can appeal to determine precisely when anxiety has crossed a threshold from something normal to something pathological, which is by no means to deny the usefulness of a distinction between normal and pathological anxiety (Horwitz 2013, 15).[4]

In addition to these more common senses of "anxiety," there is also a distinctively *philosophical* usage of the term, according to which anxiety is "an all-encompassing attitude toward the world" (Solomon 1993, 229–30) and "a form of affective anticipation . . . that is inextricable from how one's . . . surroundings appear salient" (Ratcliffe 2017, 72). Anxiety in this uniquely philosophical sense is like a mood or disposition in which certain otherwise hidden truths about human existence and finitude are brought into focus. This is the sense of "anxiety" in which, as Martin Heidegger proclaimed, "anxiety reveals the nothing" (Heidegger 1993, 101).

These three familiar senses of the word "anxiety"—(i) the ordinary emotion, (ii) the mental health disorder, and, (iii) the philosophical mood or temperament—are all represented in the chapters of this volume. In several of the contributions that follow, anxiety is considered as a commonly felt human emotion or psychological experience that can, given the right circumstances, help us better navigate a world replete with uncertainty and potential danger. For instance, Juliette Vazard argues in her contribution to the volume that "properly cultivated anxiety routinely contributes to the success of our inquiries." Anxiety is normally understood as a cognitive hindrance, an emotion or affect that usually gets in the way of clear and accurate thinking. But Vazard focuses on the "epistemically virtuous upshots of a well-calibrated anxiety." Developing the capacity to "worry well" (as Vazard puts it), can make us more responsible and effective epistemic agents. Not only can a well-cultivated anxiety help us guard against costly errors in the course of inquiry. Under the right circumstances, it can also contribute to the cultivation of intellectual virtues like inquisitiveness, scrutiny, thoroughness, humility, and a more sensitive awareness and open-mindedness about our own biases and prejudices.

The same features that make anxiety potentially epistemically advantageous also suggest that anxiety can be valuable for us as moral agents. This line of argument is pursued in Charlie Kurth's contribution. Kurth develops a Kant-inspired argument according to which, "the moral endowment of conscience is best understood as a distinctive, anxiety-driven type of moral self-regulation." Kurth defines "moral anxiety" as the "unease" we experience when confronted with "a difficult moral decision" which enables recognition of its significance and "engages epistemic behaviors" such as "reflection and information gathering." Moral anxiety, Kurth persuasively argues, is an important "affective mechanism" that helps us identify moral danger and "sounds a moral-deliberation-engaging, aversively experienced alarm when an apparent danger is found."

Michael S. Brady also accentuates the positive in his contribution to the volume, arguing that anxiety (especially when it is brought on intentionally by an agent rather than bubbling up involuntarily) can be "*attractive* or *alluring* in certain circumstances" and even "an object of desire." Most often, we call attention to the extent to which anxiety is unwanted and unpleasant. Freud himself famously singled out its "very marked character of unpleasure" as one of anxiety's defining features (Freud 1959, 60). But that, Brady has it, is only part of the story. While anxiety "tends to be a blight on our existence when it occurs" it is also frequently true, Brady argues, "that the lives of people we regard as the most admirable or exemplary of human beings (those 'who represent our highest ideals of character') are lives that will have very high levels of anxiety."

Other chapters in this volume focus specifically on anxiety understood as a mental disorder. Jesse Prinz's contribution, for instance, seeks to better understand generalized anxiety disorder (or GAD). Naturalistic analyses of psychiatric conditions explain them in biological terms while normative approaches do so in terms of displaced cultural values. Prinz offers a critique of both types of analyses and develops a hybrid social constructionist approach for GAD. Prinz's analysis centers on GAD because it is a "paradigm case of an evolved emotional response" which is possibly heritable and thus amenable to a biological account. But research also suggests that GAD is not "strongly associated" with ill-health or premature death; and under a normative view it is unclear which norms specifically are violated. Prinz concludes that, because "social forces" impact GAD's "symptoms, prevalence, and status as a disorder" GAD is instructive for our understanding of mental disorders in general, in helping to provide alternatives to the typical naturalist and normative theories that currently dominate the field.

Michelle Maiese's chapter focuses on another extremely common variety of anxiety diagnosis: social anxiety disorder (or SAD). Maiese's goal is to understand anxiety's presence in social interactions via an examination of the concepts of "affordance and habitual trust." An affordance renders some possible actions as "inviting" and others as "threatening" while "habitual trust" impacts the extent to which "agents rely on others to help them engage effectively with relevant action possibilities." In healthier cases, habitual trust remains largely intact, and agents look to others to help them regulate their attention. Anxiety allows subjects to attend to relevant social factors and regulate their engagements with the relevant affordances. In cases of social anxiety disorder, habitual trust is eroded and subjects become more attuned to "negative social stimuli" which render "interpersonal interaction" dangerous. Due to their diminished habitual trust, agents with social anxiety disorder deny themselves "social resources" and restrict interpersonal affordances as their attempts to compensate for diminished social skills "exacerbate anxiety and constrict the affordance field."

Ian Dowbiggin's contribution also considers anxiety specifically as a mental health diagnosis. Dowbiggin offers a sociohistorical analysis of anxiety disorders and diagnoses, tracing how our understanding of anxiety and its treatment has changed over time, and how this connects to our broader cultural understanding of the meaning of mental health and illness. Dowbiggin claims that his sociohistorical approach is primarily educational: not only does it shed much needed light on various factors that may "predispose populations to anxiety." It also helps us understand how previous generations developed "coping strategies for engaging with the world." Dowbiggin contends that contemporary lawmakers and policy analysts would do well to keep these "coping strategies" in mind as they think about how to negotiate the "illness-affirming" and "illness-breeding" culture he thinks we find ourselves currently inhabiting.

There are also chapters in this volume that address anxiety in the distinctively philosophical sense of the term. In the volume's opening essay, for instance, Massimo Pigliucci observes that while anxiety is and can be a "psychological condition" treatable by standard therapeutic and pharmaceutical resources, it is also an "existential condition," a fundamental feature of human existence. Pigluicci offers an examination of Stoicism (focusing especially on the Stoic philosophers from the Roman Imperial period: Seneca, Epictetus, and Marcus Aurelius), which offers a moral psychology that addresses the existential anxiety that men and women from all walks of life find themselves grappling with. Pigluicci's chapter introduces readers to a Stoic moral psychology, centering on Stoic descriptions and resolutions of anxiety, and proposes practical techniques for diminishing anxiety.

In "The Anguish of Ivan Karamazov" Mauro Rossi and Christine Tappolet also focus on anxiety in its philosophical sense. Starting with a striking passage from Dostoevski's classic 1879 novel, *The Brothers Karamazov*, in which Ivan Karamazov experiences feelings of anguish (*toska*) as he approaches his father's house, Rossi's and Tappolet's goal is to provide a philosophical account of Ivan's state of mind. Based on a brief typology of affective states, Rossi and Tappolet argue that Ivan's anguish is best characterized as an "occurrent affective state." One important observation in the chapter is that Ivan's anguish has an intentional object that he is unable to identify, something Rossi and Tappolet call an "epistemically undetermined intentional object." Such an object turns out to be the mark of a distinctive kind of nonstandard affect. Another important characteristic of Ivan's anguish is that it is productive of several meta-emotions. Ivan is vexed and irritated by the fact that he cannot put his finger on the intentional object of his anguish.

The distinctions between "normal," "pathological," and "philosophical" anxiety are also on display in the more historical chapters that make up the first half of this volume. In "Not a Moment of Worry: Confucian Views on the Value of Anxiety," Leah Kalmanson offers an examination of early Confucian texts, including the *Liji*, to explore the relationship between ritual and anxiety in Confucian moral psychology. Such a moral psychology is uniquely concerned with the relationship of our mental states to "socio-political and environmental conditions" and results in the striking conclusion that our anxiety may reflect that we bear an "unavoidable interconnectedness with others and with the world around us."

Deborah Brown's chapter focuses on an exchange between René Descartes and Princess Elisabeth of Bohemia which centered on finding putative solutions in response to her "debilitating" and "profound" anxiety. Descartes's attempts to "heal" Elisabeth accentuate intellectual and personal self-regulation, an approach countered by Elisabeth's insistence that such maneuvers were destined to fail lacking the appropriate "favorable social and political conditions." Brown considers how this important exchange illuminates the development of Descartes's moral psychology, Descartes's and Elisabeth's relationship to Stoicism, and Elisabeth's relationship to feminism. Brown shows Descartes and Elisabeth in the throes of a "modern dilemma" of how to conduct ourselves when confronted with "an unchangeable past and an uncertain and uncontrollable future."

It puts the point mildly to say that anxiety is a large and difficult topic. No volume of this kind could possibly have aspired to cover everything. Given unlimited time and space, additional chapters exploring anxiety in Hindu and Buddhist thought, for instance, or in the Epicurean tradition, or in the existentialist thought of Kierkegaard or Jean-Paul Sartre, might have plausibly been included. Many interesting questions about anxiety remain untouched by the chapters in this volume. Can nonhuman animals suffer with anxiety or can they only be afraid? Is anxiety, as Nietzsche might have put it, human all too human? Where precisely does the emotion of anxiety begin and a cluster of other nearby emotional-mental states (dread, disquiet, apprehension, worry, panic, unease, anguish, trepidation, angst, and so on) end? And many of the questions that *are* taken up in the chapters ahead—about what's happening in the brain when anxiety strikes; about anxiety's physical properties and physiological causes, about its nosology, symptoms, and evolutionary history—will always be amenable to further research.

Despite the various omissions and the need for further research, we believe that the essays in this volume, taken as a collection, provide an impressively wide-ranging exploration of the moral psychology of anxiety. Such an exploration is both interesting in its own right and timely. No age in human history has been anxiety-free, but our current age is, or so it seems, an unusually anxious one. In the end, our hope is that *The Moral Psychology of Anxiety* will be profitably read by researchers and scholars in psychology, philosophy, and various clinical fields, as well as by anyone interested in wrestling with the good, the bad, and the ugly of anxiety.

NOTES

1. On the potential epistemic and moral benefits of anxiety, some important work includes: Cabrera 2021, de Sousa 2008, Goldie 2004, Hookway 1998, Kurth 2015, Maibom 2022, Munch-Jurisic 2021, Vazard 2019, and Vazard and Kurth 2022.

2. Psychiatrist Paul Hoch noted all the way back in 1949: "Although it is widely recognized that anxiety is the most pervasive psychological phenomenon of our time, there has been little or no agreement on its definition" (Hoch 1949, v). As Judson Brewer makes essentially the same point (half-jokingly but correctly), "Anxiety is like pornography. It's hard to define, but you sure know it when you see it" (Brewer 2021, 3).

3. There is disagreement about how best to characterize the differences between anxiety and fear. One common view, advanced by Kierkegaard, Freud, and many others, is that while fear is object-directed, anxiety frequently lacks an object. Anxiety, Kierkegaard writes, "is altogether different from fear and similar concepts that refer to something definite" (Kierkegaard 1980, 42). See also Freud 1952. Joseph Ledoux thinks that recent brain science corroborates the view that Kierkegaard and Freud share. He writes: "fear states occur when a threat is present or imminent; states of anxiety result when a threat is possible but its occurrence is uncertain." He goes on to argue that "somewhat different brain mechanisms are engaged when the state is triggered by an objective and present threat as opposed to an uncertain event that may or may not occur in the future. An immediately present stimulus that is itself dangerous, or that is a reliable indicator that danger is likely to soon follow, results in fear. Anxiety may well also be present, but if the initial state is triggered by a specific stimulus, it is a state of fear. However, when the state in question involves worry about something that is not present and may never occur, then the state is anxiety. Fear can, like anxiety, involve anticipation, but the nature of the anticipation in each is different: In

fear the anticipation concerns if and when a present threat will cause harm, whereas in anxiety the anticipation involves uncertainty about the consequences of a threat that is not present and may not occur" (LeDoux 2016, 10–11).

4. See also Alessandri (2023, 145) who points out that, "The distinction between 'normal' and 'disordered' anxiety buckles once it says that 30 percent of us have an anxiety disorder. One in three may not constitute a majority, but it seems awfully close to normal."

REFERENCES

Alessandri, Mariana. 2023. *Night Vision: Seeing Ourselves Through Dark Moods*. Princeton: Princeton University Press.

Barlow, David. 2001. *Anxiety and Its Disorders: The Nature and Treatment of Anxiety and Panic*. 2nd edition. New York: Guilford Press.

Brewer, Judson. 2021. *Unwinding Anxiety*. New York: Penguin Random House.

Cabrera, Frank. 2021. "Is Epistemic Anxiety an Intellectual Virtue?" *Synthese* 199: 13471–95.

de Sousa, Ronald. 2008. "Epistemic Feelings." In *Epistemology and Emotions*, edited by George Brun, Ulvi Douoglu, and Dominique Kuenzle, 185–203. New York: Routledge.

Foulkes, Lucy. 2021. *Losing Our Minds: What Mental Illness Really Is and What It Isn't*. London: Penguin.

Freeman, Daniel, and Jason Freeman. 2012. *Anxiety: A Very Short Introduction*. Oxford: Oxford University Press.

Freud, Sigmund. 1952. *A General Introduction to Psychoanalysis*. New York: Washington Square Press.

———. 1959. *Inhibitions, Symptoms and Anxiety*. Translated by Alix Strachey. New York: W.W. Norton.

Goldie, Peter. 2004. "Emotion, Reason and Virtue." In *Emotion, Evolution, and Rationality*, edited by Dylan Evans and Pierre Cruse, 249–68. Oxford: Oxford University Press.

Heidegger, Martin. 1993. *Martin Heidegger: Basic Writings*. Edited by David Farrell Krell. New York: HarperCollins.

Hoch, Paul. 1949. *Anxiety*. New York: Grune & Stratton.

Hookway, Christopher. 1998. "Doubt Affective States and the Regulation of Inquiry." *Canadian Journal of Philosophy* 24 (supplement): 203–25.

Horwitz, Allan V. 2013. *Anxiety: A Short History*. Baltimore, MD: The Johns Hopkins University Press.

Kierkegaard, Søren. 1980. *The Concept of Anxiety*. Edited and Translated by Reidar Thomte. Princeton: Princeton University Press.

Kurth, Charlie. 2015. "Moral Anxiety and Moral Agency." *Oxford Studies in Normative Ethics* 5: 171–95.

———. 2018. *The Anxious Mind: An Investigation into the Varieties and Virtues of Anxiety*. Cambridge, MA.: MIT Press.

LeDoux, Joseph. 2016. *Anxious: Using the Brain to Understand and Treat Fear and Anxiety*. New York: Penguin.

Maibom, Heidi. 2022. "Don't Worry, Be Happy." *Synthese* 200 (67).

Munch-Jurisic, Ditte Marie. 2021. "Lost for Words: Anxiety, Well-Being, and the Costs of Conceptual Deprivation." *Synthese* 199: 13583–600.

Prinz, Jesse. 2012. *Beyond Human Nature: How Culture and Experience Shape the Human Mind*. New York: W.W. Norton.

Ratcliffe, Matthew. 2017. *Real Hallucinations: Psychiatric Illness, Intentionality, and the Interpersonal World*. Cambridge: MIT Press.

Solomon, Robert C. 1993. *The Passions: Emotions and the Meaning of Life*. Indianapolis: Hackett.

Stossel, Scott. 2013. *My Age of Anxiety: Fear, Hope, Dread, and the Search for Peace of Mind*. New York: Vintage Books.

Vargas, Manuel, and John Doris. 2022. "Introduction." In *The Oxford Handbook of Moral Psychology*, edited by Manuel Vargas and John Doris, 1-5. Oxford: Oxford University Press.

Vazard, Juliette. 2019. "(Un)reasonable Doubt as Affective Experience: Obsessive-Compulsive Disorder, Epistemic Anxiety and the Feeling of Uncertainty." *Synthese* 198: 6917–34.

Vazard, Juliette, and Charlie Kurth. 2022. "Apprehending Anxiety: An Introduction to the Topical Collection on Worry and Well-Being." *Synthese* 200: 327.

PART I

Anxiety in the History of Philosophy

Chapter 1

The Moral Psychology of Anxiety

A Stoic Perspective

Massimo Pigliucci

It may seem rather odd to talk about the *moral* psychology of emotions. After all, moral philosophy is in the business of prescribing certain attitudes or behaviors, and it is commonly assumed that emotions just are what they are, we have no control over them. So how can anyone prescribe how I *should* feel about this or that?

As it turns out, the massive body of empirical evidence and practice associated with various types of cognitive behavioral therapy, or CBT (Beck 2011), challenges the notions that emotions cannot be, in a sense, reasoned with. On the contrary, the whole idea of CBT is that we can engage in emotional regulation, develop coping strategies, and alleviate or resolve a number of psychologically debilitating conditions, including depression and anxiety. The basic CBT approach is founded on the notion that maladaptive behaviors and distortions in our thought processes play a major role in psychological disorders (Field et al. 2015). And the CBT approach works for a variety of conditions, including anxiety (e.g., DiMauro et al. 2013).

Interestingly, a number of techniques employed in CBT have originally been inspired by ancient Stoic philosophy (Margula and Díaz 2015; Robertson 2019). Stoicism itself developed as a very practically oriented philosophy of life based on a type of intuitive psychological theory of the interrelation between reason and emotion that still holds up pretty well in the light of contemporary science (LeDoux 2016). While CBT is a form of therapy, and hence prescriptive only in the limited sense of advising a patient on how to improve her condition, Stoicism is a philosophy of life, and therefore prescriptive in a much broader sense, pertaining to nothing less than the way we should live our lives. In this essay I will first summarize the basics of Stoic moral psychology. I will then proceed to examine what the ancient Stoics had to say about anxiety. I will conclude with a number of practical exercises, inspired by ancient Stoicism but brought up to date with the aid of modern cognitive science. Their goal is to help us cope with anxiety. As we should.[1]

STOIC MORAL PSYCHOLOGY, A BRIEF INTRODUCTION

Before we can meaningfully discuss the Stoic take concerning the moral psychology of emotions in general, and of anxiety in particular, we need to briefly examine the basics of Stoic psychological theory. Let us begin with one of the most famous and important passages in all extant Stoic literature, crucial in order to understand the practical import of Stoic moral psychology:

> So make a practice at once of saying to every strong impression: 'An impression is all you are, not the source of the impression.' Then test and assess it with your criteria, but one primarily: ask, 'Is this something that is, or is not, in my control?' (Epictetus, *Enchiridion* 1.5)

What exactly is an "impression," and how do we "talk" to it? First we need to talk about the Stoic treatment of emotions (Graver 2009). Stoic philosophers made a distinction between unhealthy, or disruptive emotions (*pathē*), and healthy, or constructive ones (*eupatheiai*). The way to understand their system is to appreciate that an emotion can be generated by the thought of something good or bad happening either now or in the future. These, then, are the four fundamental unhealthy emotions:

	Present	Future
Good	pleasure (*hēdonē*), an impulse toward something present now that is considered good, but isn't	appetite (*epithumia*), an impulse toward something in the future that is considered good, but isn't
Bad	distress (*lupē*), an impulse away from something present now that is considered bad, but isn't	fear (*phobos*), an impulse away from something in the future that is considered bad, but isn't

Figure 1.1. Table of Stoic Negative Emotions (Pathe)
Source: Author created.

As the figure shows, all *pathē* are the result of bad judgments. Before we proceed, please note that I will be using the key English words in the Stoic sense, which will be indicated from now on by the presence of scare quotes, in order to distinguish them from the modern, nontechnical meaning; that's also why I'm mentioning the Greek words, to dispel possible ambiguities.

For instance, "pleasure" in the figure may be the result of the misguided thought that it is good for me to stuff myself with food now that I'm having dinner, which is not true because I will later feel awful and put on some extra pounds. Similarly, "distress" may be caused by the thought that my ongoing conversation with uncle Benny is painful and unpleasant, while in reality he is a smart guy who has something to teach me, if I bothered to listen. "Appetite" might be generated by the thought that it would be good to have sex, in the near future, with that attractive married woman I just met, while in fact I would be betraying the trust of my spouse, whom I love. Finally, I could experience "fear" at the prospect of having to go to a medical checkup tomorrow, because I might discover that I have some medical condition, while it's actually good to get checked out and practice preventive medicine. All of the above *pathē* can generate anxiety, because they are about dreaded situations or unfulfilled desires.

The same general scheme (with one exception, as we will see in a moment) can be used to understand the healthy emotions:

"Joy" is the sort of thing I experience, say, in the presence of a gesture of friendship or love between two people I know. "Reasonable wishing" is a desire for a good thing to happen in the future, like racial and gender justice in our society. And "caution" is a rational tendency to shy away from things that are bad for me, such as arriving at mistaken judgments or endorsing questionable values.

As we can see, "joy" is the opposite of "pleasure" (again, note the all-important scare quotes!), "reasonable wishing" is the opposite of "appetite," and "caution" is the opposite of "fear." Moreover, there is no positive opposite of "distress." The reason is that this would have to be an impulse

	Present	Future
Good	joy (*khara*), an impulse toward something present now that is considered good and is, in fact, good	reasonable wishing (*boulêsis*), an impulse towards some future thing regarded as good, which is, in fact, good
Bad	n/a (because the only present evil is bad judgment, which is under our control)	caution (*eulabeia*), an impulse away from some future thing regarded as bad which is, in fact, bad

Figure 1.2. Table of Stoic Positive Emotions (Eupatheiai)
Source: Author created.

away from something present now that is considered bad and is, in fact, bad. This is impossible for the virtuous person, because the only present evil would be to respond unvirtuously to a given situation (externals themselves are never—for the Stoics—good or evil, they are morally indifferent to the agent). But it is always possible to respond virtuously, so the box is empty. As a reminder, here is how Epictetus defines the dichotomy of control: "Some things are up to us, while others are not. Up to us are opinion, motivation, desire, aversion, and, in a word, whatever is of our own doing; not up to us are our body, our property, reputation, office, and, in a word, whatever is not of our own doing" (Epictetus, *Enchiridion* 1.1).

Armed with the above classifications, we can now move to the three concepts that will make clear the bit from Enchiridion 1.5 that we started with. The three concepts are:

> Impressions (phantasiai, sing. phantasia), precognitive judgments originating from our previous experiences or our subconscious thinking. For example: cats are nice, or cats are selfish; the square root of 9 is 3, or the square root of 9 is 4.
>
> Assent (sunkatathesis), the confirmation, usually at a cognitive level, of the initial impression: cats are indeed selfish animals; the square root of 9 is indeed 3. (Obviously, one can deny assent to other impressions, like that cats are actually nice, or that the square root of 9 is 4.)
>
> Impulse (orgē), a movement of the will toward action that we feel because of having assented to a given impression. Note that all the emotions we examined above, both negative and positive, are impulses.

In Stoic psychology, the causal chain connecting these three phenomena looks like this:

> impression> assent> impulse

The impression, then, is involuntary. The assent, however, is the result of reflection (at least in individuals who are prone to reflect on things, otherwise it's implicit), and so the impulse is voluntary, the outcome of a specific combination of impression and assent. It is in this sense that the Stoics (and modern cognitive psychologists) hold that our emotions are voluntary, because they are the result of proto-emotions (involuntary) and cognitive (sometimes implied) judgments.

Here are some practical examples brought up by Epictetus:

> Provoked by the sight of a handsome man or a beautiful woman, you will discover within you the contrary power of self-restraint. Faced with pain, you will

> discover the power of endurance. If you are insulted, you will discover patience. In time, you will grow to be confident that there is not a single impression that you will not have the moral means to tolerate. (Epictetus, *Enchiridion* 10)

Let's take the specific case of something we are anxious about. A Stoically incorrect causal analysis of it would be:

impression: I am likely to fail at my job interview tomorrow
assent: it is awful to fail at a job interview!
impulse: I experience "fear" (phobos)

What should a good Stoic practitioner do instead? This:

impression: I am likely to fail at my job interview tomorrow
deny assent: the outcome of the interview is not up to me, and does not reflect my moral character
impulse: none, I just relax and get a good night's sleep before the interview

This, of course, is far easier said than done, which is why Epictetus warns his students:

> If from the moment they get up in the morning they adhere to their ideals, eating and bathing like a person of integrity, putting their principles into practice in every situation they face—the way a runner does when he applies the principles of running, or a singer those of musicianship—that is where you will see true progress embodied, and find someone who has not wasted their time making the journey here from home. (Epictetus, *Discourses* I, 4.20)

Because after all:

> If you didn't learn these things in order to demonstrate them in practice, what did you learn them for? (Epictetus, *Discourses* I, 29.35)

WHAT THE ANCIENT STOICS SAID ABOUT ANXIETY

Now that we have reviewed the basics of the Stoic approach to moral psychology, we are in a position to evaluate several explicit comments about anxiety made by the ancient Stoics. Some of them wrote specifically about anxiety, understood as a fully fledged, and therefore partially cognitive, emotion. Their writings in this respect can be usefully organized in a number of subtopics within the broader context of Stoic moral psychology, as I do in this section.

The Obsessive Quest for Externals

> Our stupidity may be clearly proved by the fact that we hold that "buying" refers only to the objects for which we pay cash, and we regard as free gifts the things for which we spend our very selves. These we should refuse to buy, if we were compelled to give in payment for them our houses or some attractive and profitable estate; but we are eager to attain them at the cost of anxiety, of danger, and of lost honor, personal freedom, and time; so true it is that each man regards nothing as cheaper than himself. (Seneca, Letter XLII.7)

For the Stoics the pursuit of "externals," for instance wealth and fame, is a misguided priority wrecking the life of so many human beings. The only thing that is truly worth pursuing is wisdom, or virtue, understood as the improvement of one's own character and quality of judgment. The reason for this is given by Socrates in the Euthydemus (Gifford 2013), where he argues against the sophist brothers Euthydemus and Dionysodorus, arriving at the conclusion that wisdom is the highest good, or the only intrinsic good, because the use of everything else depends crucially on whether we act wisely (or virtuously, or with good judgment) or not. Epictetus says something very similar when he equates virtue with reason and states: "What decides whether a sum of money is good? The money is not going to tell you; it must be the faculty that makes use of such impressions—reason" (Epictetus, *Discourses* I, 1.5).

What Seneca is getting at in the above quote, then, is that we simply do not realize the high price we pay—including in terms of anxiety—for our obsessive quest for externals. A quest that we wouldn't entertain for a moment if we actually realized what it costs us, if somehow that price could be quantified in terms of familiar currency. A corollary of this conclusion is articulated in another letter by Seneca to his friend Lucilius: "Everything conducive to our well-being is prepared and ready to our hands; but what luxury requires can never be got together except with wretchedness and anxiety" (Seneca, Letter CXIX.15).

Our actual needs can be taken care of with little effort, but once we cross the boundary into luxury, understood as anything more than is really necessary to our body and mind, then there are no boundaries. This is because nature sets limits in terms of the size of our body and the capacity of our mind. We need shoes to walk, but do we need ten pairs of them? We need food to nourish us, but do we need to import it at great cost from the other side of the world? We enjoy and learn from reading books, but do we need a personal library that contains many times the volumes we may hope to read in a lifetime? Once we go beyond our natural needs there is no stopping point: more is always "better," and this never-ending quest for more is a major factor underlying our existential anxiety. Epictetus says that we fool ourselves in that regard:

> People to whom such things [i.e., externals] are still denied come to imagine that everything good will be theirs if only they could acquire them. Then they get them: and their longing is unchanged, their anxiety is unchanged, their disgust is no less, and they still long for whatever is lacking. Freedom is not achieved by satisfying desire, but by eliminating it. (Epictetus, *Discourses* IV, 1.174–75)

This observation, made almost two millennia ago, is backed up by plenty of modern empirical research into what psychologists call the "hedonic treadmill" (Larsen and Prizmic 2008; Mancini et al. 2011). That is why Epictetus advises us to eliminate our desires for externals, rather than constantly trying to satisfy them. This does not mean that we should embrace an ascetic lifestyle, like the one practiced by the Stoics' close cousins, the Cynics (Desmond 2006). The Stoics did think that externals have *axia*, i.e., value, other things considered. For instance, Epictetus:

> If I can make money while remaining honest, trustworthy and dignified, show me how and I will do it. But if you expect me to sacrifice my own values, just so you can get your hands on things that aren't even good—well, you can see yourself how thoughtless and unfair you're being. (Epictetus, *Enchiridion* 24.3)

Money is not an (intrinsic) "good," it is simply preferred, so long as one doesn't act unvirtuously either in acquiring or in using it. The Stoics referred to externals with the deliciously, but only apparently, oxymoronic phrase of "preferred indifferents," accompanied by a mirror category of "dispreferred indifferents," like poverty, sickness, and so forth. These things are preferred or dispreferred, and therefore can be reasonably pursued or avoided, but they are indifferent to our moral worth, because they don't make us better or worse human beings. On the contrary, it is our character as moral agents that makes such things preferred or dispreferred. Money is preferred for a virtuous person who uses it to help others, but dispreferred for a tyrant who uses it to oppress his people.

The category of externals is not limited just to material things, like wealth, or to physical states, like health or sickness. It also encompasses mental states, as in the following: "It was Antigonus who was anxious before their meeting. Naturally—he wanted to make a good impression, which was beyond his control. Zeno, for his part, had no wish to please the king; no expert needs validation from an amateur" (Epictetus, *Discourses* II, 13, 15). The episode refers to the meeting between Zeno of Citium, the founder of the Stoic sect, and King Antigonus Monophthalmus, one of the successors of Alexander the Great. The king had not as yet internalized the fundamental Stoic concept of the dichotomy of control that we have encountered above (Epictetus, Enchiridion 1.1): some things are up to us and other things are not up to us, and it is wise to focus on the former and accept the latter with equanimity. Specifically, the king wanted something that was not under his control: to make a good impression on the philosopher. Instead, he should have focused on preparing for the meeting in the best way he could. Which, of course, is an approach that would, likely (but not certainly) result in impressing Zeno. Anxiety, according to Epictetus, is often caused by the fact that we disregard the dichotomy of control, as in this case:

> Take a lyre player: he's relaxed when he performs alone, but put him in front of an audience, and it's a different story, no matter how beautiful his voice or how well he plays the instrument. Why? Because he not only wants to perform well, he wants to be well received—and the latter lies outside his control. (Epictetus, *Discourses* II, 13.2)

Imagine how much less performance anxiety we would all experience if we followed Epictetus's advice!

Countering Fortune

> Reasons for anxiety will never be lacking, whether born of prosperity or of wretchedness; life pushes on in a succession of engrossments. We shall always pray for leisure, but never enjoy it. (Seneca, *On the Shortness of Life*, XVII)

For Seneca the source of our anxieties is the fact that we hand our happiness over to Fortune, which is by nature fickle. Fortune is understood by the Stoics as the sum total of the web of cause-effect that is not the result of our judgments and decisions to act or not to act. By definition, all externals—including health, wealth, reputation, etc.—depend on Fortune. Of course we can influence all those things in terms of outcomes, but ultimately such outcomes are determined by things that are not up to us.

It follows that if we stake our happiness on externals we are asking for trouble. In Letter IV.7 Seneca reminds us that on the very same day that we think Fortune has smiled on us she could turn around and sink us into an abyss. As I pointed out above, this does not imply that the Stoic does not care about externals. But what it does imply is that we should work toward cultivating a very different attitude toward them. If the web of cause-effect makes it so that we enjoy some good luck, we should take advantage of it without getting too cocky, because we realize that much of it is not the result of our own doing, and the situation could change in an instant. Conversely, if the web of cause-effect hands us a period of bad luck, we should console ourselves because this, too, shall pass, and at any rate being lucky or unlucky in any particular endeavor is not what truly matters, because externals do not contribute—either positively or negatively—to our character.

In a strong sense, then, the Stoics, and Seneca in particular, are telling us that we should work toward emotional self-sufficiency, as clearly indicated by the quotes in the next section.

Self-sufficiency

> For the mass of mankind consider that a person is at leisure who has withdrawn from society, is free from care, self-sufficient, and lives for himself; but these privileges can be the reward only of the wise man. Does he who is a victim of anxiety know how to live for himself? What? Does he even know (and that is of first importance) how to live at all? (Seneca, Letter LV.4)

Without emotional self-sufficiency there is no escape from anxiety. Seneca is not talking about self-sufficiency tout court, which is impossible for any human being. Elsewhere (IX.3) he explicitly says that even the ideal Stoic sage requires the help of others when it comes to material things, since the sage is, after all, still a human being. Indeed, the wise person desires friends, neighbors, and associates (Letter IX.3). She just does not depend on them for her own happiness.

In the quote, Seneca goes so far as to argue that someone who is in the thrall of anxiety, because she has not internalized the notion discussed above that happiness does not depend on externals, in a sense does not know how to live at all. People are mistaken if they think that leisure and being free from care are the things that lead one to be free of anxiety. On the contrary, those privileges can only be enjoyed by someone who has already freed herself of anxiety because she has rejected the common value system that emphasizes externals at the expense of internally generated serenity and peace of mind. Precisely because it flouts societal pressures and expectations the Stoic attitude requires courage: "And what is bravery? It is the impregnable fortress for our mortal weakness; when a man has surrounded himself therewith, he can hold out free from anxiety during life's siege; for he is using his own strength and his own weapons" (Seneca, Letter CXIII.27).

Seneca here invokes the same concept that a later Stoic, the emperor-philosopher Marcus Aurelius, referred to as "the inner citadel" (Marcus Aurelius, *Meditations*, VIII.48; Hadot 2001). If we let it, life becomes a siege on our inner tranquility, and the way to resist the siege is, again, to distance ourselves from externals and focus on who we are and what kind of human being we wish to be.

That said, most of us are not sages (Brouwer 2014), which according to Seneca are as rare as the phoenix (Letter XLII.1), the mythological bird that emerges from its own ashes every five hundred years. So how do we manage to build our impregnable fortress, or at least to learn how to live a life without anxiety? Part of the answer is: by associating with the right people and distancing ourselves from the wrong ones, just like our parents told us when we were kids. Hence the next topic:

Keeping the Right Company

> We should live with the quietest and easiest-tempered persons, not with anxious or with sullen ones: for our own habits are copied from those with whom we associate, and just as some bodily diseases are communicated by touch, so also the mind transfers its vices to its neighbors. . . . Virtues do the same thing in the opposite direction, and improve all those with whom they are brought in contact. (Seneca, *On Anger*, III.8)

Who we are influences who we choose to associate with, and in turn our associations with other human beings has dramatic effects on who we become. Plenty of modern research supports this early Stoic insight. For instance, De Vries et al. (2018) have shown that being reminded of one's friends helps in self-control and curtails people's compulsive buying behavior. Effects of friendship networks are also evident in teenagers, as demonstrated by Huang et al. (2014) when examining the co-evolution of friendships and peer influences in adolescents in terms of risk behaviors and use of social networks. The authors found significant shifts in both drinking and smoking behavior as a result of network dynamics.

So Seneca was onto something when he stated that vices get worse and virtues improve as a function of who we choose to associate with. Hence the importance of friendship in Stoic training, as emphasized by Seneca himself in his third and ninth Letters to his own friend, Lucilius.

Death

Finally, the last—and perhaps both most obvious and most consequential—source of existential anxiety is, of course, our own mortality. The Stoics have a lot to say on death and how to approach it, and for Seneca preparing oneself for the last test of character is what philosophy does all along. But it is Epictetus that nails the underlying problem: "Because we're the only animals who not only die but are conscious of it even while it happens, we are beset by anxiety" (Epictetus, *Discourses* II, 6.14). Precisely. But, as always in Stoic philosophy, the issue is not with the thing itself, but with our attitude toward it. We can choose to look at death as the ultimate catastrophe, too horrible to even contemplate. Or we can choose to regard it as an inevitable natural process that need not concern us, because once it has occurred we will not be there to experience it or to suffer any consequence (on this, the Stoic view was essentially identical to the Epicurean one).

Once again, this is easier said than done. But Stoicism is unusual among the philosophies of life that have been proposed over the millennia in both the Western and Eastern traditions, because it puts a marked emphasis on the regular practice of its precepts. Over time, Stoics have developed a number of techniques to help the "prokopton" or "prokoptousa" (the one who makes progress, male or female, respectively) in their path of ethical and philosophical self-improvement. My friend and collaborator Gregory Lopez and I have compiled a collection of Stoic exercises inspired by the ancient sources and updated on the basis of modern scientific research (Pigliucci and Lopez 2019). In the next section I will briefly present a subset of these exercises that deal expressly with anxiety.

HOW TO COUNTER ANXIETY, STOICALLY SPEAKING

Exercise 1: Discover What's Really under Your Control

A major source of anxiety is the feeling that we are not in control of things, that something terrible may happen despite our best efforts. Recall the quote above from Epictetus, in *Enchiridion* 1.1. The idea is that what is "up to us" is actually quite limited, and the sooner we realize this and internalize the notion, the better we will position ourselves for a happy and serene life. Specifically, the Stoics believe that the only things truly up to us are our own judgments ("thought"), decisions to act ("impulses"), and what we consciously decide to pursue or to stay away from ("will to get and will to avoid"). Everything else, including our health, wealth, reputation, and career, we are in a position to influence, but ultimately depends on other people and circumstances.

In order to help internalize this concept, sometimes referred to as the Stoic fork, Greg and I suggest taking time to analyze potentially anxiety-inducing situations in the following way. Draw a table with two columns: "up to me" and "not up to me." Then think carefully about a specific issue you either have faced recently or are likely to face in the near future. For instance, an upcoming job interview. Then begin to fill out your table, as illustrated in Table 1.1.

And so on. The more detailed the table, the better. The idea is that explicitly putting things in writing will help us better analyze a potentially anxiety-causing situation and preempt, or at least alleviate the anxiety by repeatedly going over the table itself, directing our attention and efforts to

Table 1.1: An example of application of Epictetus's fundamental rule to the situation presented by a forthcoming job interview. The left column presents a partial list of things that are up to the agent, the right column a partial list of things that are not up to the agent.

Up to me	*Not up to me*
Doing my best to be competitive for the position	Whether I actually am competitive, depending on who else is applying for the job
Putting together a good résumé	How the interviewer will receive the résumé
Preparing for a good performance during the interview	How my performance will be received
Conscious thoughts, what I tell myself	Automatic thoughts, whatever my subconscious comes up with
The intention to show up on time	Whether I actually show up on time, which depends also on traffic, or public transport
The intention to stay focused during the interview	Whether the environment will be conducive or disruptive to maintaining focus

the left column, and reminding ourselves that we need to accept the items on the right with the serenity that comes from the knowledge that we have done our best.

Exercise 2: Premeditation of Future Adversity

Modern cognitive behavioral therapy uses a modified version of a technique that was commonly recommended by the ancient Stoics: (pre)meditating on the possibility of a specific future adversity as a way, again, to prepare mentally (i.e., both cognitively and emotionally) for something that might trigger anxious thoughts. Seneca summarizes the idea:

> If an evil has been pondered beforehand, the blow is gentle when it comes. To the fool, however, and to him who trusts in fortune, each event as it arrives "comes in a new and sudden form," and a large part of evil, to the inexperienced, consists in its novelty. This is proved by the fact that people endure with greater courage, when they have once become accustomed to them, the things which they had at first regarded as hardships. Hence, the wise man accustoms himself to coming trouble, lightening by long reflection the evils which others lighten by long endurance. We sometimes hear the inexperienced say: "I knew that this was in store for me." But the wise man knows that all things are in store for him. Whatever happens, he says: "I knew it." (Seneca, *Letters to Lucilius*, 76.34–35)

There are different ways to carry out this exercise. My favorite involves writing things down, as in Table 1.2.

As Seneca says, if an evil has been pondered beforehand, the blow is gentle when it comes.

Table 1.2: An example of a Stoic exercise employing premeditation on possible adversities. The contemplation of the goal (first column) is accompanied by questions (columns 2, 3, and 4) aimed at better preparing the agent in case things don't go as expected or planned.

Goal	*How could it go wrong?*	*If it does go wrong, what would be up to me?*	*What could I do or say to myself if my plan goes wrong?*
Do my taxes	I might discover that I don't have all the forms or documents I need	My thoughts about the outcome, as well as planning my next step	The worst that might happen is a financial penalty

Exercise 3: Take a Broader Perspective

One reason we become anxious is because we lose a sense of perspective on things, thinking that if something doesn't go the intended way this is somehow a huge problem. Cognitive behavioral therapists call this attitude "catastrophizing," and we need to train ourselves not to indulge in it. Marcus Aurelius wrote:

> The agitations that beset you are superfluous, and depend wholly upon judgments of your own. You can get rid of them, and in so doing will indeed live at large, by embracing the whole universe in your view and comprehending all eternity and imagining the swiftness of change in each particular, seeing how brief is the passage from birth to dissolution, birth with its unfathomable before, dissolution with its infinite hereafter. (Marcus Aurelius, *Meditations*, 9.32)

Again there are different ways to carry out the exercise. We could focus, as Marcus does in the above passage, on the vastness of time, or of space. My preference is for a version that focuses on the relative size of the problem at hand. Whatever is bothering me, almost certainly will have been experienced by other people, who have been able to overcome or endure the situation. So why can't I?

In practice I write in my philosophical journal, describing the problem in some detail. For instance, the fact that I am in the middle of a pandemic (at the time of writing) and I'm getting anxious about not being able to travel while at the same time not getting any younger. Time is running out! Then I write down a series of reminders of the fact that: (i) most of the rest of humanity is in my same exact predicament; and (ii) in fact, I am lucky, since—although I cannot travel—I am in good health, none of my close relatives or friends have gotten sick, I am living with a supportive partner, and I retained my job, which means I have something productive to do and I can pay my bills. Once you go through the exercise, multiple times if necessary, it becomes increasingly embarrassing that you were so worried about your initial problem.

Exercise 4: Challenge Your Anxious Thoughts

Anxiety tends to focus our attention on negative possibilities. While we're caught up in fantasizing about an awful future, we fail to realize that in the present moment, everything's okay. The pain people experience from anxiety comes solely from the mind, according to the Stoics. This is how Seneca puts it:

> How am I to know whether my sufferings are real or imaginary?' Here is the rule for such matters: We are tormented either by things present, or by things to come, or by both. As to things present, the decision is easy. Suppose that your person enjoys freedom and health, and that you do not suffer from any external injury. As to what may happen to it in the future, we shall see later on. Today there is nothing wrong with it. 'But,' you say, 'something will happen to it.' First of all, consider whether your proofs of future trouble are sure. . . . It is likely that some troubles will befall us, but it is not a present fact. How often has the unexpected happened! How often has the expected never come to pass! And even though it is ordained to be, what does it avail to run out to meet your suffering? You will suffer soon enough, when it arrives, so look forward meanwhile to better things." (Seneca, *Letters to Lucilius*, 13.7–10)

This isn't a Pollyannish approach to life, but rather a very sensible one. Let us focus our energy and resources on what we have to tackle right now. There is no guarantee of future troubles, and indulging in negative thinking does not help us, and indeed may impair any sensible preemptive action we may otherwise contemplate.

The proposed exercise includes a three-step process, and again may be best carried out (in part) in writing. The first step is to check in with the present moment. This is because, when we're worried about something, the present isn't what's causing our distress—our thinking is. If the present moment is comfortable for you, then you can relax into it. You can do so by using techniques rooted in modern mindfulness. One technique is to focus your attention on the sensations of breathing, in the places where the sensations are most prominent (often around the nostrils or belly).

After you've grounded yourself for a few moments, consider whether there is anything actually wrong right now. Sometimes there is. If you are not free, or not healthy, or in pain now, this exercise may not be appropriate, and you really need to take care of whatever the issue is. But if nothing is wrong, then you can move on to step two. That consists in clearly laying out the outcome you are worried about. What do you think will happen? Making your worry concrete will make it easier to question. Then ask what strong evidence you have that the outcome you are worried about will actually occur. After you weigh the evidence for the feared outcome, ask the same question for the feared outcome not happening: is there any evidence that it won't happen? Another possible way to challenge your anxiety is to brainstorm other outcomes besides the one you fear. This could help you think of alternatives that you weren't previously considering since you were only focused on the worst-case scenario.

The final step is to ask a pragmatic question: is this worry doing me any good right now? Whether or not the feared outcome will happen, how is worrying helping you in the present moment? If you find that it's not, then consider putting the worry to the side for now. A worry could be useful, though, if it suggests an action you can take. While outcomes are never completely under your control, if you can come up with a plan of action, then implement it.

There are a number of other, related or complementary, exercises that are available to modern Stoic practitioners. The point to remember is that, except in extreme pathological cases that may require professional psychological or psychiatric intervention, there is a lot you can do to challenge your anxieties. Indeed, according to the Stoics, you *ought* to challenge them, for the sake of your happiness and of the well-being of those around you.

NOTE

1. Citations to works by Seneca, Epictetus, and Marcus Aurelius are all from the public domain, *Delphi Classics* editions of their complete works. More particularly, references to Seneca are quoted from the *Complete Works of Seneca the Younger* (East Hastings, Sussex, UK: Delphi Publishing, 2014). References to Epictetus are quoted from the *Complete Works of Epictetus* (2018, East Hastings, Sussex, UK: Delphi Publishing, 2018), and citations to Marcus Aurelius are quoted from the *Complete Works of Marcus Aurelius* (East Hastings, Sussex, UK: Delphi Publishing, 2014).

REFERENCES

Beck, Judith S. 2011. *Cognitive Behavior Therapy: Basics and Beyond*. New York: Guilford Press.

Brouwer, René. 2014. *The Stoic Sage: The Early Stoics on Wisdom, Sagehood and Socrates*. Cambridge: Cambridge University Press.

De Vries, Eline L. E, Bob M. Fennis, Tammo H. A. Bijmolt, Gert J. T. Horstc, and Jan Bernard C. Marsman. 2018. "Friends with Benefits: Behavioral and fMRI Studies on the Effect of Friendship Reminders on Self-control for Compulsive and

Non-Compulsive Buyers." *International Journal of Research in Marketing* 35: 336–58.

Desmond, William D. 2006. *The Greek Praise of Poverty: The Origins of Ancient Cynicism*. Notre Dame, IN. University of Notre Dame Press.

DiMauro, Jennifer, Janine Domingues, Geraldine Fernandez, and David F. Tolin. 2013. "Long term Effectiveness of CBT for Anxiety Disorders in an Adult Outpatient Clinic Sample: A follow-up study." *Behavior Research and Therapy* 51: 82–86.

Field, Thomas A., Eric T. Beeson, and Laura K. Jones. 2015. "The New ABCs: A Practitioner's Guide to Neuroscience-Informed Cognitive-Behavior Therapy." *Journal of Mental Health Counseling* 37: 206–20.

Gifford, Edwin Hamilton. 2013. *The Euthydemus of Plato: With Revised Text, Introduction, Notes and Indices*. Cambridge: Cambridge University Press.

Graver, Margaret. 2009. *Stoicism and Emotion*. Chicago: University of Chicago Press.

Hadot, Pierre. 2001. *The Inner Citadel: The Meditations of Marcus Aurelius*. Cambridge, MA.: Harvard University Press.

Huang, Grace C., Daniel Soto, Kayo Fujimoto, and Thomas W. Valente. 2014. "The Interplay of Friendship Networks and Social Networking Sites: Longitudinal Analysis of Selection and Influence Effects on Adolescent Smoking and Alcohol Use." *American Journal of Public Health* 104: 51–59.

Larsen, Randy J., and Zvjezdana Prizmic. 2008. "Regulation of Emotional Well-Being: Overcoming the Hedonic Treadmill." In *The Science of Subjective Well-Being*, edited by Michael Eid and Randy J. Larsen, 258–89. New York: Guilford Press.

LeDoux, Joseph. 2016. *Anxious: Using the Brain to Understand and Treat Fear and Anxiety*. London: Penguin.

Mancini, Anthony D., George A. Bonanno, and Andrew E. Clark. 2011. "Stepping Off the Hedonic Treadmill. Individual Differences in Response to Major Life Events." *Journal of Individual Differences* 32: 144–52.

Marguia, Edward, and Kim Díaz. 2015. "The Philosophical Foundations of Cognitive Behavioral Therapy: Stoicism, Buddhism, Taoism, and Existentialism." *Journal of Evidence-Based Psychotherapies* 15: 39–52.

Pigliucci, Massimo, and Gregory Lopez. 2019. *A Handbook for New Stoics—How to Thrive in a World Out of Your Control. 52 Week-by-Week Lessons*. New York: The Experiment.

Robertson, Donald. 2019. *The Philosophy of Cognitive-Behavioral Therapy (CBT): Stoic Philosophy as Rational and Cognitive Psychotherapy*. New York: Routledge.

Chapter 2

Not a Moment of Worry

Confucian Views on the Value of Anxiety

Leah Kalmanson

Every morning, before I leave the house, I briefly touch the knob on the oven to make sure it is set to the "off" position. Also, every morning, on my way out the door, I briefly touch the mezuzah case on my doorpost and then kiss my fingers. The latter habit supposedly indicates my religiosity, while the former, I suspect, indicates my diagnosis of "generalized anxiety disorder." However, given that I am not particularly religious, I have often wondered whether the mezuzah habit is but a sublimated expression of the same obsessive tendencies prompting my vigilance over the oven. With this in mind, I open the following brief exploration of the relation between ritual and anxiety in what we might call a Confucian "moral psychology."

The *Liji* 禮記 or *Book of Rites*, a canonical text dating back to the Warring States period (475–221 BCE), advises that the exemplary person will have "a lifetime of anxiety, but not a moment of worry" (故君子有終身之憂，而無一朝之患) (*Liji* 2011, "Tan Gong I" 檀弓上, passage 9). Here, the context concerns the care and preparation that a good son devotes to his father's funeral arrangements, so as to avoid any preventable mistakes in the ritual attention given to mourning in the Confucian tradition. The key term *you* 憂 is commonly translated as "anxiety." It carries connotations of being apprehensive, concerned, mournful, or weighed down by cares. In these senses, the larger message of the *Liji* passage seems to regard the value of anxiety as a mode of solicitude or apprehensive watchfulness to be cultivated in all matters, but especially in matters of ritual. Moreover, notably, in the Chinese cultural context, ritual has both moral and metaphysical dimensions.

We begin with this broader philosophical framework before moving on to a closer look at the discussions of anxiety in several early texts, including the *Liji*. As we will see, a Confucian "moral psychology" is undergirded by what we will call a moral-metaphysical realism that links our inner states to outer conditions (both sociopolitical and environmental), making anxiety a reasonable response to our unavoidable interconnectedness with others and with the world around us.

THE RUIST CONTEXT

The term "Confucianism" gives the somewhat misguided impression that the historical figure of "Confucius" (Kongzi 孔子, 551–479 BCE) is the founder of a religious or philosophical movement. In fact, the tradition known in Chinese as *rujia* 儒家 predates the life of Kongzi, and Kongzi himself denies being an innovator (*Lunyu* 論語 2011, 3.14).[1] Master Kong was a member of the "lineage" or "family" (*jia* 家) of the *ru* 儒, a term better translated as "scholar" or "literati." The *ru* were members of China's educated elite: they were often employed as educators or government officials, they were versed in the classic scholarly and literary texts of Chinese culture, and they were qualified to preside over various state rites and civic ceremonies as well as the rituals performed at ancestral shrines. Throughout this chapter, I use the alternative English terms "Ruism" and "Ruists" to refer to the tradition and its members.

One could argue that the Ruist tradition, and Chinese philosophy in general, avoids the dilemma that Western philosophy refers to as the "fact–value distinction." According to this distinction, so-called bare facts about the world consist in its material, chemical, or biological features, and so forth, and these bare facts are not evaluated by moral standards—mere facts are neither "right" nor "wrong" but simply "are." In contrast, in the Chinese context, the efficacious functioning of the cosmos is "good" just as the efficacious functioning of the human heart-mind is "good," and both senses of "good" have a moral valence. Or, as the contemporary historian Tze-Ki Hon comments, "As part of the ceaseless flow of qi in the universe, morality is understood metaphysically" (2005, 97). The key term here, i.e., qi 氣, has been translated into English as, for example, "vital stuff" (Angle and Tiwald 2017), "psychophysical stuff" (Gardner 1990), or "lively material" (Ivanhoe 2016). All such terms seek to capture the sense in which qi can refer to material as well as mental and spiritual phenomena: qi can be condensed and palpable, as in physical objects; or dispersed and fluid, as in the mental energies of human thoughts and feelings; or ethereal, as in the energies of ghosts and spirits. It is precisely because of this confluence of material and mental realities that our discussion of moral psychology necessarily travels into cosmological and metaphysical territory.

Reflecting this confluence, analytic philosopher JeeLoo Liu uses the term "*qi*-realism" to capture the sense in which qi "constitutes everything and is responsible for all changes" (2011, 62). Whether we speak of chemical reactions, biological processes, moral values, or existential meaning, we can express it all through the nature and functioning of qi. As such, like Hon, Liu associates the qi-based worldview with what she calls a "moral metaphysics" (2018, 2–3) in which anything that exists can be considered morally, or at least axiologically, significant.

I note here that this "moral-metaphysical realism" (to borrow from Liu's formulation) is not the result of intentional design by a transcendent creator. Rather, our cosmological source is usually attributed to the underlying nature of reality itself, which is said to be beginningless. This cosmic origin can be described in terms of supreme unity (*taiyi* 太一) or supreme ultimate (*taiji* 太極), as limitless (*wuji* 無極) or chaotic (*hundun* 混沌), or even personified as a great ancestor Shangdi 上帝 as in the Shang Dynasty (1600–1045 BCE). In the Daoist context, the origin may be described in terms of void, absence, or emptiness (e.g., *xu* 虛, *wu* 無, *kong* 空); whereas in the Ruist context, it may be more commonly referred to as primordial *qi* (*yuanqi* 元氣), unified *qi* (*yiqi* 一氣), or the unnameable state that precedes formless qi, where negative terms like void or emptiness are descriptive markers (i.e., the cosmic source is void of distinctions, or empty of forms, and so forth).[2]

From this cosmic source, itself beginningless, comes the initial distinction into yin 陰 and yang 楊 and, eventually, all the myriad things of existence as we know it. Here, the tendency of formlessness to produce form and the tendency of the cosmic origin to give rise to life are both parts of the foundational natural patterns observable in reality broadly. These underlying patterns can be understood as the "way" or dao 道 of existence or as the principles or structures that reflect overarching cosmic order (*li* 理). Two important points follow, for our purposes here. Firstly, similar patterns are observable on microcosmic and macrocosmic scales. This reflects what is often described as the "correlative cosmology" of the qi-based worldview.[3] According to this, certain correspondences can be mapped between phenomena of similar structures or constitutions. In particular, the five phases (*wuxing* 五行) of water, fire, wood, metal, and earth can be associated with specific bodily organs, seasonal changes, human affairs, and so forth, influencing practices as diverse as medicine, agriculture, politics, and pedagogy

All such microcosmic and macrocosmic levels are mutually interdependent—success in one aspect reinforces success in all others, and likewise disorder at one level will often have repercussions elsewhere. The mechanism by which correlated phenomena exert influence upon each other is referred to as *ganying* (感應), translated literally as "response-stimulus" or the mutual resonance of similarly structured phenomena. Of note here is that *ganying* is also invoked to explain ritual efficacy in the Chinese context broadly. Ritual behaviors are efficacious precisely because they bring similar structures into attunement with each other, thereby linking personal, social, environmental, and even cosmic orders. In the Buddhist context, *ganying* might be used to describe a bodhisattva's responsiveness to prayer.[4] In a Ruist context, it is the explanatory framework that links the heart-mind of the sage to sociopolitical and spiritual conditions in the surrounding world.

This leads to our second point: The primordial forces that birthed the universe are not just features of our cosmic origins but remain with us in the present, accessible via specific self-cultivation practices such as meditation or, especially for Ruists, scholarly study. These practices are important precisely because they develop the human capacity for efficacious action via qi-based correspondences and resonances. For example, as Joseph Adler comments, "there is a moral imperative for learning, and the process of learning is a psycho-spiritual transformation that refines and clarifies one's *qi*" (2004, 132). Fully clarified qi results in the attainment of "spirit": "In human beings, spirit [*shen* 神] is a quality of mind—specifically mind-qi in its finest, most free-flowing state. . . . To embody this epistemological potential . . . is to be a fully authentic (*cheng*) human being, a Sage" (141).[5]

To be utterly clear, the qi-based energy of the heart-mind has efficacious reach into the surrounding world. As the contemporary scholar Yung Sik Kim explains, in the Ruist view, an individual's mental life is not simply an internal experience, nor is it restricted to the confines of her physical body: "Mind . . . was really nothing but *qi*, its 'essential and refreshing' (*jingshuang* 精爽) or 'numinous' (*ling* 靈) portion, to be more specific. Thus, *qi* was endowed with qualities of mind, and could interact with the mind. The mind-*qi* interaction was not restricted to man's *qi* and his own mind, but was extended to the *qi* of the outside world and to the minds of others" (2015, 129). Here, the well-developed heart-mind, via its spiritual or "numinous" aspect, is able to directly influence other people, the shared social world, and even the physical environment. Given this, any "moral psychology" in the Ruist context must take into account the transpersonal scope of psychical energies and the techniques used to modify them and control their external reach. Ritual is one such technique, and we turn next to the special relationship between anxiety and ritual in early Ruist thought.

ANXIETY, WORRY, AND RITUAL IN THE *BOOK OF RITES* AND *ANALECTS*

We return now to our opening passage from the *Liji*: the exemplary person will have "a lifetime of anxiety, but not a moment of worry" (故君子有終身之憂，而無一朝之患). The partner concept to *you* or "anxiety" is the near-synonymous term "worry" (*huan* 患), which contemporary scholar Michael Ing defines as the kind of concern that arises due to our personal failings or inadequate efforts, such as a lack of self-discipline or negligence in meeting our obligations. In contrast, he says, *you* refers to anxiety arising from a more fundamental vulnerability (2012, 195). In other words, even the most disciplined and well-prepared person is still vulnerable to the unforeseen vicissitudes of life. Hence, the *Liji* passage seems to recommend perpetual vigilance regarding those events that are, indeed, beyond our control.

That said, the *Liji*'s message is complicated by the fact that Kongzi says various contradictory things about *you* throughout his collected sayings in the *Lunyu* 論語 or *Analects*. Some of his comments seem to directly oppose the *Liji*, as in *Lunyu* 9.29: "Those that are wise are not confused, those that are humane are not anxious, those that are brave are not fearful" (知者不惑，仁者不憂，勇者不懼).[6] Elsewhere, however, in 14.28, he explicitly places this level of attainment beyond of the reach of most people: "The way of the exemplary person is threefold, but it is beyond my reach: to be humane and not anxious, wise and not confused, brave and not fearful" (君子道者三，我無能焉：仁者不憂，知者不惑，勇者不懼). And, finally, in 7.3, Kongzi discusses his own anxieties: "That I have not cultivated my moral power, that I have not explained what I have learned, that I have not aligned with what I know to be appropriate, and that I have been unable to change what is not good—these are what cause my anxiety" (德之不脩，學之不講，聞義不能徙，不善不能改，是吾憂也). Here, for Kongzi at least, the line between his personal failings and larger existential uncertainties remains ambiguous.

For this very reason, speculates Ing, Kongzi appears as an exemplary but relatable figure in Chinese traditions: "Confucius, in this sense, is fully human and stands in for us as we stand in for him" (2012, 203). Speaking more generally, Ing suggests that the Ruist tradition encourages us to manage our anxieties so that they contribute to what he calls "productive disorientations," which arise when there is a mismatch between the way we expect the world to work and the way events actually unfold: "The Confucian project sets out to order the world; yet the anxiety associated with this project's contingency on governmental structures beyond the control of Confucians is never fully resolved" (197). This is, we might say, the basic "existential anxiety" of the Ruist worldview—that even our best efforts cannot sway the tide of impending disorder, that the cosmos is not especially receptive to our interventions, and above all that our moral exemplars are as ineffective as the rest of us.

This disorientation is "productive," in Ing's sense, because it drives us to reengage with circumstances that seem out of hand and to develop new strategies for establishing order. As he says, the *Liji* traces the origin of ritual itself to the overwhelming disorientation of human mortality and bodily vulnerability. For example, he quotes the following passage from the "Liyun" (禮運) chapter, which speculates about the origin of ritual itself: "Ritual originated . . . when someone died. [The living] climbed up to the rooftop and called [after them] saying: 'Alas! You [must] come back!'" (quoted in Ing 2012, 195). This is the *Liji*'s own explanation for why the traditional mourning rites require family members to climb to the roofs of their homes and call out for the deceased. The ritual works in accord with our own heartfelt tendencies, while channeling our emotions and helping us to manage their overwhelming force. In this way, as Ing explains, ritualized actions are deeply related to fundamental human anxieties:

> A central theme [in the *Liji*] is that human beings naturally have feelings that well up within themselves as a result of encountering certain circumstances in life. Without ritual, these feelings will be directionless. They will manifest themselves in random—and likely destructive—actions. . . . Rituals are the tools for providing direction and cultivating a habituated sense of proper performance. (2012, 32–33)

All in all, Ing helps us to think of rituals as what we might call existential coping strategies. They make use of preexisting tendencies—in this case, our raw emotions—while shaping and developing our capacity to endure otherwise overwhelming anxieties.

To put this in the context of moral psychology, we might say that, when functioning optimally, anxiety and ritual work together to guide us effectively through our ethical, social, and political deliberations. Our constant sense of foreboding directs our attention to the important matters of concern and alerts us to possible dangers, mistakes, or inauspicious tidings. Simultaneously, our familiarity with ritual protocols helps us determine the right course of action to meet these challenges, where "right" will always mean, at least in part, "ritually correct." Of course, as we saw earlier, ritual correctness is not a mere formality but has metaphysical implications that are important to bear in mind so as to appreciate the true stakes of ritual action here. On this note, we turn to one more early text for additional perspective on these connections between anxiety, ritual, and the moral-metaphysical realism underlying Ruist moral psychology.

Inner Tranquility and Outer Attentiveness in the *Guanzi*

The *Guanzi* 管子 is a syncretic text, bearing marks of Ruist, Daoist, and Legalist influences. The chapter on "Inner Workings" (*nei ye* 內業) in particular contains some of the earliest instructions for Daoist contemplative practices such as "grasping the one" (*zhiyi* 執一), through which the mind is returned to its originally formless and potent state. Yet, in one notable passage, the text also presents a characteristically Ruist concern for ritualistic matters as well the scholarly pursuits of music and poetry, thus distinguishing it from other early Daoist texts that adopt overtly anti-ritualistic rhetoric as part of a larger critique of Ruist formalism. I will note that scholarly consensus seems to be that the passage in question is a later addition, but nonetheless the commentary on ritual and anxiety is illuminating for our purposes here, as it shows Ruist interest in mental cultivation techniques for the sake of sagely development.[7] As we see, the passage moves from the Daoist-inflected advice that we empty our minds of specific forms (in this case, specific feelings) to a markedly Ruist recommendation that we adopt ritual formality and an attitude of "reverence" or "attentiveness" (*jing* 敬):

> Generally, people's vitality must be a matter of balance and good alignment. The loss of this [vitality] must be due to pleasure, anger, anxiety, and worry. Therefore, for halting anger, nothing is better than poetry. For casting off anxiety, nothing is better than music. For moderating music, nothing is better than ritual. For preserving ritual, nothing is better than reverent attentiveness. For preserving reverent attentiveness, nothing is better than tranquility. Inwardly tranquil and outwardly attentive—then you can revert to your original nature. And that nature will be completely stable (凡人之生也，必以平正；所以失之，必以喜怒憂患，是故止怒莫若詩，去憂莫若樂，節樂莫若禮，守禮莫若敬，守敬莫若靜，內靜外敬，能反其性，性將大定). (*Guanzi* 2011, passage 8)[8]

How, asks the text, do we attain the balance and alignment needed to nurture our own vital powers? The answer: when the mind is beset with chaotic forms that disrupt its tranquility, then we rely on practiced forms to effectively reset, as it were, the mind's inner state. To counter the disorder of anger, we turn to the rhythmic formal language of poetry. To counter the disorder of anxiety, we turn to the composed structure of music. And, for the most effective poetic and musical structuring, we rely on ritual formalism and a reverential demeanor. Through this, we pass through our anger and anxiety to arrive back at the originally formless and tranquil state of mind that is the source of our deepest stability.

To put this again in the context of moral psychology, anxiety is a disturbance in the body-mind ecology that can be addressed by certain therapeutic techniques, including the ritualized scholarly practices of Ruism that reestablish mental order. Here, perhaps, anxiety has the expectedly negative valence. It is one of the vicissitudes of mental life that must be addressed and corrected via appropriate strategies. Nonetheless, as we saw with the *Liji* and *Lunyu* above, anxiety and ritual still stand in a mutually informative relationship. Disordered mental forms such as anger and anxiety are little signs that the microcosm of the mind's inner ecology is out of balance, and our guide in deciding how to remedy the situation still lies, as above, in Ruist scholarly and ritual pursuits.

Moreover, undergirding the importance of remedying disorder is the moral-metaphysical realism that links inner states to outer conditions. This begins, in the *Guanzi*, with the link between the inner mind and the outer body: "When a complete mind lies within, it cannot be concealed. It may be ascertained from one's bearing and observed from one's complexion" (Rickett, trans., 1998, 49). Notably, this is a two-way process, in that maintaining proper demeanor also effectively regulates the inner mind: "Maintain a dignified appearance and respectful attitude [and the mind's] vital essence will itself become stable" (45). This stability allows the sage to serve as the locus of energy around which all others revolve. The text frequently contrasts the true power of the sage with physical or brute force:

> Meet people with good *qi*, and they will be close to you like siblings. Meet people with bad *qi*, and they will harm you with their weapons. The unvoiced sound may be more startling than thunder. The form of the mind's *qi* is more illuminating than the sun and moon, more discerning than even a father or mother. Rewards are not enough to encourage goodness, and punishments are not enough to prevent mistakes. But when *qi*-based awareness is attained, the whole world submits. When the mind's awareness is stable, the whole world obeys (善氣迎人，親於弟兄。惡氣迎人，害於戎兵。不言之聲，疾於雷鼓。心氣之形，明於日月，察於父母。賞不足以勸善，刑不足以懲過。氣意得而天下服。心意定而天下聽). (*Guanzi* 2011, passage 6)[9]

On the one hand, the takeaway points from this moral-metaphysical realism are perhaps less than comforting. Our anxieties, it seems, are not so safely contained within our so-called inner lives. Indeed, it would appear that untrained people regularly unleash their disordered emotions upon the surrounding world, resulting in social strife and, if the underlying realism is to be taken seriously, metaphysical imbalances. On the other hand, the *Guanzi* expresses a characteristically Ruist optimism regarding the spiritual charisma of the one who puts in the time and effort to refine their psycho-spiritual energies. Such refined energies constitute the true power of the sage, whose inner stability serves as the spiritual anchor that brings harmony to the world.

CONCLUSION

Despite this optimism over the possibility of moral self-cultivation, I have lingering concerns about the scope of ritual efficacy we find in the Ruist context, especially as this relates to the topic of anxiety. Let us return to the opening example of my own time and effort dedicated to checking my oven. One might say that a qi-based understanding of those spiritual resonances underlying ritual efficacy too easily feeds into precisely such obsessive tendencies. In other words, I am intellectually aware that double-checking the stove does not ritually stave off a house fire, yet I am unable to dispense with the gesture even when I know full well that the stove is not on. Regardless of what I know, I *feel* the ritual to be efficacious, and underlying this feeling is surely some vague intuition about unseen channels of causality that accounts, I suspect, for much of my anxious ideation. From this perspective, an uncritical appropriation of qi-based energy correspondences would only exacerbate these tendencies that I am paying a therapist good money to avoid exacerbating.

However, the Ruist approach to ritual efficacy is nuanced and complex. Ultimately, ritual behaviors that exacerbate anxiety can be critiqued for relying on either an overly mechanistic or overly fastidious understanding of ritual correctness. For example, resisting a naively mechanistic understanding of ritual divination, the *Guanzi* asks. "Without oracle bones and yarrow stalks, can you yet know bad and good fortune?" (能無卜筮而知吉凶乎) (*Guanzi* 2011, passage 6). Common divination methods involved heating bones or tortoise shells to cause cracks, which could then be deciphered, or tossing yarrow stalks to consult passages in the *Yijing* 易經 or *Book of Changes*. Although the *Guanzi* passage seems to reject such practices, this nonetheless does not mark a disenchanted view on spiritual correspondences and ritual efficacy. The passage goes on to say: "Think about it. Think about it. And, again, think about it. You think about it but cannot get through to it, while ghosts and spirits can get there. This is not because they are especially forceful, but because the purest *qi* goes the farthest" (思之思之，又重思之。思之而不通，鬼神將通之，非鬼神之力也，精氣之極也). Here, the counterpoint to mechanistic ritual practice is not the disenchanted view that, for example, all ritual is mere superstition. Rather, the key distinction the text makes is between, as we saw above, brute force (*li* 力) and the true power and efficacy that results from qi-based cultivation. Ghosts and spirits here are understood precisely as rarefied or numinous, and hence potent, aspects of qi. The text thus privileges ritual practices that accomplish the inner work of purifying qi over those practices that rely on mechanistic procedures. The difference lies in whether the ritual form results in the transformation of anger and anxiety that is evidence of successful moral self-cultivation.

Similarly, in the next great Ruist work after the *Lunyu*, the *Mengzi* 孟子, we meet Chunyu Kun 淳于髡, who asks Mengzi: "That men and women should not touch in handing something to one another—is this the ritual?" When Mengzi answers in the affirmative, Chunyu Kun replies: "If your sister-in-law were drowning, would you pull her out with your hand?" A seemingly irritated Mengzi retorts that only a beast would not have the discretion to use his hands to save his sister-in-law from drowning (Van Norden, trans. 2001, 4A17). Here, the concern is with an overly fastidious attitude toward ritual correctness that overrides other moral considerations or commitments.

Both examples give us tools for navigating obsessive or anxious tendencies that might privilege ritual form above all else. With these examples, and throughout this brief exploration of ritual and anxiety in the Chinese philosophical context, we have seen the Ruist tradition balance the positive and negative effects of anxiety on moral psychology. On the one hand, anxiety is a warranted response to insurmountable uncertainties, and maintaining an openness to anxiety can help us forestall preventable mishaps. On the other hand, anxiety is a disordered inner energy that can indeed have negative effects on external conditions, and hence it must be moderated and transformed via ameliorative practices. But, across both registers, anxiety and ritual work together in the process of moral self-cultivation that results, ideally, in the wisdom and spiritual charisma of the sage.

NOTES

1. In this passage, Kongzi famously declares himself a follower of the ways of the Zhou dynasty (1046–256 BCE).

2. For more on the question of nothingness in Chinese context, and the operation of related terms in the pre-Buddhist context, see JeeLoo Liu 2014.

3. For a discussion of the history of this term in studies of China, see Puett 2004, 146.

4. On *ganying* and a bodhisattva's responsiveness, see Chiew Hui Ho (2017), 1127–29. See also Charles B. Jones 2000, 63.

5. Bracketed material is mine.

6. For translations of this passage and the several that follow, I rely on *Lunyu* 2011 and Roger Ames and Henry Rosemont, trans., 1998.

7. See Harold D. Roth 1999, 30–33; and W. A. Rickett trans., 1998, 32, n40.

8. My translation. See Roth 1999, 88; Rickett, trans., 1998, 52–53.

9. My translation. See Roth 1999, 80; Rickett, trans., 1998, 49–50.

REFERENCES

Adler, Joseph. 2004. "Varieties of Spiritual Experience: Shen in Neo-Confucian Discourse." In *Confucian Spirituality* Vol. 2, edited by Tu Wei-ming and M. E. Tucker, 120–48. New York: Crossroad.

Ames, Roger T., and Henry Rosemont Jr., trans. 1998. *The Analects of Confucius: A Philosophical Translation*. New York: Random House.

Angle, Stephen C., and Justin Tiwald. 2017. *Neo-Confucianism: A Philosophical Introduction*. Cambridge: Polity Press.

Chiew Hui Ho. 2017. "Sinitic Buddhist Narratives of Wonders: Are There Miracles in Buddhism?" *Philosophy East and West* 67 (4): 1118–42.

Gardner, Daniel K., trans., 1990. *Learning to Be a Sage: Selection from the Conversations of Master Chu, Arranged Topically, by Chu Hsi*. Berkeley: University of California Press.

Guanzi 管子. 2011. "Nei Ye" 內業. In *Chinese Text Project*, edited by Donald Sturgeon. https://ctext.org/guanzi/nei-ye.

Hon, Tze-Ki. 2005. *The Yijing and Chinese Politics: Classical Commentary and Literati Activism in the Northern Song Period, 960–1127*. Abany: SUNY Press.

Ing, Michael David Kaulana. 2012. *The Dysfunction of Ritual in Early Confucianism*. New York: Oxford University Press.

Ivanhoe, Philip J. 2016. *Three Streams: Confucian Reflections on Learning and the Moral Heart-Mind in China, Korea, and Japan*. Oxford: Oxford University Press.

Jones, Charles B. 2000. "Mentally Constructing What Already Exists: The Pure Land Thought of Chan Master Jixing Chewu 際醒徹悟 (1741–1810)." *Journal of the International Association of Buddhist Studies* 23 (1): 43–70.

Kim Yung Sik. 2015. "Zhu Xi on Scientific and Occult Subjects: Defining and Extending the Boundaries of Confucian Learning." In *Returning to Zhu Xi: Emerging Patterns within the Supreme Polarity*, edited by David Jones and Jinli He, 121–46. Albany: SUNY Press.

Liji 禮記. 2011. In *Chinese Text Project*, edited by Donald Sturgeon. https://ctext.org/liji/zh.

Liu, JeeLoo. 2011. "The Is-Ought Correlation in Neo-Confucian Qi-Realism: How Normative Facts Exist in Natural States of Qi." *Contemporary Chinese Thought* 42, no. 1 (Fall): 60–77.

Liu, JeeLoo. 2014. "Was There Something in Nothingness? The Debate on the Primordial State between Daoism and Neo-Confucianism." In *Nothingness in Asian Philosophy*, edited by JeeLoo Liu and Douglas L. Berger, 181–96, New York: Routledge.

Liu, JeeLoo. 2018. *Neo-Confucianism: Metaphysics, Mind, and Morality*. Malden, MA: Wiley.

Lunyu 論語. 2011. In *Chinese Text Project*, edited by Donald Sturgeon. https://ctext.org/analects/zh.

Puett, Michael J. 2004. *To Become a God: Cosmology, Sacrifice, and Self-Divinization in Early China*. Cambridge: Harvard University Press.

Rickett, W. Allyn, trans. 1998. *Guanzi: Political, Economic, and Philosophical Essays from Early China*. Vol. 2. Princeton: Princeton University Press.
Roth, Harold D. 1999. *Original Tao*. New York: Columbia University Press.
Van Norden, Bryan W., trans. 2001. *Mengzi* (*Mencius*). In *Readings in Classical Chinese Philosophy*, edited by Philip J. Ivanhoe and Bryan W. Van Norden, 115–59. Indianapolis: Hackett.

Chapter 3

Anxiety, Curiosity, and the Fracturing of the Self

Descartes and Princess Elisabeth

Deborah J. Brown

INTRODUCTION

Anxiety—excessive worry or apprehension about the future—operates at both the microcosmic (personal) and macrocosmic (sociopolitical) level and the two are interconnected.[1] Sociologically, anxiety has been linked with modernity and Western culture, with its emphasis on competition, control, risk appetite, and a self-proclaimed tolerance for uncertainty and ambiguity. Modernity's contradictory reliance on expert systems combined with an individualistic drive toward each person becoming a critical "self-expert," informed by dubious and inconsistent sources of freely available information, has been identified as itself a source of anxiety, undermining the very trust in expertise and authority upon which so many Western societies now depend (Giddens 1991; Beck 1992; Foucault 1983; Rebughini 2021). This fracturing of the body politic is mirrored in the fractured self of the individual sufferer of pathological or generalized anxiety disorder, which, according to DSM 5,[2] is a persistent rather than occurrent response to threat, with debilitating physical and psychological effects, including sleeplessness, irritability, muscle fatigue, and excessive, uncontrollable worry that impairs functioning in social, occupational, or other important areas of life. If indeed personal and cultural anxiety are interconnected, what these trends suggest is that anxiety should not be defined as a mood disorder affecting individuals in isolation from their social and cultural circumstances, and that its treatment is a much more complex matter than we hitherto might have thought. As Rebughini (2021, 560) points out, the "cultural injunction to self-government: that is, a psychological attitude of self-accountability whereby the single individual is required to find a solution, or to take a decision, also in regard to problems outside his/her range of control or comprehension" is likely only to exacerbate rather than alleviate an individual's tendency toward anxiety.

This paper concerns a relatively brief moment in the history of European responses to anxiety—an exchange between René Descartes (1596–1650) and Princess Elisabeth of Bohemia (1618–1680) prompted by a prolonged illness of Elisabeth's affecting her spleen and lungs.[3] It was then diagnosed as melancholy—a catchall term encompassing every form of sorrow or grief of a transitory or habitual nature that causes a person to become sad, dull, vexed, anguished, and isolated.[4] But it was more Elisabeth's profound anxiety that she found debilitating and Descartes's initial endeavors to live up to his Hippocratic oath as her appointed "best doctor for my soul" (AT 3, 662; Shapiro 2007, 62) bear many of the marks and tensions of modern methods for treating anxiety through an individualized form of self-government. Her resistance to Descartes's remedies anticipate what would become a core principle of later feminist theorizing—that happiness and the good "in this life" cannot be obtained in the absence of favorable social and political conditions—although whether Elisabeth's reasoning qualifies as distinctively feminist is a further matter.[5] I consider their exchange through the lens of this focus on anxiety, how it influenced the development of Descartes's moral psychology culminating in *The Passions of the Soul* (1649), and how to read both Descartes's and Elisabeth's relationship to Stoicism and Elisabeth's relationship to feminism. Three themes emerge from their exchange that are particularly important for understanding their relationship to Stoic ethics. The first is that anxiety is rooted in an inappropriate affective relationship to time. The second is that uncertainty is symptomatic of a misalignment between microcosm and macrocosm. A third, more subterranean theme, is how Elisabeth's curiosity for knowledge shines through as an antidote for anxiety. It is for this latter reason that it is she, not Descartes, who is more sympathetic to "reason-dominant" remedies for mood disorders. Despite her confirmation that there are "passions that carry us to reasonable actions" (AT 4, 290; Shapiro 2007, 111), it is the good use of her intellect and will that she experiences as providing the best relief for anxiety.[6] There is no inconsistency here, for anxiety, being an excess of fear produced by "some vapours," is among the defects of the passions that both she and Descartes can agree affect the ability of reason to perform its natural functions (AT 3, 685; Shapiro 2007, 68; AT 4, 201–2; Shapiro 2007, 87). Overall, an investigation into how Descartes and Elisabeth navigate the subject of anxiety shows them to be grappling with a very modern dilemma—how to live well in the face of an unchangeable past and an uncertain and uncontrollable future. Grounded in a very real problem of praxis—how to apply in practice the theoretical understanding of the passions she and Descartes develop together to repair the psychological damage caused by her circumstances—their exchange reveals many of the tensions present in ancient and modern deliberations concerning anxiety and its ills.

ANXIETY: HISTORY AND MECHANISMS

Historically, anxiety has a much longer history than that to which modernity can lay claim. Crocq (2015, 320) finds it implicitly referred to in Hippocrates's description of phobias such as nocturnal terrors and explicitly discussed in Cicero's *Tusculan Disputations*, where anxiety (*angor*, from the verb, *ango*, "to constrict") is listed among the *aegritudines*—disorders or maladies of the soul. For Seneca, anxiety afflicts those who put themselves in fortune's power. "We ought to make ourselves adaptable, so that we do not become too fond of the plans we have formed . . . for obstinacy, from which fortune often wrests some concession, must needs be anxious and unhappy" (*De tranquillitate animi*, 14.1; Inwood and Gerson 1988, 243). For both the Stoics and Epicureans, attaining freedom from anxiety (ataraxia), particularly, anxiety toward death, was the path toward tranquility of the soul (*tranquillitas animi*). The solution to anxiety was to withdraw the mind "from all externals into itself," live in the present, for "nothing happens to the wise man contrary to his expectations," even when his desires are frustrated because he has not promised himself success (*De tranquillitate animi*, 13.3; Inwood and Gerson 1988, 243).

The interest in anxiety within the Hellenistic schools is important for evaluating the correspondence dating from around July 1644 between Princess Elisabeth and Descartes. Elisabeth, the eldest daughter of the protestants, Frederick V, nicknamed "Winter King" for his short-lived reign in 1620, and Elizabeth Stuart, daughter of James I, had good reason to suffer chronic anxiety. As Shapiro (2007, 7 16) notes, Elisabeth's happiness was marred by the family's exile from the Palatinate following her father's defeat in 1620 at the hands of Catholic forces at the start of the Thirty Years War. The family sought refuge at The Hague with Frederick's maternal uncle, Maurice of Nassau. Elisabeth undertook to manage many of her family's affairs, hoping to restore their fortunes but without success. Several of her siblings died young or in tragic circumstances. One brother, Edward, converted to Catholicism, outraging Elisabeth, and another, Philip, stabbed a suitor of his mother, causing Elisabeth, who defended him, to be sent away. Elisabeth played an active political role, corresponding on behalf of the family, advocating for her brothers fighting for Charles I in the English Civil Wars, one of whom, Rupert, was imprisoned, and negotiating her siblings' marriages. Following unsuccessful marriage negotiations which would have required Elisabeth to convert, Elisabeth entered the Lutheran convent at Herford in 1660, assuming the role of abbess in 1667 and successfully managing the convent's estates until her death. When her correspondence with Descartes turns to the subject of her ill-health, including a nasty and persistent cough, and to their shared interest in Stoicism, it is in connection with the melancholy induced by her family affairs.

Much has been written about Elisabeth's melancholy and how it served as the catalyst for what many see as Descartes's Neo-Stoic theorizing about the passions, virtue ethics, and analysis of happiness (true or sovereign contentment).[7] Melancholy was a prominent subject for discussion in the early modern period, bringing into sharp focus the perceived clash between passion and reason. Popular books such as Thomas Wright's *The Passions of the Minde in Generall* (1598) and Robert Burton's encyclopaedic *The Anatomy of Melancholy* (1621) associated melancholy primarily with a failure of reason: an excessive and irrational fear and sorrow resulting in the production of too much black bile in the spleen that infects the blood, stomach, bowels, and heart (Jeffery 2017). Thus, melancholy was essentially a psychosomatic disorder requiring both cognitive and somatic remedies. Symptoms of melancholy included abulia (diminished motivation), languor, inactivity, timidity, and depression. But melancholy was also associated with delusions, phobias, and excessive fear. It is not sadness alone but the sadness-fear pathway that defines and sustains melancholy, suggesting that anxiety and melancholy are intimately connected. As Burton writes (cited in Crocq 2015, 326): "Cousin-german [first cousin] to *sorrow*, is *fear*, or rather a sister, *fidus Achates,*[8] and continual companion—an assistant and a principal agent in procuring of the mischief; a cause and symptom as the other." In diagnosing and treating melancholy, it was thus considered important to consider both elements—fear and sorrow.

From Elisabeth's description of her ailments, we can discern that she had been diagnosed by her doctors as melancholic and that she was prepared to accept their diagnosis as reflecting a *temperamental* condition—i.e., what Burton (1621/1927, 125) would refer to as "habitual" melancholy, ingrained and difficult to remove. She attributes her indisposition both to her circumstances—"the interests of her house"—and to the "weakness" (AT 4, 208; Shapiro 2007, 88) and "curse" (At 4, 234; Shapiro 2007, 94) of her sex. Melancholy is the diagnosis most commentators, including me,[9] have accepted. This almost exclusive interest in Elisabeth as a melancholic is, however, questionable, for at least two reasons. First, Elisabeth is a somewhat atypical melancholic. She is busy, not still, energetic, not dull, taking charge of the complex affairs of her family, complaining that she does not have time for the rest that Descartes and her doctors prescribe. She proclaims that she does not know "how to avoid [thinking about her misfortunes] without sinning against my duty" (AT 4, 234; Shapiro 2007, 93), baulking at Descartes's suggestion that she find repose from her misfortunes through the exclusive use of her senses and imagination diverted toward objects that will cause joy and pleasure. She professes to need the distraction of study and intellectual stimulation, not laziness, to avoid dwelling on misfortune, and to finding the "antidote to melancholy" in her epistolary friendship with Descartes (AT 4, 233; Shapiro 2007, 93). All of this is highly interesting, for it reveals the strength of Elisabeth's curiosity for knowledge, even if she does not label it as such, and given the nature of curiosity, it makes sense that she would find in it the antidote she needs. Curiosity—an emotion that initiates the search for truth or knowledge—is a positive emotional response to uncertainty; anxiety, its negative evil twin.[10] Far from being timid or her reason diminished, she feels the "inconvenience of being but a little rational" which prevents her from finding "pleasures in common with those among whom I must live" and who are thus better able to make use of the sensory-based relaxation techniques that Descartes and her doctors prescribe (AT 4, 234; Shapiro 2007, 94).

Second, it is not so much melancholy that Elisabeth describes as debilitating as its attendant anxiety:

> I will continue by confessing to you also that, although I do not rest my felicity on things which depend on fortune or on the will of men at all, and although I do not judge myself to be absolutely wretched knowing I will never see my house in order or those near to me away from misery, I still do not know how to consider the injurious accidents that befall them under any other notion than that of evil, nor how to consider the useless efforts I make in their service without some sort of anxiety. This anxiety is no sooner calmed by reasoning than a new disaster produces another anxiety. If my life were entirely known to you, I think the fact that a sensitive mind, such as my own, has conserved itself for so long amidst so many difficulties, in a body so weak, with no counsel but that of her own reason and with no consolation but that of her own conscience, would seem more strange to you than the causes of this present malady. (AT 4: 209; Shapiro 2007, 89)

This passage, worth quoting in full, draws together a number of important themes. First, it is precisely the *cycle* of anxieties that Elisabeth finds exhausting and detrimental to her health. Whatever solution to her anxiety she chooses will have to be one that prepares her to meet any contingency with the right measure of its worth, which she later complains to Descartes is impossible in the absence of an "infinite science" (AT 4, 289; Shapiro 2007, 110; AT 4, 405; Shapiro 2007, 134). Even if she uses her reason wisely to deal with any one anxiety, another is soon upon her. Advocating that Elisabeth cast her eyes to the goods that can never be taken away from her, including the good use of her reason and freedom of the will (AT 4, 201–4; Shapiro 2007, 87–88), Descartes accepts the Stoic ideas about the independence of virtue and happiness from fortune. This relates to a second theme in the above passage, namely, that while it is true that Elisabeth expresses many anti-Stoic sentiments (Shapiro 2007, 89, n.47), she is committed both to the independence of happiness from fortune and to the power of reason to conserve the body, however "weak" or "cursed" hers may be. Rather than this being an inconsistency in Elisabeth's analysis (between her commitment to both the independence of virtue and happiness from fortune and her commitment to the obstructing force of external circumstances), her comments reflect more the common gap between espoused and enacted values, a problem of praxis which Descartes later in his correspondence attempts to address. But at this earlier point in their exchange, Descartes proceeds only to reassure Elisabeth that he is "not one of those cruel philosophers [i.e., Stoics] who want their sage to be insensible" (AT 4, 201; Shapiro 2007, 87). His subsequent recommendations are focused not on trying to eradicate her anxiety but to managing its consequences—a distinctively Stoic technique.[11] It is not necessary to eradicate passions to be happy or virtuous: "it suffices that we render them subject to reason, and when we have thus tamed them they are sometimes the more useful the more they tend to excess" (AT 4, 287; Shapiro 2007, 109). The question then is how to tame a passion when it depends on movements of the animal spirits in the body over which the soul has no direct control.[12]

There is, Descartes tells Elisabeth, only one remedy for "domestic enemies": "to divert one's imagination and one's senses as much as possible and to employ only the understanding alone to consider them when one is obliged to by prudence" (AT 4, 218; Shapiro 2007, 91). The use of cognitive exercises to construct new associations between "useful" thoughts and movements of the spirits was widely accepted in both the medical and philosophical literature and generally thought of as characteristically Stoic. Epictetus taught his students how to engage in imaginative exercises to understand unfortunate situations without distress and to use premeditation to imagine worst-case scenarios to reduce the element of surprise that is often a trigger for distress.[13] In an illuminating passage, Descartes goes further, however, explaining how this technique addresses anxiety in terms consistent with his mechanical philosophy. In *The Passions of the Soul* he asserts that unlike his predecessors he will approach the passions "en physicien"—i.e., as a physicist (AT 11, 325). Somatically, anxiety is grounded in a constriction of the heart (hence, its etymological root in the verb *ango*). In the person disposed to tragedies and the sorrows they cause, the heart closes up, blocking circulation, presumably because of a muscular contraction, a tensing up, that reduces heat.[14] This, in turn, causes larger particles of blood to compact and get caught in the spleen, while smaller, more fiery particles agitate the lungs, causing a dry cough. These effects "in the long term would give good cause for fear" (AT 4, 219; Shapiro 2007, 91). This, for Descartes, is the sorrow-fear pathway bridging melancholy and anxiety. By contrast, the person who turns her imagination away from cares to objects of joy and regards them "without passion," except when prudence demands, can reduce these effects on the heart (AT 4, 219; Shapiro 2007, 92). It is thus only in the context of the sorrow-fear pathway that Descartes's remedies as remedies to anxiety make sense. Although the doctor's remedies for flushing out the spleen and lungs (e.g., the waters of Spa, diet, and exercise) will "cure the part of the blood that causes the obstructions," they will not address the root cause of anxiety and its effects on the heart and so must be combined with a therapy to "clear the mind of all unhappy thoughts" (AT 4, 220; Shapiro 2007, 92). The undergirding mechanical analysis provides the foundation for his subsequent emphasis on the need for Elisabeth to address the philosophical bases for her anxiety. But while she acknowledges Descartes's suggestion that it is the imagination (not understanding or reason) that represents things as upsetting, she objects that she cannot eliminate the element of *surprise* in misfortunes, even when they are foreseen. It is the surprise factor of the unending sequence of crises that she has to endure that always affects her for "several months" (AT 4, 234; Shapiro 2007, 93). To address this, Descartes suggests, she needs to rethink what constitutes an effective way to spend time.

TEMPORAL THEMES

The cycle of anxieties Elisabeth describes suggests a misalignment between her conception of living and its relationship to time. She views her "life" (e.g., "*If my life were entirely known to you*"; AT 4, 208; Shapiro 2007, 89) as the culmination of her past experiences and events and all the calamities with which she has had to deal. She views taking time out from her service to her family by diverting her imagination and senses to things that do not require thinking about as "sinning against her duty" (AT 4, 233; Shapiro 2007, 93). Descartes tries to steer her back, pointing out that using the imagination and senses to think about pleasant subjects "*is not to waste time but to employ it well*" (AT 4, 220; Shapiro 2007, 92; my emphasis). These comments imply that Descartes sees Elisabeth as wasting time by using her understanding excessively in the service of her family when it only leads to melancholy and anxiety. In a letter of October 6, 1645, he admonishes her for comparing herself to those who give her cause to complain (those "men who commit errors") instead of those who give her satisfaction, but the point is put in terms that suggest it is her sense of wasting time on these matters that is making her unnecessarily anxious:

> The constitution of our nature is such that our mind needs a lot of rest so that it can usefully devote a few moments to seeking the truth, and it will be numbed instead of polished if it is applied in too much study, and so we ought not to measure the time we were able to use in instructing ourselves by the number of hours we have to ourselves. Rather, it seems to me, we should measure it by the example of what we see commonly occurring with others, as being a mark of the ordinary comportment of the human mind. (AT 4, 307; Shapiro 2007, 116–17)

It is only in the context of Elisabeth's chronic anxiety that we can make sense of Descartes's recommendation that they read Seneca's *De Vita Beata*. Stoic philosophy would have seemed to anyone in the period as addressing precisely the anxiety produced by constant misfortune and an unpredictable, uncertain, and uncontrollable future. Descartes recommends this text to help make his thoughts on the matter more exact (AT 4, 252; Shapiro 2007, 96). The exercise initially disappoints both. Descartes is disappointed because Seneca does not clarify what *vivere beata* means or distinguish *beatitude* (true happiness) from *vivre heureusement*—living happily. Living happily could be construed as dependent on good fortune. In his more extended exposition, Descartes approves of Seneca's warnings against following custom and example more than reason in the matter of how to live and of his advice to use judgment in taking the advice of the wisest (AT 4, 271–73; Shapiro 2007, 101–2). But he finds Seneca inexact on the question of what it is to live in accordance with nature. For Descartes, this is living in accordance with the order of nature established by God, but that too needs explication. He finds most merit in the suggestion that the *truly happy person is one, who by benefit of reason, neither desires nor fears,* but sees this recommendation as lacking in reasons why this should be so (AT 4, 274; Shapiro 2007, 103). In the end, Descartes finds it necessary to distinguish true happiness from the sovereign good, the former being a consequence of the latter and that which attracts us to the sovereign good. Later, we learn that the sovereign good is nothing distinct from the exercise of virtue (Brown 2006, 19).

Elisabeth, meanwhile, is disappointed because she reads Seneca as sloppy in his method and as preaching that "riches and luxury" like his own do not prevent one from attaining true happiness rather than showing the "shortest path" to it. But a deeper level, Elisabeth is also unconvinced of the possibility of rising above one's circumstances or social expectations without passion. Citing Epicurus's struggle to convince his friends that he felt no pain from his kidney stones, Elisabeth claims that he could not escape his role as a philosopher or the dictates of his hedonism, but that on these occasions "regret seems to me inevitable, and the knowledge that to err is human is as natural as it is to be sick cannot protect us" (AT 2, 270; Shapiro 2007, 100).

We will come back to Descartes's and Elisabeth's reading of Seneca. For the moment, it is apt to consider that in suggesting that they read *De Vita Beata*, Descartes has possibly chosen the wrong book. *De Brevitate Vitae* would have been a better choice for investigating how to live well in the face of inevitable uncertainty—the root cause of Elisabeth's anxiety. Seneca is there concerned to show how living—or rather not living—can be affected by the wrong attitude toward time—a theme which permeates the exchange between Descartes and Elisabeth.

First, there is in both Seneca and Descartes an analogy between time and commodities like money—finite resources that can be spent well or badly. Recall: "*This is not to waste time but to employ it well.*" As a commodity, time requires careful self-management. In *De Brevitate Vitae*[15] (2014, 110, sec. 1.4), Seneca writes:

> Just as impressive and princely wealth is squandered in an instant when it passes into the hands of a poor manager, but wealth however modest grows through careful deployment if it is entrusted to a responsible guardian, just so our lifetime offers ample scope to the person who maps it out well.

Anxiety is one sure way to waste time: "how much time has been lost *to groundless anguish*, foolish pleasure, greedy desire, the charms of society; how little is left to you from your own store of time. You'll come to realize that you're dying before your time" (2014, 112, sec. 3.2; my emphasis). Preoccupation with affairs is antithetical to living. Quoting the "greatest of poets,"[16] Seneca notes (2014, 111, sec. 2,2): "'Scant is the part of life in which we live.' All the rest of existence is not living but merely time." What, for Seneca, is the antidote to this kind of not living? Answer: To live in the present, properly understood. "The greatest impediment to living is expectancy, which relies on tomorrow and wastes today. You map out what is in fortune's hand but let slip what's in your own hand. What are you aiming at? What's your goal? All that's to come lies in uncertainty: live right now" (2014, 119, sec. 9.1). To live in the present does not mean ignoring either the past or the future—preoccupation with the present is also a vice—but to be one's best self in the present.

> It takes a tranquil and untroubled mind to roam freely over all the parts of life; but preoccupied minds, as if under the yoke, cannot turn around and look backward. Their life therefore disappears into an abyss; and just as it does no good to pour any amount of liquid into a vessel if there's nothing at the bottom to receive and keep it, so it makes no difference how much time we are given if there's nowhere for it to settle, and it's allowed to pass through the cracks and

> holes in the mind. . . . So the preoccupied are concerned with the present alone, and it is so fleeting that it can't be grasped, and even that little amount is stolen away from them because they're pulled in many different directions. (2014, 120–21, sec. 10.5)

To be one's best self in the present requires minimizing the extent to which one's satisfaction depends on the satisfaction of one's desires, of being in a state of constant "expectancy." It is also to embody the lessons of the past, keeping them active in one's present decision-making and retained in memory, like liquid in a waterproof jar. "Living right now" thus does not rely on an "absence of representations of the future" (Rebughini 2019, 560) as if uncertainty can be managed away, but rather on using one's experience to moderate one's desires while tempering one's expectations by accepting the uncertainty of the future. In *De Tranquillitate Animi*, Seneca gives the following examples of tempered expectations: "*I shall set sail unless something intervenes.*" . . . "*I shall become praetor unless something hinders me*." It is in making plans qualified by an appropriate understanding of contingency that one insures oneself against disappointment and the disruptive effects of surprise which Elisabeth notes is a key element of her own anxieties. Thus, it was that when Zeno heard all his possessions had been lost in a shipwreck, he responded: "fortune bids me to follow philosophy bearing a lighter load" (*De tranquillitate animi*, 14.2; Inwood and Gerson 1988, 244).

For similar reasons, Descartes recommends to Elisabeth that she not reflect on the causes of her past anxieties as evil, that she instead reflect—after sleep has calmed her emotions, (another example of using time well)—to see all the benefits she has derived from her mishaps. She should consider especially how adversity has provided her more occasions to cultivate her mind than have those with great prosperity, to think how her life now is richer for her past adversities (AT 4, 237; Shapiro 2007, 94–95). Where Elisabeth thinks she requires infinite knowledge of all the contingencies of life to avoid anxiety, Descartes thinks it is sufficient to use one's imagination to imagine the worst outcomes and be prepared to suffer them (AT 4, 411; Shapiro 2007, 137). The independence of the "sovereign felicity" from fortune (AT 4, 252; Shapiro 2007, 96) is an idea that both Descartes and Elisabeth profess to accept, but Descartes suspects that Elisabeth is not able to put this idea into practice. Yet, it is hard to see how by not engaging her understanding and instead distracting herself through her senses and imagination, Elisabeth can be guided to close this theory-practice gap.

In the *Discourse on Method*, the correspondence with Elisabeth, and subsequent *Passions of the Soul*, these ideas about what it is to live well in time form the backbone of Descartes's account of how we can remain happy, despite the capriciousness of fortune. In the *Discourse*, they are contained in

Descartes's three rules of conduct: (1) to make the best use of one's mind; (2) to execute what reason demands with a "firm and constant resolution"; and (3) to keep in mind that the goods one does not possess are outside one's control and to limit one's desires accordingly. These messages are repeated in the correspondence with Elisabeth, where it is argued that by these means one can mitigate regret and repentance, which Elisabeth identified as among "the principal obstacles to true happiness" (AT 4, 288; Shapiro 2007, 110).[17] Anxiety is not itself classified a basic emotion in *The Passions of the Soul*, most likely because it is an excess of fear directed at a future object, and thus a defect of basic passions (sadness and desire) in combination.[18] Desire is a future-oriented passion, one which we cannot as embodied creatures dependent on our environments live without. In *The Passions of the Soul*, Descartes defines desire as an "agitation of the soul caused by the spirits, which disposes the soul to want for the future the things it represents as agreeable" (AT 11, 392). Regret, repentance, and remorse pertain to the past—regret is for goods lost; repentance for one's mistaken past actions; and remorse for mistaken past actions resulting from irresolution. These passions are, however, interconnected and connected to anxiety. Because the future is unknowable and because in this embodied state, vain desires are unavoidable,[19] anxiety about the future and subsequent regret, remorse, and repentance about the past, seem inevitable.

In many respects, Descartes's proposal for how to break the cycle of vain desires, regret, repentance, remorse, and anxiety, is a classically Stoic one—to make "a virtue of necessity" (AT 6, 26). These negative, backward-looking emotions are premised on a false metaphysical picture related to time and possibility. The principle of alternative possibilities makes us think that we could have chosen to act differently and that the way the universe unfolded could have been otherwise and would have been better for it. But this is to fail to understand how providence works. In a providential system, things always happen of necessity and for the best (Brown 2006, 172). Phenomenologically, irresolution contributes to our false assumptions about possibilities because it makes us experience our indecisiveness as if we were operating in a garden of forking paths. There is no such garden. We should recognize that there is only one outcome at any point in time and try our best to align our desires with what God wills for us (AT 4, 294; Shapiro 2007, 113).

> I am persuaded that resolution and promptness are virtues very necessary for matters already begun. One does not have cause to fear what one does not know, for often things about which we have been most apprehensive before knowing them turn out to be better than those we desired. Thus, the best thing in this case is to trust oneself to divine providence and to let oneself be led by it. (AT 4, 415; Shapiro 2007, 138)

"A firm and constant resolution" to act always in the way we judge best is hence the only preventative for minimizing regret, remorse, and repentance. This will be so, Descartes assures Elisabeth, even if we are mistaken on occasion about what we ought to do. "It is . . . not necessary that our reason never been mistaken. It suffices that our conscience testifies that we have judged to be the best. Thus, virtue alone is sufficient to make us content in this life" (AT 4, 266–67; Shapiro 2007, 99) If fortune opposes us, "we will at least have the satisfaction of having lost nothing by our fault" (AT 4, 285; Shapiro 2007, 108). The self-satisfaction derived from using our reason and will to the best of our ability is one way to live well in time despite the chance of failure. But it is also, you might now suspect, a far cry from Descartes's initial sensory-based remedies.

Embracing one's place in the providential order, accepting that what did not come to pass was never intended by God, is one way to stop oneself from investing too much in the success of desires that depend for their satisfaction on conditions outside our control. There are, Descartes tells Elisabeth, only two things required to judge well, and in explicating these things, he makes clear their remedial effects for anxiety. Simply, these are to know the truth and to make a habit of remembering and acquiescing in this knowledge whenever the occasion requires. The truth in question is threefold: that there is a God on whom all depends, whose perfections are infinite and decrees infallible; that the nature of the mind is more noble than that of the body, which is necessary to avoid fearing death and to detach one's affection from worldly things; and to understand the vast extent of the universe. To want to control one's future is simply the "impertinent assumption" of those who want to counsel God on how to conduct the world, which only leads to "*an infinity of anxieties and annoyances*" (AT 4, 293; Shapiro 2007, 12; my emphasis). That our vain desires and anxieties are implicated in this sort of thinking is grounds for taking stock. All the passions, he writes, "represent to us the goods they incite us to seek as much greater than they actually are, and that the pleasures of the body are never as lasting as those of the mind." Hence, we should, where possible, suspend judgment until the passion abates to avoid being deceived by false appearances. But this knowledge, Descartes realizes, is not sufficient for praxis—for practicing the truth one preaches. For that one needs a "firm habit of believing" and habituating ourselves to attach positive thoughts to our feelings, which can only come through the exercise of virtue (AT 4, 295–96; Shapiro 2007, 113).

Elisabeth, for her part, is unsure of the theory, not just the practice. "In running from repentance," she responds, "we run the risk of losing the desire to correct ourselves" (AT 4, 322; Shapiro 2007, 123). She objects to the usefulness of this knowledge, even if it is based in philosophical truths. The truth of God, she says, cannot console us about the evils of men arising from their free will. Knowledge of the immortality and nobility of the soul could make us seek death as easily as despising it. And if the knowledge of the universe contained in Descartes's physics detaches our affections from what we see, it also detaches the idea of providence from the idea of God (AT 4, 303; Shapiro 2007, 114–15). It is unclear what exactly Elisabeth is alluding to in this last point, whether it is an allusion to Descartes's rejection of final causality which perhaps robs us of the ability to wonder at the natural world as the works of God in quite the same way,[20] or whether she is alluding to the controversy over whether providence operates only at the global level (*sub specie aeternitatis*) or must work out locally as well, which for her, it appears not to be doing. In any case, Descartes denies all three of Elisabeth's retorts, objecting to the idea that the decisions of men are independent of God's will[21]; that reason could instruct us to prefer death since it cannot know whether life after death is more felicitous; and that considering the extent of the universe could separate providence from the idea of God when the former concerns finite, expendable powers, and God, infinite (and thus greater) power (AT 4, 314–16; Shapiro 2007, 120–21). Elisabeth stands her ground on many of her objections, especially on what she sees as the incoherence of Descartes's compatibilism,[22] and the discussion lapses into a stalemate.

Obtaining the right balance between microcosm and macrocosm is a larger undertaking, and despite Descartes's insistence that Elisabeth practice the arts of self-government to alleviate her anxiety, the exercise of virtue requires that she turn her attention more to the macrocosms of which she is a part.

WHOLES AND PARTS AND FRACTURED SELVES

It was suggested above that *De Vita Beata* was an odd selection for Descartes and Elisabeth to read in the context of attempting to alleviate Elisabeth's anxiety and chronic ill-health. But it does enable them to reflect on the nature of the good, and its relationship to happiness. Seneca is there attempting to navigate a path between Zeno, who argued that virtue must be independent of pleasure, and Epicurus's hedonism, on the relationship between the sovereign good (virtue) and true contentment (beatitude). Descartes entangles himself on the ancient question of what Epicurus means by pleasure (*voluptas* in Seneca)—whether it consists in the titillations produced by the senses or the more moderate and sober pleasures associated with the exercise of virtue. Descartes thereby skirts around the deeper question raised by Seneca, who, holding that only the sage possesses true pleasure, denies that one can act virtuously if pleasure is conceived of as the end or goal of action (Dyson 2010). Interestingly, Descartes connects the view represented by Zeno and Seneca with the very psychosomatic illness—melancholy—Elisabeth has been diagnosed with, writing that only "melancholic people or minds entirely detached from bodies" would be able to follow Zeno's conception of the good, which is virtue without pleasure (AT 4, 276–77; Shapiro 2007, 104).

Anxiety, trouble, and repentance often accompany false pleasures, Descartes continues, which is why Epicurus is mistakenly thought to teach vice. What Seneca should have realized, Descartes's suggests, is that virtue and contentment instead must work together, like aiming at a bull's-eye (virtue) for the sake of the prize (contentment). We cannot, he suggests, aim our action directly at virtue without its promise of the sovereign contentment, for virtue alone cannot motivate an embodied being. But neither can we aim directly at contentment without virtue, for that leads us both to false pleasures and to a false kind of happiness. This discussion, reminiscent of the exchange in the Middle Ages between Henry of Ghent and Godfrey of Fontaines on the question of whether if one is motivated by happiness to do the right thing, one can be said to act for the right reason and thus virtuously, elude Descartes and will not detain us here. What is interesting for our purposes is the similarity implied between melancholics and "minds entirely detached from bodies." Both represent a fracturing of the self—the disembodied mind because of a metaphysical separation and the melancholic because of a psychosomatic mood disorder that deprives a person of the capacity to derive pleasure from acting virtuously. Those whose reason is mistress of their passions can take pleasure even in the worst of their afflictions, in a way similar to how we enjoy tragedies as much as comedies even when they bring us to tears (AT 4, 202–3; Shapiro 2007, 87; AT 4, 118; Shapiro 2007, 118).[23] Taking Descartes at his word that virtue is impossible without true contentment, it follows that the melancholic should be incapable of virtue. It is thus imperative that Elisabeth get the house of her body in order because "perfect health" is "the foundation of all the other goods one can have in this life" (AT 4, 220; Shapiro 2007, 92). Nor can there be any simple rationalist solution to maladies like melancholy or anxiety. Pitting reason against one's "weak" or "cursed" body is part of the problem, not the solution.

Descartes is sometimes accused of rendering happiness and virtue entirely independent of other people, and this indeed is one point Elisabeth challenges him on, but this is not quite fair.[24] First, friendship is important and often motivates courageous self-sacrifice (AT 4, 203; Shapiro 2007, 87). In *The Passions of the Soul*, the mechanism underwriting friendships and other social unities is love:

> Love is an emotion of the soul . . . that incites it to join itself by will [*se joindre de volonté*] to objects that seem suitable [*convenables*] to it. . . . By the word "will," I mean here not desire—which is a different passion, directed to the future—but the assent [*consentement*] by which you consider yourself from this

> very moment so joined to what you love that you imagine a whole of which you think yourself but one part, and the object of your love the other (AT 11, 387; CSM 1, 356).[25]

Second, in their correspondence, the existence of social wholes is taken as a precondition for judging and acting well, and thus, for true contentment:

> After having recalled the goodness of God, the immortality of our souls and the greatness of the universe, there is also one more truth the knowledge of which seems to me quite useful. This is that, even though each of us is a person separate from others and, by consequence, with interests that are in some manner distinct from the rest of the world, one must, all the same, think that one does not know how to subsist alone and that one is, in effect, one part of the universe and, particularly even, one part of this earth, one part of this state, and this society, and this family, to which one is joined by his home, by his oath, by his birth. It is always necessary to prefer the interests of the whole, of which one is a part, to those of one's person in particular, though with measure and discretion. For one would be wrong to expose oneself to a great evil in order to procure only a small good for one's parents or country. . . . But if one related everything to oneself, one would not fear harming other men greatly when one wanted to take something small for oneself. One would have no true friends, no faithfulness, and in general no virtue. On the other hand, in considering oneself as part of the public, one takes pleasure in acting well toward everyone, and one does not fear exposing one's life for the service of others when the occasion occurs. That is, one would lose one's soul, if one could, in order to save others. And so this consideration is the source of all the most heroic actions. (AT 4, 293; Shapiro 2007, 112)

Descartes's social mereology mirrors at the macrocosmic level the unity of mind and body at the microcosmic level. As an individual person becomes separated from others with whom they form a social whole, so too does their mind behave as if it were distinct from the body. Each member of these pairs is, however, in some sense "incomplete" without the other (AT 7, 222; CSM 2, 156–57). While the above passage suggests that the body politic is a matter of choice in that whether one relates everything to oneself or not is in some sense up to each of us, a later comment suggests that, for Descartes, it is part of the institution of nature. A person needs only prudence (practical rationality or rational self-interest) to act for the sake of the whole:

> For God has so established the order of things and conjoined men together in so tight a society that even if each person related himself wholly to himself, and had no charity for others, he would not ordinarily fail to work for them in everything that would be in his power, so long as he used prudence, and principally

> if he lived in a time when mores were not corrupted. (AT 4, 316–17; Shapiro 2007, 122)

The impossibility of any real divergence between what is good for an individual and good for the whole is a characteristically Stoic idea, tracing originally from Plato's idea of the cosmos as a living animal (*Timaeus* 30a6-c1) through Democritus to Seneca (2015) and Marcus Aurelius (2013). It is what distinguishes, as it does for Descartes, the apotheosis of virtue—heroic virtue—from the cardinal virtues. There is, moreover, reciprocity between acting heroically—living pro bono publico, as the Stoics would say—and acting for the sake of one's own interests. What is good for the whole is always good for the part—a maxim by which one ought to live according to Marcus Aurelius: "What is brought by the nature of the whole and what maintains that nature is good for each part of nature. Just as the changes in the elements maintain the universe, so too do the changes in the compounds. Let these things satisfy you; let these always be your doctrines" (Marcus Aurelius 2013, 10).

For her part, again, Elisabeth is resistant to Descartes's social mereology providing her with a solution to her problems. While acknowledging that seeing oneself as part of a larger whole is the "source of all generous actions," she finds it little help when it comes to calculating how much one should risk oneself for the sake of the whole and how to overcome the fact that the evils one brings against oneself will seem greater because of the distinctness of its idea, compared to the benefit that might accrue to the whole. A particularly telling example she gives is that of acting in accordance with the "impertinent established laws of civility" while residing in the country when she would prefer to write letters, study, and enjoy her private leisure (Shapiro 2007, 115). Descartes's response is to point out that if we consider ourselves as part of the whole, we partake in the goods of the whole as well as in those of our part, whereas, since evil is a privation, we risk nothing because we do not thereby partake in any defect in which evil in the whole consists. We can always therefore derive the satisfaction of virtue, exercised in the form of Christian charity, in helping to alleviate the sadness and suffering of others with whom we are joined (Shapiro 2007, 117). Reason, he admits, cannot be very precise about the degree to which we ought to be interested in the public good, but this is not essential. When we have the capacity for prudence, conscience, and acting in such a way that we esteem ourselves neither too much nor too little, we can always derive some satisfaction (AT 4, 316–17; Shapiro 2007, 121–22). That one might restore the unity of one's self, fractured by melancholy and anxiety, through identification with and service to the larger wholes of which one is a part, is a message that Elisabeth is perhaps simply too jaded by her circumstances to hear.

CONCLUSION: INFLUENCES, STOICISM, FEMINISM

There is no doubt, as many commentators have pointed out, that Descartes's developed thoughts on the passions and ethics would not have had the sophistication that they do without the challenges Elisabeth raised. In *The Passions of the Soul*, the developed account of virtue—generosity, or legitimate self-esteem—is part of a picture that offers the reader a way to calibrate the esteem one has for objects outside oneself against the supreme value of the will used well in accordance with reason. There is, as Jacqueline Broad and I have argued,[26] a social dimension to Descartes's account of generosity, which ensures an internal, not merely contingent connection between the esteem we hold ourselves in because of our free wills and the goodwill we have toward others. There is also some recognition of the need for equitable social conditions to make virtue truly possible, although these ideas are only developed with any satisfaction by later, feminist authors who saw in Descartes's ethics liberation from assumptions about the weakness of their sex. The themes explored in Descartes's response to Elisabeth's anxiety—developing the right attitude toward uncertainty, freeing oneself from vain desires relying on fortune for their success, relying on providence to avoid debilitating regret and repentance, figure prominently in *The Passions of the Soul*, as do the cognitive exercises by which reason can gain, albeit indirectly, dominion over unruly passions. To read Elisabeth as anti-Stoic and Descartes as Neo-Stoic is too simple. Both rely on Stoic ideas when it suits, and while there are clearly other influences, including that of Aristotle, on the issue of how to deal with anxiety, it is the Stoics who have more to say and more to offer in helping Elisabeth navigate her problems of practice.

Is Elisabeth in her resistance to Descartes's theorizing about reason and the passions exhibiting a feminist attitude? She cannot see how to free herself from the sadness, frustration, and anxiety caused by not being able to put her house in order, but these are not couched as problems peculiar to women. It has been pointed out that hers is a standpoint of a woman trying to operate in ways that many would see in the period as "above her sex," and there can be no denying this.[27] To my mind, however, she is more a feminist by example than by letter, and I have offered her indefatigable curiosity for knowledge as a case where she transcended social expectations for her sex and made herself a role model to others. Her curiosity for knowledge as a woman is perhaps more relevant to feminist theorizing about the period than her challenges to Descartes's assumptions about self government, for it shows her commitment to the value and necessity to health for both sexes of education and intellectual stimulation. The latter remained for her the only truly effective antidote to what would otherwise have been a crippling cycle of anxieties.

NOTES

1. Funding for this research was supported by an Australian Research Council (ARC) Discovery Grant (DP190100019)—*The Philosophical Foundations of Women's Rights: A New History, 1600–1750*. I am grateful for the support of the ARC and the University of Queensland, an editor of this volume, David Rondel, to the audience of the *Reinventing Women's Nature: Early Modern Feminism and its Roots* conference at UCLA in 2023 for their feedback, and to Calvin Normore, the best doctor for *my* soul.

2. American Psychiatric Association (2013).

3. All references to the correspondence are drawn from Lisa Shapiro's (2007) translation with original Adam and Tannery (1909) numbers. Additional translations indicated by "CSM" numbers are from Cottingham, Stoothoff, and Murdoch (1984–1985) translations of Descartes's philosophical writings. If not otherwise indicated, they are my own.

4. Robert Burton's (1621/1927, 125) definition reads: "*Melancholy*, the subject of our present discourse, is either in disposition or in habit. In disposition, is that transitory *Melancholy* which goes and comes upon every small occasion of sorrow, need, sickness, trouble, fear, grief, passion, or perturbation of the mind, any manner of care, discontent, or thought, which causes anguish, dulness, heaviness and vexation of spirit, any ways opposite to pleasure, mirth, joy, delight, causing forwardness in us, or a dislike. In which equivocal and improper sense, we call him melancholy, that is dull, sad, sour, lumpish, ill-disposed, solitary, any way moved, or displeased. And from these melancholy dispositions no man living is free, no Stoic, none so wise, none so happy, none so patient, so generous, so godly, so divine, that can vindicate himself; so well-composed, but more or less, some time or other, he feels the smart of it. Melancholy in this sense is the character of Mortality. . . . This *Melancholy* of which we are to treat, is a habit, a serious ailment, a settled humour, as Aurelianus and others call it, not errant, but fixed: and as it was long increasing, so, now being (pleasant or painful) grown to a habit, it will hardly be removed."

5. A move that some (e.g., Schneck 2019) see as a return to Peripatetic ideas about the relationship between happiness and fortune and contrary to a feminist interpretation like Broad's (2002, 15). Most commentators now agree, however, that Elisabeth is a philosopher in her own right, not merely a muse to Descartes. See Shapiro (1999).

6. Even late in their correspondence when she is feeling healthy and restored (29 November 1646; AT 4578–79; Shapiro 2007, 151), Elisabeth insists on how she has used knowledge and reason over her "occult imagination" to preserve the felicity of her mind.

7. On Elisabeth's relationship to Stoicism, see Shapiro's Introduction (2007, 33–35; 46–48), Alanen (2004), Rutherford (2004; 2014), Kambouchner (2014).

8. Burton R. (1621/1826, v. I: 142–43) Achates was the faithful [*fidus*] follower of Aeneas (Virgil Aeneid, 6. 158). From Crocq (2015, 321).

9. Brown 2006, 18ff.

10. Descartes's attention to wonder, the first of all passions, and recognition of its essential role in motivating and sustaining scientific investigation, is a dominant

theme in *The Passions of the Soul*. See Schmitter (2002) and Brown (2006, c.6). I prefer to use "curiosity" in this context, even though Descartes seems to display an Augustinian distrust of the term, confusing it with an insatiable lust for knowledge (AT 10, 499–500). Descartes's notion of wonder is ambiguous between wondering at something great (which may be already known) and wondering whether something is the case (which is not yet known), and thus I use "curiosity" to signify specifically the emotional drive toward acquiring knowledge.

11. The Stoics do not deny that the sage will feel the involuntary movements of the passions or 'first motions'; they deny only that the sage will voluntarily assent to them. For example, on a ship in a storm at sea, the sage will feel the first motions of fear but not accept that it poses any evil. On Stoic detachment, see Knuuttila (2004).

12. See also *Passions of the Soul*, art. 41 (AT 11, 359–60).

13. See Descartes's advice to Elisabeth (AT 4, 411); Knuuttila (2004); Galen (1963); and Brown (2006, 33–34).

14. See AT 4, 312–13 on how the tightening of the openings of the heart retards the circulation of the blood and excites the passion of fear.

15. Likely written for Seneca's father-in-law, Paulinus, urging him to retire from public office. See Williams's introduction to Seneca (2014, 107).

16. It is not clear to whom Seneca is referring. It could be either Virgil or Homer, but the reference can be traced to neither. See Williams's comments in Seneca (2014, 135).

17. For discussion on the significance of Elisabeth's views on regret, see Shapiro (2014).

18. Mertz-Weigel (2005, 175) surmises that Descartes would not want to list negative affects within his taxonomy as if implying that there are natural conditions that are essentially negative and debilitating. All the primary passions are, for Descartes, natural and good. Only their excess or defect can be problematic.

19. See Elisabeth to Descartes (April 25, 1646) on how since one cannot foresee all the accidents that can afflict one, one cannot prevent oneself desiring things for the conservation of one's self that one has no control over (AT 4, 405; Shapiro 2007, 134).

20. Thanks to Jacqueline Broad for this suggestion.

21. Actually, Descartes vacillates on this question in the same letter (6 October, 1645), saying at AT 4, 307, that we are responsible only for our thoughts but at AT 4, 313, that all the effects that depend on the free will of humans, including presumably their thoughts, also depend on God as cause.

22. See her letters of 30 November, 1645 (AT 4, 336; Shapiro 2007, 127) and 25 April, 1646 (At 4, 405; Shapiro 2007, 133–34).

23. Elisabeth responds that the pleasure in tragedies is explained by the fact that we can enjoy being moved knowing that the sadness will not be so violent to lead us to "extravagances" or "corrupt our health" (AT 4, 322; Shapiro 2007, 123).

24. It is too strong to assert as Schneck (2019, 755) does that "In order to be content, he [Descartes] claims, one has to make oneself emotionally independent of other people, as well as of external circumstances not in one's control."

25. For further discussion about these "larger than life" social wholes, see Brown and Normore (2019, c. 7).

26. See Brown and Broad (2022a).

27. See Brown and Broad (2022b) for an overview of how in the period women acting heroically or politically was widely viewed as involving a transcendence of their feminine sex and femininity.

REFERENCES

Alanen, Lilli. 2004. "Descartes and Elisabeth: A Philosophical Dialogue?" In *Feminist Reflections on the History of Philosophy*, edited by Lilli Alanen and Charlotte Witt, 193–218. Dordrecht: Kluwer Academic Publishers.

American Psychiatric Association. 2013. *Diagnostic and Statistical Manual of Mental Disorders*.5th ed. Arlington, VA: American Psychiatric Association.

Beck, Ulrich. 1992. *Risk Society: Towards a New Modernity*. London: Sage.

Broad, Jacqueline. 2002. *Women Philosophers of the Seventeenth Century*. Cambridge: Cambridge University Press.

Brown, Deborah J. 2006. *Descartes and the Passionate Mind*. Cambridge: Cambridge University Press.

Brown, Deborah J., and Calvin G. Normore. 2019. *Descartes and the Ontology of Everyday Life*. Oxford: Oxford University Press.

Brown, Deborah J., and Jacqueline Broad. 2022a. "The Social Dimension of Generosity in Descartes and Astell." *Journal of the History of Philosophy* 60: 409–27.

———. 2022b. "Petticoat Power? Mary Astell's Appropriation of Heroic Virtue for Women." *Journal of the American Philosophical Association*: 1–20.

Burton Robert. *The Anatomy of Melancholy. 1621/1826.* Reprinted. London, UK: Thomas McLean.

———. 1621/1927. *The Anatomy of Melancholy*. London: Thomas McLean.

Crocq, Marc-Antoine. 2015. "A History of Anxiety: From Hippocrates to DSM." *Dialogues in Clinical Neuroscience* 17: 319–25.

Descartes, René. 1909. *Oeuvres de Descartes*. Edited by Charles Adam and Paul Tannery, 12 vols. Paris: Léopold Cerf.

———. 1984–1985. *The Philosophical Writings of Descartes*, vols. 1 and 2. Edited and translated by John Cottingham, Robert Stoothoff, and Dugald Murdoch. Cambridge: Cambridge University Press.

Dyson, Henry. 2010. "Pleasure and the Sapiens: *Seneca De vita Beata 11.1*." *Classical Philology* 105: 313–18.

Foucault Michel. 1983. "Hypomnemata." *Corps Ecrit* 5: 3–23.

Galen, Claudius. 1963. *On the Passions and Errors of the Soul*. Translated by Paul. W. Harkins. Columbus: Ohio State University Press.

Giddens, Anthony. 1991. *Modernity and Self-Identity: Self and Society in the Late Modern Age*. Cambridge: Polity.

Inwood, Brad, and L Lloyd P. Gerson1997. *Hellenistic Philosophy: Introductory Readings*, 2nd ed. Indianapolis: Hackett.

Jeffery, Renée. 2017. "The Origins of the Modern Emotions: Princess Elisabeth of Bohemia and the Embodied Mind." *History of European Ideas* 43: 547–59.

Kambouchner, Denis. 2014. "Le cas Élisabeth: Générosité et Mélancolie." In *Élisabeth de Bohême face à Descartes: Deux philosophes?*, edited by Delphine Kolesnik-Antoine and Marie-Frédérique Pellegrin, 1139–53. Paris: J. Vrin.

Knuuttila, Simo. 2004. *Emotions in Ancient and Medieval Philosophy*. Oxford: Clarendon Press.

Marcus Aurelius. 2013. *Meditations*. Translated by Christopher Gill. Oxford: Oxford University Press.

Mertz-Weigel, Dorothée. 2005. *Figuring Melancholy: From Jean de Meun to Molière, Via Montaigne, Descartes, Rotrou and Corneille*. Columbus: Ohio State University Press.

Rebughini, Paola. 2021. "A Sociology of Anxiety: Western Modern Legacy and the Covid-19 Outbreak." *International Sociology* 36: 554–68.

Rutherford, Donald. 2004. "On the Happy Life: Descarte vis-à-vis Seneca." *In Stoicism: Traditions and Transformations*, edited by Steven K. Strange and Jack Zupko, 177–97. Cambridge: Cambridge University Press.

———. 2014. "Reading Descartes as a Stoic: Appropriate Actions, Virtue, and the Passions." *Philosophie Antique* 14: 129–55.

Schmitter, Amy. 2002. "Descartes and the Primacy of Practice: The Role of the Passions in the Search for Truth." *Philosophical Studies* 46: 99–108.

Schneck, Ariane Cäcilie. 2019. "Elisabeth of Bohemia's Neo-Peripatetic Account of the Emotions." *British Journal for the History of Philosophy* 27: 753–70.

Seneca, Lucius Annaeus. 2014. *Hardship and Happiness*. Translated and edited by Gareth D. Williams. Chicago: University of Chicago Press.

———. 2015. *Letters on Ethics: To Lucilius*. Edited and translated by Margaret Graver and A. A. Long. Chicago: University of Chicago Press.

Shapiro, Lisa. 1999. "Princess Elizabeth and Descartes: The Union of Soul and Body and the Practice of Philosophy." *British Journal for the History of Philosophy* 7: 503–20.

———. 2014. "Je ne Regrette Rien: Élisabeth, Descartes et la Psychologie Morale du Regret." In *Élisabeth de Bohême face à Descartes: Deux philosophes?*, edited by Delphine Kolesnik-Antoine and Marie-Frédérique Pellegrin, 155–69. Paris: J. Vrin.

Shapiro, Lisa (ed. and trans.). 2007. *The Correspondence Between Princess Elisabeth of Bohemia and René Descartes*. Chicago: University of Chicago Press.

Chapter 4

The Anguish of Ivan Karamazov

Mauro Rossi and Christine Tappolet

INTRODUCTION

Affective states that concern danger come in different guises.[1] Hence it is not a surprise that we have a rich vocabulary to capture the fine-grained distinctions among such states. Think of anguish, anxiety, dread, fear, fright, horror, panic, phobia, terror, trauma, and scare. Other cultures make further distinctions. There is for instance the *megatu* of the Ifaluk people, an emotion that seems to be close to fear, but which is positively valued, or else the Chinese fear of cold and wind, *pa-leng*.[2] In this chapter, we will focus on yet another non-Western emotional concept, the Russian concept of *toska*, which we will refer to by the term "anguish."[3]

The concept of *toska* figures prominently in a tantalizing passage from *The Brothers Karamazov*, Fyodor Dostoevski's last novel:

> And Ivan Fyodorovich, on parting from Alyosha, went home to Fyodor Pavlovich's house. But, strangely, an unbearable anguish suddenly came over him, and, moreover, the closer he came to home, the worse it grew with every step. The strangeness lay not in the anguish itself, but in the fact that Ivan Fyodorovich simply could not define what the anguish consisted of. He had often felt anguish before, and it would be no wonder if it came at such a moment, when he was preparing, the very next day, having suddenly broken with everything that had drawn him there, to make another sharp turn, entering upon a new, completely unknown path, again quite as lonely as before, having much hope, but not knowing for what, expecting much, too much, from life, but unable himself to define anything either in his expectations or even in his desires. And yet at that moment, though the anguish of the new and unknown was indeed in his soul, he was tormented by something quite different. "Can it be loathing for my father's house?" he thought to himself. "Very likely. I'm so

> sick of it, and though today I shall cross that vile threshold for the last time, still it makes me sick . . . " But no, that was not it. Was it the parting with Alyosha and the conversation he had had with him? "For so many years I was silent with the whole world and did not deign to speak, and suddenly I spewed out so much gibberish!" Indeed, it could have been the youthful vexation of youthful inexperience and youthful vanity, vexation at having been unable to speak his mind, especially with such a being as Alyosha, on whom he undoubtedly counted a great deal in his heart. Of course there was that, too, that is, this vexation, there even had to be, but it was not that either, not that at all. "Anguish to the point of nausea, yet it's beyond me to say what I want. Perhaps I shouldn't think . . ."
>
> Ivan Fyodorovich tried "not to think," but that, too, was no use. Above all, this anguish was vexing and annoyed him by the fact that it had some sort of accidental, completely external appearance; this he felt. Somewhere some being or object was standing and sticking up, just as when something sometimes sticks up in front of one's eye and one doesn't notice it for a long time, being busy or in heated conversation, and meanwhile one is clearly annoyed, almost suffering, and at last it dawns on one to remove the offending object, often quite trifling and ridiculous, something left in the wrong place, a handkerchief dropped on the floor, a book not put back in the bookcase, or whatever. At last, in a very bad and irritated state of mind, Ivan Fyodorovich reached his father's house, and suddenly, glancing at the gate from about fifty paces away, he at once realized what was tormenting and worrying him so.
>
> On the bench by the gate, idly enjoying the cool of the evening, sat the lackey Smerdyakov, and Ivan Fyodorovich realized at the first sight of him that the lackey Smerdyakov was also sitting in his soul, and that it was precisely this man that his soul could not bear. It all suddenly became bright and clear. Earlier, with Alyosha's story of his encounter with Smerdyakov, something gloomy and disgusting had suddenly pierced his heart and immediately evoked a reciprocal malice. Later, during their conversation, Smerdyakov was temporarily forgotten, but remained in his soul nonetheless, and as soon as Ivan Fyodorovich parted with Alyosha and headed for home alone, the forgotten feeling at once began suddenly and quickly to reemerge. "But can it be that this worthless scoundrel troubles me so much!" he thought with unbearable malice. (Dostoevski 1879–1880/1990, part II, book V, chapter 6)

This is how Dostoevski describes Ivan Karamazov's state of mind while he returns to his father's house for the last time, shortly before the murder of his father. This description follows Ivan's intense conversation with his brother Alyosha and precedes the dialogue between Ivan and his stepbrother Smerdyakov, where the latter subtly hints at his plan to murder their father Fyodor Karamazov. Smerdyakov is looking to establish an implicit agreement between Ivan and himself, in order to make Ivan an accomplice of the crime he plans to commit. At that moment, Ivan does not fully grasp what

Smerdyakov is up to—this will only become evident to him in retrospect—but he perceives the sinister undertone of Smerdyakov's words.

Ivan has grown suspicious of and disturbed by Smerdyakov before their momentous dialogue. In the excerpt with which we started, Dostoevski masterfully introduces us to the darkness of Ivan's thoughts and the intensity of his mental distress. Ivan is indeed deeply affected, and Dostoevski describes his state of mind with a series of suggestive terms—"anguish," "torment," "loathing," "sickness," "nausea," "annoyance," "very bad and irritated state of mind," "worry," "gloom," "disgust," "trouble," and "unbearable malice"—thereby building a crescendo that reaches its climax when Ivan suddenly realizes that it is Smerdyakov who is responsible for what he feels.

Dostoevski's description is a remarkable piece of literary work. Yet, it is also particularly interesting from the point of view of affective science and philosophy. Ivan's state of mind raises, indeed, a number of questions. Clearly, Ivan goes through several distinct states in the process of reaching his father's house. But it seems that the dominant state, the state that most fully pervades Ivan's mind is a state that Dostoevski characterizes as "anguish" (*toska*).[4] What sort of state is it?

The goal of our paper is to provide a philosophical account of Ivan's state of mind that aims at specifying the kind of affective state it consists in. We believe that our account will allow a better grasp of the depth and richness of anguish and similarly danger-oriented affective states, such as anxiety. We proceed as follows. We start, in section 2, by providing a brief typology of affective states, distinguishing between occurrent and dispositional affective states. We argue that the anguish that Ivan experiences is best characterized as an occurrent affective state. The question is which kind of occurrent affective state Ivan's state of mind exactly consists in. We consider two main options. In section 3, we examine whether Ivan's anguish should be conceived of as an emotion. We offer reasons to think that Ivan's anguish is neither a standard emotion nor a nonstandard emotion of the sorts that are typically discussed in the literature. In section 4, we examine whether Ivan's anguish should instead be conceived of as a mood. Ivan's anguish does not fit any of the standard accounts of moods. What makes Ivan's anguish especially interesting is that it seems to have not a just a specific cause, but also a proper object, yet Ivan appears unable to identify the object of his anguish. In section 5, we argue that this makes Ivan's anguish either a mood, provided that one adopts a nonstandard account such as the account that one of us has recently defended (Rossi 2021), or an access-unconscious emotion, or a sui generis affective state. Independently of the question of which of these accounts is correct, what matters most is that Ivan's state of mind is characterized by the fact that it has an epistemically undetermined intentional object. We end with the suggestion that by generating meta-emotions, states of mind such Ivan's not only inform the individual that there is an unknown source of danger but also prepare them to deal with a kind of evasive threat that appears particularly worrisome.

Before we start, let us make clear that even though the discussion is structured around the distinction between emotions and moods, this distinction should be taken with a grain of salt. On many accounts, moods are a kind of emotions. As we will explain below, some view the difference as being simply a matter of degree along some dimension, like intensity or duration, while others hold that moods and emotions merely differ in terms of their intentional objects. What is important for us in this paper is less the question of whether Ivan's anguish is an emotion or a mood than the general question of what its central features are.

IS IVAN'S ANGUISH AN OCCURRENT OR A DISPOSITIONAL AFFECTIVE STATE?

It seems clear that Ivan's anguish is an affective state, where the term "affective state" refers to the most general category encompassing emotions, moods, sentiments, etc. It is custom in the literature to distinguish between occurrent and dispositional affective states. The first difference between them is that the former are mental episodes, i.e., they occur at particular times, whereas the latter are more stable mental conditions, which may or may not manifest themselves into occurrent affective states.[5] A second difference is that occurrent affective states typically have a phenomenological character, i.e., there is something that being in those states "feels like," whereas dispositional affective states do not have any phenomenological character over and beyond the phenomenology of the occurrent affective states that manifest them.

Emotions, or more precisely emotional episodes, are the paradigmatic example of occurrent affective states. Emotional episodes such as the disgust you feel while smelling a rotten tomato, the fear you experience at a dog running toward you, or the joy that pervades you at the birth of your child, are momentary states, which typically have a relatively short, though variable, duration. They also have a rich phenomenology. It is an open question whether all emotional episodes have a phenomenological character. Arguably, some emotional episodes may occur unconsciously. In any case, there is no question that Ivan's state is phenomenally conscious. By this, we mean that there is something that Ivan feels like while being in the state. Given this, in what follows we will consider only phenomenally conscious emotional episodes.[6]

Emotional episodes should be distinguished from emotional dispositions.[7] These are dispositions to experience particular emotions. For instance, if a dog attacked you when you were a child, you might have developed a disposition to experience fear every time you encounter a dog. The underlying state is a dispositional affective state: it is a disposition to experience fear in particular circumstances. It is a relatively stable mental state, e.g., it is part of you since you were attacked by the dog. By itself, however, it has no phenomenology. You only experience the feeling of fear when you encounter actual dogs, that is, when your disposition manifests itself into actual episodes of fear.

Emotional dispositions are not the only dispositional affective states. Sentiments, such as love, care, hate, hostility, are typically considered to be another important kind of such states (see Naar 2018). What distinguishes sentiments from emotional dispositions is that the former are "multi-track dispositions," i.e., dispositions to experience instances of a specific variety of emotion types, rather than of a single emotion type, in different contexts. Thus, for example, a sentiment of love for your partner may manifest itself into episodes of joy at your partner's promotion, anger at a person insulting your partner, sadness at your partner's illness, and so on.

Moods present us with a trickier case from the taxonomical point of view. In the literature, they are sometimes categorized as dispositional states (e.g., Lormand 1985, Griffiths 1997, Sizer 2000, Siemer 2009), sometimes as occurrent affective states (e.g., Armon-Jones 1991, Solomon 1976/1993, Frijda 1994, Goldie 2000, Prinz 2004, Price 2006, Mendelovici 2013, Tappolet 2018). In each of these two camps, moreover, there exist several different accounts, something that greatly complicates the task of categorizing moods. For our part, however, we think that moods should be conceived of as distinct occurrent affective states. Consider paradigmatic moods such as irritability, anxiety, elation, peacefulness, boredom, excitement, sulkiness, suspicion, longing, melancholia, discouragement, and depression. Generally speaking, these moods seem to have a phenomenology of their own.[8] Thus, for instance, there seems to be something that "feels like" being irritable, which does not reduce to the phenomenology of the emotion that supposedly manifests irritability, namely, the emotion of anger. In other words, while there is certainly a close relation between irritability and anger, *each* of these states seems to have a distinctive phenomenology.

In what follows, then, we will take moods to be occurrent affective states. Like emotions, moods can be grounded in affective dispositional states. Following Haybron (2008), we will call the dispositions to experience instances of specific mood types "mood propensities." It is an open question whether there also exist multitrack mood dispositions, i.e., dispositions to experience instances of a variety of distinct mood types, which would be the equivalent for moods of what sentiments are for emotions. Perhaps such multitrack mood dispositions could be conceived as stable and long-lasting conditions akin to personality traits.

With this taxonomy of affective states in hand, we can go back to the question we are concerned with: what kind of affective state is Ivan in, while he walks back to his father's house? As stated in the introduction, Ivan is described as experiencing, or having recently experienced, several different affective states, including emotions such as annoyance and disgust, moods such as gloom and irritability, and sentiments, such as dislike of his father's house, of which he says "I am so sick of it." This suggests that Ivan has developed particular emotional and mood dispositions, as well as some sentiments, which manifest themselves in various ways. However, as we have also remarked, the state that mostly dominates Ivan's mind is anguish. This is the state with which Ivan is struggling and that consumes him up to the moment when he meets Smerdyakov. Now, one thing is clear: Ivan's anguish is phenomenologically salient. Dostoevski describes it as "unbearable," growing worse "with every step," "to the point of nausea," "vexing," and annoying. There is no doubt, therefore, that Ivan's anguish is an occurrent affective state; an experience that weighs heavily on his mind; a kind of affective episode that is not entirely new to him, but that, in those particular circumstances, is strange and disconcerting.

If Ivan's anguish is an occurrent affective state, which kind of state is it? Is it an emotional episode? Is it a mood? Or is it something else, perhaps a sui generis affective state? We consider these questions in the next two sections, starting with emotional episodes, which we call, for short, "emotions."

IS IVAN'S ANGUISH AN EMOTION?

The first option we want to consider is that Ivan's anguish is a standard emotion, belonging to the same family of negative emotions as fear and anger. A brief analysis of the main features of standard emotions reveals, however, that Ivan's anguish is a rather different affective state. Earlier on, we have described emotions by reference to two important features: they are mental episodes and they possess a phenomenological character. In fact, standard emotions have a third important feature: they are *about* something, in the sense that they are *directed at* something. Consider typical instances of fear, such as your fear of a bear or your fear that it will rain. In both of these cases, you are afraid *of* something, i.e., of a bear and that it will rain, respectively. In other words, your fear is directed at specific objects and is about them. The same is true of other standard emotions. For example, one is angry *with* a politician; one is joyful *at* a friend's winning a regatta; one is surprised *to* receive a prize, and so on.

This feature of standard emotions is often described by saying that standard emotions have *intentional objects*. There exist different types of intentional objects (see de Sousa 1987, Deonna and Teroni 2012, Scarantino and de Sousa 2018). For example, one common distinction is between target objects and propositional objects. Roughly, the target of an emotion is the particular entity the emotion is about, whereas the propositional object of an emotion is the fact or the state of affairs which the emotion is directed at. No matter the type, the intentional objects of standard emotions have three important characteristics that are relevant for present purpose. First, they typically are specific, e.g., specific individuals, items, or states of affairs. Second, they are objects of which the individual experiencing the emotion is aware and that they are capable of identifying. Third, and relatedly, they are objects that shape the individual's attentional focus. To illustrate, consider again your fear of the dog attacking you. Your emotion is directed at a specific dog, of which you are aware as attacking you, and whose behavior captures your attention.

When assessed against this characterization, Ivan's anguish does not appear to be a standard emotion. In fact, one of these three things seems true of Ivan's anguish: *either* it has no specific intentional object *or*, if it has one, it is an object that Ivan is incapable of identifying, *or* it has an object that does not narrow Ivan's attentional focus down on anything specific. At this stage, we can leave it open which of these descriptions is more appropriate for Ivan's anguish. Either way, we get to the conclusion that Ivan's anguish is not a standard emotion, since it lacks at least one of the features that characterize such emotions.

This brings us to a second option. Perhaps Ivan's anguish is simply a *non*standard emotion. A first possibility is that Ivan's anguish is an *objectless* emotion, that is, an emotion without an intentional object. Notice, as this will be relevant later on, that this option does not say only that Ivan's anguish lacks a *specific* intentional object, or that it has an object that Ivan is unable to identify; it says that Ivan's anguish lacks an intentional object *altogether*. According to this reading, then, Ivan experiences a particular negative feeling, i.e., a feeling of anguish, but his emotion is not directed at any object, individual, or state of affairs; in fact, his anguish is not about anything at all.

What should we make of this option? For a start, it is not clear whether the idea of an objectless emotion makes full sense. It is true that some authors have defended the existence of objectless emotions. For instance, in describing an alleged instance of objectless fear, Peter Goldie writes that "your fear on waking may have no very specific object—the dark, the shape of the curtains, the strange noise which woke you—but it is still an emotional experience and not a mood" (Goldie 2000, 17–18). Considering a case of panic on a plane, Carolyn Price similarly claims that the content of an objectless fear such as this is something like the following: "Things are extremely threatening in that I am trapped inside a flimsy container high above the ground; make sure that I am not injured now, by fleeing now, or by lashing out now, or by cowering now" (Price 2006, 63). It may be argued, however, that neither case presents us with a genuine instance of objectless fear. In Goldie's case, fear might be directed at any of these things: the dark, the shape of the curtains, and the strange noise which woke you. Likewise, in Price's case, there is arguably something your fear is about, namely, being aboard an airplane high above the ground.

However, even if the idea of an emotion that entirely lacks an intentional object could be defended, it is doubtful that Ivan's anguish is such an emotion. The reason is that Ivan's anguish does not appear to lack an intentional object. At this stage, we can leave it open what exactly this object is. We can simply say, provisionally, that it bears some relation to Ivan's stepbrother Smerdyakov. All through his way toward his father's house, Ivan repeatedly tries to understand what his anguish is *about* or, in Dostoevski's own words, what it "consisted of." That is, he tries to zoom in on the intentional object of his affective state. Only when he reaches his father's house and sees Smerdyakov does he realizes that his anguish has to do with his stepbrother.

Another type of nonstandard cases is constituted by emotions that are responses to uncertainty. This type of emotions has recently been highlighted by Charlie Kurth (2018a, 2018b). According to Kurth, the emotion of anxiety is a response to uncertainty about a possible threat or challenge. As he puts it, "when one feels anxious, one sees one's situation as involving a threat or challenge whose potential is unpredictable, uncontrollable or otherwise open to question" (2018a, 96). One of his examples involves anxiety regarding social interaction, such as when you are worried that you might say something silly and are uncertain about the negative outcome that could result from your performance. Unlike fear, which Kurth sees as involving a defensive response that engages specific actions (e.g., fight/flight/freeze), such anxiety is thought to involve general patterns of risk assessments and risk-minimization behavior.

Does Ivan's anguish fit the model of the emotion of anxiety? It does not. According to Kurth, anxiety is directed at particular, identified objects (e.g., a person, one's circumstances, a decision), which are seen as potentially threatening or challenging, as a result of the individual being uncertain about certain features of the situation that are related to the objects of their anxiety (see Kurth 2018b, 10). For instance, in cases of *practical anxiety*, an individual may be anxious about a particular decision in virtue of the fact that they ignore which norms apply in the situation. Or, in cases of what Kurth calls "punishment anxiety," an individual may be anxious about other people's judgments after a public performance because they ignore how well their performance went (see Kurth 2018b, 69).[9] Ivan's anguish does not seem to have these characteristics. It is true, as we have seen, that Ivan's anguish appears to have an intentional object and that Ivan is in a state of uncertainty. However, his uncertainty does not concern the features of the context that trigger his anguish, as it does in Kurth's examples of anxiety. Ivan's uncertainty concerns the object of his anguish. Put differently, his anguish is not a response to uncertainty regarding some aversive possibility, nor uncertainty about the aversive features possessed by the object of his emotion. Rather, the anguish involves uncertainty about its very object.

An additional point confirms this verdict: nothing in the passage suggests that Ivan's behavior is marked by patterns that aim at assessing and reducing the risk involved in some threat, challenge, or more generally the possibility of some negative outcome. While experiencing anguish, Ivan simply continues to walk toward the house of his father. It might be argued here that the mere fact that Ivan tries to pinpoint the object of his anguish is proof that he aims at mitigating the uncertainty of some negative outcome. However, what upsets Ivan appears to be the fact that he cannot identify what bothers him in the first instance, not the possibility of a negative outcome related to this object. Thus, Ivan is looking for the object of his anguish and not for the aversive possibilities that this object might involve.

We have seen that there is reason to believe that Ivan's anguish is directed at an object. What could this be? Here are two other options. The first is that Ivan's anguish is an emotion with an intentional, yet not specific, object, e.g., a generalized object, of which Smerdyakov is somehow part. The second is that Ivan's anguish is an emotion with a specific intentional object, yet one that does not come with a specific attentional focus, e.g., a modal object such as the possibility of something troublesome happening, where this possibility is somehow related to Smerdyakov. These two options refer to mental states that are often characterized as moods in the literature. For this reason, we will consider them in the next section.

IS IVAN'S ANGUISH A MOOD?

The answer to the question of whether Ivan's anguish is a mood obviously depends on what moods are taken to be. In section 2, we have rejected the views that conceive of moods as dispositional affective states. This still leaves us with a variety of different views that conceive of moods as occurrent affective states. Some hold that moods share the main features of standard emotions, but differ from them at the level of duration (Oatley and Johnson-Laird 1990, Owens and Maxmen 1979) or intensity (DeLancey 2006). If so, we should conclude that Ivan's anguish is not a mood. Indeed, since his anguish is not a standard emotion, it is not, a fortiori, a less intense or longer-lasting standard emotion either. However, because it is easy to come up with counterexamples, such as short-lasting or intense moods, these views are not especially promising accounts of moods, so we can leave them aside. Moreover, they do not explain some of the main features of moods. It is useful to remind what these are before continuing.

One of the central features of moods is that they lack a specific intentional object. It is often said, for instance, that moods seem to be about everything and nothing at the same time (e.g., Goldie 2000). This is an important difference between moods and standard emotions. There are others. Moods tend to have a typical phenomenology, which is often characterized in terms of a kind of "diffuseness."[10] Moods differ from standard emotions also at the level of their dispositional properties. Even if moods can result in expressive behavior, moods do not motivate the subject to perform actions. In particular, moods are not associated with any specific behavioral tendencies or motivational effects. For instance, contrary to an emotion of fear, which typically motivates an individual to perform actions such as fleeing, fighting or freezing, a mood of anxiety does not reliably motivate an individual to perform any particular action.[11] At the same time, moods are productive of more global effects than standard emotions on an individual's psyche. For instance, moods involve expressive behavior, cause particular emotions and evaluative beliefs, and trigger bodily as well as mental processes such as memory, self-attention, and categorization.[12]

Nevertheless, moods also have some important similarities with standard emotions. For many paradigmatic mood types—consider, for example, irritability, anxiety, and elation—there are corresponding emotion types—respectively, anger, fear, and joy.[13] In fact, moods such as irritability, anxiety, and elation are often defined in terms of their corresponding emotions. Such pairs of moods and emotions also seem to have a similar, though not necessarily identical, phenomenology,[14] and to involve similar expressive and physiological reactions.[15] This explains why even the authors who think that moods are not just particular kinds of standard emotions do not typically conceive of moods as completely different states from standard emotions.

Amongst the accounts that are compatible, at least prima facie, with these features of moods, the most popular is perhaps the account of moods as generalized emotions (e.g., Solomon 1976/1993, Goldie 2000, Prinz 2004). This account holds that, while moods lack a *specific* intentional object, they have an intentional object nonetheless. It is just that their object is either a general or a plural object.[16] In most versions, the object of moods is the "world as a whole," or else most things in the environment of the individual experiencing the mood. Thus, Jesse Prinz argues that "moods refer to things or situations quite generally," the mood of anxiety, for instance, representing general peril, as opposed to a specific danger (Prinz 2004, 185). This specific intentionality is invoked to explain the other differences between moods and emotions, particularly their more diffuse phenomenology and their different dispositional properties. At the same time, by construing moods as generalized emotions, this account can also explain the many similarities between moods and standard emotions.

Should we think that Ivan's anguish is a generalized emotion of this sort? This is doubtful. For Ivan's anguish seems to be much more localized than what this account of moods would construe it to be. Consider this passage: "Above all, this anguish was vexing and annoyed him by the fact that it had some sort of accidental, completely external appearance; this he felt. *Somewhere some being or object was standing and sticking up*" [our italics]. This clearly suggests that Ivan's anguish has a more specific object than the world "as a whole." It is an object that Ivan cannot fully identify yet, but that appears to him—he feels it—like an external object, "some being or object" out there, that is obtruding his mind.

Finally, there is another account of moods which might work better. According to this account, moods are occurrent states, but by contrast to emotions, which concern actual evaluative states of affairs, moods concern possible evaluative states of affairs.[17] More precisely, moods would consist in perceptual or quasi-perceptual experiences of evaluative possibilities that are taken to be likely, and which are characterized by a certain amount of indeterminacy. For instance, your anxiety would amount to a sense of looming danger, that is, a sense of the likely possibility that something or other will harm you.

Whether this is a plausible account of moods or not, the question is whether it fits Ivan's anguish. It might well seem so, for it seems undeniable that Ivan is haunted by a sense of looming danger—who would not, given the context? Thus, it might well seem that his anguish amounts to a feeling that some threatening possibility or other is about to materialize. As we have argued earlier on, however, it does not seem right to assume that Ivan's anguish concerns threatening possibilities and their likelihood. If it had that kind of content, it would be very difficult to make sense of Ivan's realizing that it is his stepbrother Smerdyakov who is the person "that his soul could not bear." There is a directedness in Ivan's affective state, which the account of moods in terms of possibilities fails to capture.

AN EPISTEMICALLY UNDETERMINED OBJECT?

To make progress, we suggest that one should focus on the undetermined character of Ivan's mental state. What we propose is that the object of Ivan's anguish is in fact an *epistemically undetermined* object, an object that Ivan is unable to identify, but that he eventually comes to recognize as being Smerdyakov. We can further specify this idea by means of a distinction we introduced above, namely, the distinction between target object and propositional object. It seems clear that Ivan's anguish is about a particular individual, i.e., Smerdyakov, rather than a state of affairs. If so, it is an instance of an affective state that has a non-identified target as its intentional object.[18]

According to our account, in experiencing anguish, Ivan experiences *something* as having evaluative relevance, i.e., he experiences an epistemically undetermined target as having evaluative relevance.[19] This suggestion works well when one assumes either a perceptual account of affective states (see inter alia Prinz 2004, Tappolet 2016)[20] or a receptive account (see Tappolet 2022, Rossi forthcoming-b).[21] According to both accounts, when experiencing an affective state, an individual has an experience that represents an object as possessing some evaluative property. The main difference between them has to do with how they conceive the relevant experience: according to the former, it is a perceptual experience; according to the latter, it is a nonperceptual experience that involves an analog representation.

These accounts can be applied to standard emotions as well as to Ivan's anguish. Consider a standard emotional episode, such as the fear an individual feels at a dog attacking them. In this case, the individual has an experience that represents a given object, i.e., the dog attacking, as fearsome. In his episode of anguish, Ivan also has an experience that represents an object as possessing a particular evaluative property, i.e., being troublesome or threatening, or maybe more precisely but less informatively being such as making anguish fitting.[22] However, the object of his anguish is a non-identified item. Thus, the difference between standard emotions and Ivan's anguish concerns the epistemic determinedness of their objects. Unlike standard emotions, which have epistemically determined objects, Ivan's anguish has an object that is epistemically *un*determined—it fails to be epistemically determined.[23]

This, we believe, is a plausible account of Ivan's anguish, as it goes a long way in explaining what Ivan is going through. First, it explains Ivan's doxastic frame of mind. Ivan experiences the situation as evaluatively charged, but his experience is not that of an individual who simply judges his situation to be troublesome or threatening. Rather, Ivan *feels* that something is troublesome or threatening, he intuits it, he "perceives" it. Second, it explains Ivan's inquisitive self-reflecting behavior, that is, the fact that Ivan repeatedly tries to identify the epistemically undetermined object of his anguish by considering various candidates as potential objects of his anguish. Third, it explains the character of Ivan's realization that his anguish had to do, all this time, with Smerdyakov. Consider this passage: "Ivan Fyodorovich realized at the first sight of him that the lackey Smerdyakov was also *sitting in his soul*, and that *it was precisely this man that his soul could not bear*" [our italics].

And consider his final thought: "'But can it be that *this* worthless scoundrel troubles me so much!'" [our italics]. Ivan seems to realize, with clarity yet with surprise, that the epistemically undetermined object of his anguish, the object that he could not put his finger on, was no one else but his stepbrother Smerdyakov. In other words, Smerdyakov was that "something" that Ivan perceived as troubling him, without being able to identify. Thus, there is good reason to hold that Ivan's anguish is a kind of evaluative experience of an epistemically undetermined object—more specifically, of an epistemically undetermined target—as possessing some negative evaluative feature such as being troublesome or threatening.

Does this make Ivan's anguish a mood? The answer depends on whether this account is plausible as a general account of moods. One of us has argued that it is (see Rossi 2021). According to this account, what unifies moods as a class of mental states is indeed the fact that moods are evaluative perceptions of epistemically undetermined objects, that is, perceptual experiences that represent epistemically undetermined objects (either undetermined targets or undetermined propositional objects) as possessing specific evaluative properties. On this account, for instance, irritability consists in a perceptual experience of an epistemically undetermined object as offensive.

We will not fully rehearse all the arguments in favor of this view here.[24] The main gist is that this view seems to well capture all the main features of moods. For instance, it explains why moods seem to lack a specific intentional object, without denying that they lack an intentional object altogether. It also explains the similarities between emotions and moods. Both emotions and moods are evaluative experiences, i.e., experiences of evaluative properties. Insofar as their phenomenology is tied to the evaluative properties they represent, then each emotion and mood that represent the same evaluative property will have a similar phenomenology. At the same time, since moods have epistemically undetermined objects, they will not be associated with any specific behavioral tendencies or motivational effects, but they will physiologically prepare the individual for a wider range of responses that may be called for by the state of uncertainty the individual is in. If all this is true, then Ivan's anguish counts as a paradigmatic type of mood. In fact, Dostoevski's description of Ivan's predicament appears to offer a vivid illustration of the account of moods understood as evaluative experiences of epistemically undetermined objects.

One may argue against this view of moods by claiming that emotions too can have epistemically undetermined objects. If this is true, then it seems that the present account of moods does not adequately distinguish between moods and emotions. Various replies are possible, but two of them are especially salient for present purposes. One option is to say that moods are indeed a particular kind of *nonstandard* emotions, namely, emotions with epistemically undetermined objects. This reply preserves a distinction between moods and standard emotions, all the while identifying moods with the entire class of evaluative perceptions of epistemically undetermined objects.

The second salient option takes as a starting point the recognition that there are at least two ways in which the object of an affective state can be epistemically undetermined. One is when the subject has not yet individuated the object of their affective state. The other is when such an object is simply not available to the individual's conscious awareness. Based on this distinction, one may argue that, while the former case is representative of moods, the latter case describes a distinct kind of nonstandard emotions, namely, emotions that are phenomenally conscious, but involve access-unconscious objects. Put differently, Ivan's anguish would be an occurrent emotion that comes with feeling, but whose content lies below the threshold of awareness.[25] This would again make it a nonstandard emotion.

When this position is applied to the issue at stake, then the question is whether Ivan's anguish is more similar to a state of the former type or to a state of the latter type. Textual evidence is insufficient to adjudicate the matter. But we can at the very least acknowledge that the second option is a reasonable alternative. In fact, it seems to capture well the phenomenology of Ivan's anguish, particularly the sense of epiphany that accompanies Ivan's recognition that it was Smerdyakov who was "sitting in his soul," as if Smerdyakov was suddenly emerging over the threshold of awareness as the object of Ivan's anguish.

An alternative option, if one rejects the previous accounts, consists in saying that Ivan's anguish is neither a mood nor a nonstandard emotion, but a sui generis affective state, one that targets epistemically undetermined intentional objects. Whatever the final word is on how to categorize affective states, let us stress that our main claim is that Ivan's anguish consists in an experience that represents an epistemically undetermined object as troublesome or threatening.[26] This is what makes Ivan's anguish an especially interesting affective state and which distinguishes it as a distinct kind of affective state. In fact, whether it is conceived as a mood, a nonstandard emotion, or a sui generis affective state, Ivan's anguish appears to belong to a specific class of affective states, i.e., the class of affective states that have an epistemically undetermined object, which does not reduce either to the class of standard emotions or to that of moods as traditionally conceived.

A salient characteristic of Ivan's anguish on which we did not comment as yet is that it is accompanied by negative meta-emotions. Ivan is deeply irritated by the fact that he cannot put his finger on the intentional object of his anguish. "Somewhere some being or object was standing and sticking up," but even if salient this being or object resisted identification, like "something left in the wrong place, a handkerchief dropped on the floor, a book not put back in the bookcase, or whatever" that annoyingly sticks up in front of one's eyes even if one fails to notice it. This, we are told, made the anguish especially worrisome and "vexing."

By generating negative meta-emotions, which themselves give rise to an intense reflection process aimed at identifying the intentional object of his affective state, Ivan's anguish not only informs the individual that there is an unknown source of danger; experiencing that kind of affective state also helps the individual mentally preparing to deal with a hard to specify threat, something that involves spelling out the different possible threats at stake. There is reason, therefore, to hold that the function of affective states that have epistemically undetermined objects as their targets is to alert individuals and prepare them for confronting hard to specify instantiations of evaluative properties. When things get out of control, however, there is the possibility that an individual loses himself in anxious rumination, reminiscent of Ivan's illness and delirium toward the end of the novel.

CONCLUSION

We have focused on the anguish that Ivan Karamazov experiences while walking toward his father's house after an intense dialogue with his brother Alyosha. We have considered the question of what kind of mental state Ivan's anguish is. We have argued that his anguish is not a standard emotion, or an objectless emotion, or an emotion that arises as a response to uncertainty about contextual features. We have also shown that Ivan's anguish does not fit any of the standard accounts of moods. We have argued that the most plausible account of Ivan's anguish conceives of it as an evaluative experience of an epistemically undetermined target. This makes Ivan's anguish either a mood, according to a recent account of moods put forward by one of us, or a phenomenally conscious, but access unconscious, emotion, or a sui generis occurrent affective state. Independently of this labelling issue, what is important is that Ivan's anguish is an experience of an epistemically undetermined target as troublesome or threatening. This, we believe, allows us to better grasp the depth and richness of Ivan's anguish and similarly danger-oriented affective states. In particular, it shows that one has to distinguish between Ivan's anguish and danger-oriented affective states that have epistemically determined intentional objects.

One might wonder whether these claims have any relevance outside of the world of fiction. After all, what is true of Ivan as Dostoevski imagined him might have no counterpart in the real world. Because the case appears psychologically plausible, however, there is reason to believe that affective states involving epistemically undetermined objects are perfectly possible. More work would be needed to make the case that Ivan's anguish has real life counterparts, but ordinary experience seems amply to confirm that we can experience affective states regarding epistemically undetermined objects.

NOTES

1. We would like to thank Anna Berman for information concerning the translation of the passage we quote, and in particular concerning the meaning of the word "toska." Thanks to Juliette Vazard, Charlie Kurth, and Ariana Pismenny for their comments. We also are grateful to audiences at the University of Lund, at the EHESS (Paris), at the Université de Neuchâtel, and at Union College.

2. For *megatu*, see Lutz (1988), for *pa-leng*, see Kleinman (1980).

3. We follow the Pevear and Volokhonsky translation of *The Brothers Karamazov*. Often considered to be untranslatable, "toska," which roughly means melancholy-cum-yearning, appears to blend many aspects, since it can be rendered by terms as varied as "melancholy," "anguish," "pangs," "depression," "ennui," "boredom," "longing," "yearning," "nostalgia," and "homesickness," among others. Regarding the meaning and the importance of *toska* in Russian culture, see Wierzbicka (1992) Note that the term *anguish*, which goes back to the twelfth century, means acute bodily or mental suffering. It is derived from Old French *anguisse*, *angoisse*, which means choking sensation, distress, anxiety, rage, and, from Latin *angustia* (plural *angustiae*), which means tightness, straitness, narrowness, or else, figuratively, distress, difficulty, from *ang(u)ere*, which means to throttle, torment (from the root *angh-, meaning tight, painfully constricted, painful) (see https://www.etymonline.com/search?q=anguish).

4. The term *toska* appears no fewer than six times in the first paragraph of the passage we quote.

5. In ontology, it is common to distinguish between two ways of occupying time: "occurrences" are entities, such as events and processes, that extend through time and have different temporal parts, while "continuants," such as states, persist through time. See Naar (Forthcoming). In this paper, we remain neutral regarding these ontological issues and use the term "state" in a noncommittal way.

6. It is standard in the literature to distinguish phenomenal consciousness from access consciousness (see Block 1995). Access consciousness has to do with the access that an individual has to the content of a mental state and to its availability for reasoning and rational guidance. Given this, it is possible for a mental state to be phenomenally conscious, without being access-conscious. We will come back to this possibility in relation to Ivan's anguish in section 5.

7. This is a common distinction. See for instance Lyons (1980) and Deonna and Teroni (2012)

8. As we have both argued elsewhere, see Tappolet (2018), Rossi (2021).

9. Kurth mentions a third type of anxiety, i.e., "environmental anxiety," where the individual is anxious about potential physical dangers in their environment, but uncertain about the nature of the threat.

10. See, for instance, Morris (1989); Frijda (1994); Sizer (2000); Siemer (2009); Kind (2013).

11. See, for instance, Goldie (2000); Price (2006); and Kurth (2018b).

12. See, for instance, Lormand (1985); Morris (1989); and Siemer (2009).

13. See, for instance, Price (2006); and Tappolet (2018).

14. See, for instance, Sizer (2000); and Price (2006).

15. See, for instance, Goldie (2000); and Price (2006).

16. For more details about the distinction between general and plural objects, see Rossi (2021).

17. See Tappolet (2018), who draws on Price (2006), according to whom moods concern evaluative likelihoods.

18. That an affective state can have an intentional epistemically undetermined object appears psychologically plausible. One can wonder how this can be the case. In particular, the question is what mechanism allows a mental state to have an intentional object about which one appears to have no clue.

19. It is important to note that an undetermined object is not the same as an *indeterminate* object. The latter is a vague object, which lacks clear boundaries, but which the individual may still be in a position to identify. By contrast, an undetermined object may be determinate, yet remains unidentified. See Rossi (2021).

20. Such an account of emotion is made plausible by the important similarities between emotions and sensory perceptions. Because there are also important differences between the two kinds of states, such as the fact that emotions depend on cognitive bases, it is premised on a liberal take on what counts as a perception. Absent such a liberal take, the account is better described as quasi-perceptual.

21. The receptive account holds that the representational content of emotions is to be modelled on the content of analog magnitude representations. See Beck (2012).

22. The exact evaluative property that is perceived in an episode of anguish depends on how anguish is construed. More specifically, it depends on whether one takes anguish to be more similar to an emotion of worry, and thereby being directed at troubling objects, or to anxiety, and thereby being directed at threatening objects.

23. More specifically, Ivan is not in a position to identify the object of his anguish *as what possesses the relevant evaluative property*, whereas, in the case of standard emotions, the individual can identify the object of their emotions *as what possesses the relevant evaluative property*.

24. For more details, see Rossi (2021).

25. Thanks to Juliette Vazard for suggesting this option.

26. His anguish has fittingness conditions: it is fitting if and only if there really is a troublesome or threatening object. And in this case, there really is: Smerdyakov.

REFERENCES

Armon-Jones, Claire. 1991. *Varieties of Affect*. Toronto: University of Toronto Press.

Beck, Jacob. 2012. "The Generality Constraint and the Structure of Thought." *Mind* 121: 563–600.

Block, Ned. 1995. "On a Confusion About a Function of Consciousness." *Behavioral and Brain Sciences* 18: 227–87.

de Sousa, Ronald. 1987. *The Rationality of Emotion*. Cambridge, Massachussetts: MIT Press.

DeLancey, Stephen C. 2006. "Basic Moods." *Philosophical Psychology* 19: 527–38.

Deonna, Julien A., and Fabrice Teroni. 2012. *The Emotions: A Philosophical Introduction*. Abington: Routledge.

Dostoevski, Fyodor. 1879–1880/1990. *The Brothers Karamazov*. Translated by Richard Pevear and Larissa Volokhonsky. New York: Farrar, Straus and Giroux.

Frijda, Nico H. 1994. "Varieties of Affect: Emotions and Episodes, Moods and Sentiments." In *The Nature of Emotion: Fundamental Questions*, edited by Paul Ekman and Richard J. Davidson, 59–67. Oxford: Oxford University Press.

Goldie, Peter. 2000. *The Emotions: A Philosophical Exploration*. Oxford: Oxford University Press.

Griffiths, Paul E. 1997. *What Emotions Really Are: The Problem of Psychological Categories*. Chicago: University of Chicago Press.

Haybron, Daniel M. 2008. *The Pursuit of Unhappiness: The Elusive Psychology of Well-Being*. New York: Oxford University Press.

Kind, Amy. 2013. "The Case Against Representationalism About Moods." In *Current Controversies in Philosophy of Mind*, edited by Uriah Kriegel, 113–34. New York: Routledge.

Kleinman, Arthur. 1980. *Patients and Healers in the Context of Culture*. Berkeley: University of California Press.

Kurth, Charlie. 2018a. "Anxiety: A Case Study on the Value of Negative Emotions." In *Philosophical Perspectives on Negative Emotions: Shadows of the Soul*, edited by Christine Tappolet, Fabrice Teroni, and Anita Konzelmann Ziv. New York: Routledge.

———. 2018b. *The Anxious Mind: An Investigation into the Varieties and Virtues of Anxiety.* Cambridge, MA: MIT Press.

Lormand, Eric. 1985. "Toward a Theory of Moods." *Philosophical Studies* 47: 385–407.

Lutz, Catherine. 1988. *Unnatural Emotions: Everyday Sentiments on a Micronesian Atoll and Their Challenge to Western Theory*. Chicago: University of Chicago Press.

Lyons, William. 1980. *Emotion*. Cambridge: Cambridge University Press.

Mendelovici, Angela. 2013. "Intentionalism about Moods." *Thought: A Journal of Philosophy* 2:126–36.

Morris, W. N. 1989. *Mood: The Frame of Mind*. Berlin: Springer.

Naar, Hichem. 2018. "Sentiments." In *The Ontology of Emotions*, edited by Hichem Naar and Fabrice Teroni, 149–68. Cambridge: Cambridge University Press.

———. Forthcoming. "What Ontology for Emotions?" In *Emotion Theory: The Comprehensive Routledge Guide*, edited by Andrea Scarantino. New York: Routledge.

Oatley, Keith, and P. N. Johnson-Laird. 1990. "Semantic Primitives for Emotions: A Reply to Ortony and Clore." *Cognition and Emotion* 4: 129–43.

Owens, Howard, and Jerrold S. Maxmen. 1979. "Mood and Affect: A Semantic Confusion." *The American Journal of Psychiatry* 136: 97–99.

Price, Carolyn. 2006. "Affect Without Object: Moods and Objectless Emotions." *European Journal of Analytic Philosophy* 2: 49–68.

Prinz, Jesse J. 2004. *Gut Reactions: A Perceptual Theory of the Emotions*. New York: Oxford University Press.

Rossi, Mauro. 2021. "A Perceptual Theory of Moods." *Synthese* 198: 7119–47.

———. Forthcoming a. "An Evaluativist Theory of Sensory Pleasures."

———. Forthcoming b. "What is Loneliness? Towards a Receptive Account."

Scarantino, Andrea, and Ronald de Sousa. 2018. "Emotion." In *Stanford Encyclopedia of Philosophy*, edited by Edward N. Zalta. https://plato.stanford.edu/entries/emotion/.

Siemer, M. 2009. "Mood Experience: Implications of a Dispositional Theory of Moods." *Emotion Review* 1: 256–63.

Sizer, Laura. 2000. "Towards a Computational Theory of Mood." *British Journal for the Philosophy of Science* 4: 743–70.

Solomon, Robert C. 1976/1993. *The Passions: Emotions and the Meaning of Life*. Indianapolis: Hackett Publishing Company.

Tappolet, Christine. 2016. *Emotions, Values, and Agency*. Oxford: Oxford University Press.

———. 2018. "The Metaphysics of Moods." In *The Ontology of Emotions*, edited by Hichem Naar and Fabrice Teroni, 169–86. Cambridge: Cambridge University Press.

———. 2022. *Philosophy of Emotion: A Contemporary Introduction*. New York: Routledge.

Wierzbicka, Anna. 1992. *Semantics, Culture, and Cognition: Universal Human Concepts in Culture-Specific Configurations*. New York: Oxford University Press.

Chapter 5

Prescription for Anxiety

A Sociohistorical Analysis

Ian Dowbiggin

On October 12, 2022, World Mental Health Day, the head of the World Health Organization (WHO) announced that the globe faced an epidemic in anxiety and depression. Anxiety rates had been on the rise prior to the COVID-19 pandemic, Tedros Ghebreyesus stated, but the coronavirus itself had "triggered at least a 25 percent increase in anxiety and depression." "Profound social and economic consequences," Ghebreyesus declared, were bound to follow (Jeffay 2022).

The United States have not been immune to this global trend. Studies show that anxiety is the most common mental disorder in the United States, affecting 40 million adults. Three out of ten Americans experience one of the varieties of anxiety disorder at least once in their lives. Women are twice as likely to be affected by anxiety as men. The overall cost of anxiety to Americans is $34 billion.

With numerous signs of an economic recession beyond 2022 and evidence that COVID-19 is here to stay for the immediate future, it is highly unlikely that anxiety rates will decline any time soon. What, then, can be done to make people less anxious? Clear-cut clinical answers to this question are beyond the scope of this chapter. However, a historical perspective can shed light on the factors that predispose populations to anxiety and point educators, entertainers, law-makers, business leaders, and other opinion-makers in directions which might help to mitigate the crippling effects of anxiety on schools, boardrooms, shop floors, courts, families, hospitals and the like. History can show how things have rarely been perfect in the past, yet earlier generations in their encounters with emotional challenges learned from their experiences how to adopt coping strategies for engaging with the world. History can also inform lawmakers whose policies can help to improve a sense of community and strengthen families and neighborhoods at a time when mental health concerns have never been higher.

What does history tell us? There is no denying that this upsurge of anxiety and its various symptoms is linked to genetics or other medical conditions such as heart disease or substance abuse. But equally important are two other basic reasons: populations in industrialized countries such as Canada and the United States live in "illness-breeding" as well as "illness-affirming" societies. Illness-breeding factors refer to the high stress conditions of twenty-first century life, such as pressures in the workplace, the growing inequities in income and wealth, increasing political polarization, and the dramatic effects of digital technology, chiefly social media. Overall, in the words of Canadian journalist Patricia Pearson, herself a victim of anxiety, modern culture encourages in-your-face hucksterism, a value system which emphasizes unsettling self-promotion and fierce competition, as seen in television shows such as *Survivor* and *American Idol.* "There is no shame in shamelessness," Pearson writes. "No shame need be felt about behaving badly or rudely" (Pearson 2007, 129).

Illness-affirming factors refer to what historians call "therapism," a doctrine that, in the words of philosopher Christina Hoff Somers and physician Sally Satel, "extols openness, emotional self-absorption, and the sharing of feelings." Therapism "encompasses the assumption that vulnerability rather than strength characterizes the American psyche." According to therapism, all "suffering is a pathology in need of a cure" and the mental health needs of the populace require "a vast array of educators, counsellors, psychologists, workshoppers and other healers" who presume to guide the public through the emotional challenges of everyday life. Therapism privileges what the former *New York Times* science writer Daniel Goleman in 1995 called "emotional intelligence," a necessity for protecting mental well-being (Hoff, Somers, and Satel 2005).

According to Tara Isabelle Burton in the *New York Times,* in 2022, the march of therapism has culminated in a "therapy culture" which is saturated with its own kind of language and imagery. The overall impact of therapism on Americans, argue critics, is to breed a kind of self-centeredness that expands at the expense of communal obligations and diminishes old fashioned notions such as virtue, duty, or self-reliance. Rather than assist in healing, therapism disables Americans' innate abilities to cope with life's problems. In the twenty-first century, it is supremely difficult to avoid therapism's reach, which extends into our homes, schools, offices, courtrooms, workplaces, our everyday language, and even our churches. Equally alarmingly, recent events indicate that therapism has become itself politicized and contributes to the partisan divisiveness that afflicts everyday life in today's America.

ILLNESS-BREEDING CULTURE

Awareness of anxiety in Western world has existed for centuries, but prior to the nineteenth century the prevailing view was that most social anxiety was a normal feature of everyday life, and even an asset in various situations which called for vigilance. Additionally, the bashfulness that often accompanied anxiety was seen in various cultures as a mark of modesty, and so shyness was widely praised in women. But there were others who noted the steep psychological toll exacted by severe anxiety. In 1844, the Danish philosopher SørenKierkegaard wrote that "no Grand Inquisitor has in readiness such terrible torture as has anxiety" (Tone 2009, xii).

In the nineteenth century, physicians began describing patients who reported that in certain social situations they suffered from breathlessness, headaches, a racing heart, sweating palms, tingling limbs, and the like. One historian has written that the first signs of clinical anxiety coincided with the "age of progress," a time period when starvation, epidemic disease and high rates of infant mortality seemed to be abating in severity, leaving people to fret about less immediate concerns. In other words, the healthier people became, the more they worried about their personal health (Zeldin 1981).

The heyday of the psychoanalytic theories of the Viennese neurologist Sigmund Freud, whose ideas dominated American psychiatry between the 1940s and 1970s, saw anxiety reduced to a "neurotic reaction" to sexual frustration. Freudian theory stated that symptoms of anxiety were secondary to deep-rooted psychological mechanisms that held the key to analytic treatment. At the time, US psychiatrists, influenced by Freudian themes, were largely uninterested in classifying nervous diseases according to symptoms. Things would change in the 1970s as psychiatrists revived the notion that mental diseases were natural, biological entities and that symptoms were crucial to identifying them and pointing toward appropriate drug therapy. Meanwhile, however, Freudianism held sway, and anxiety, even when it seemed to cripple patients, was typically viewed as something that masked an underlying conflict over sex. In any case, psychoanalysis involved lengthy and expensive treatment which placed it far beyond the resources of most Americans, whose anxiety levels were rising disturbingly after the 1950s.

The two world wars of the twentieth century were a major watershed in the history of anxiety, which became a commonplace term after 1945. In 1950, American composer Leonard Bernstein named his Second Symphony after W. H. Auden's 1947 Pulitzer Prize winning poem "The Age of Anxiety." Pundits such as David Riesman and Arthur Schlesinger Jr., described Americans as gripped by fear and anxiety and out of touch with their authentic selves. In Sloan Wilson's 1955 best-selling novel *The Man in the Gray Flannel Suit*, the central character, who worked in media and public relations, was unhappy as he tried unsuccessfully to balance the needs to conform and resist. As critic James Wolcott observed when the novel was reissued in 2022, the book "captured and bottled a floating anxiety, a sour malaise, that belied the preppy froth of Patti Paige records and TV jingles" in the 1950s (Self 2022).

The 1960s, seventies, eighties and nineties were years of troubling events and trends, including the buildup of nuclear weapons, the Vietnam War, energy crises, the outbreak of Acquired Immunodeficiency Syndrome (AIDS), and horrific crimes against humanity, such as the mass killings in Rwanda and the former Yugoslavia. Coverage of these stories spread alongside the coming of cable television systems, satellite television news channels, and the twenty-four-hour news cycle. CNN, for example, began broadcasting in 1980, and journalists were quick to point out that the fierce competition for audience share among similar news channels fostered, among other things, sensationalist coverage and the viewpoint that news should be entertainment rather than a sober reporting of verifiable facts. (Kovach and Rosenstiel 1999) Exposed to such broadcasting, millions of TV viewers increasingly believed they lived in a world of killer diseases, mounting violence, and diminishing natural resources.

The terrorist attacks on the World Trade Center and the Pentagon on September 11, 2001, and later jihadist bombings in London, Madrid, and Paris increased mistrust and suspicion among people, especially travelers. Polls confirmed what psychologists were saying more and more in the new millennium: the fearful suspiciousness bred by terrorism was causing acute distress. Between 2002 and 2006 the number of patients in the United States seeking medical help for anxiety jumped from 13.4 million to 16.2 million. In November 2001, the *New England Journal of Medicine* worried that "ongoing media coverage" of terrorism might "serve as a traumatic reminder, resulting in persistent [psychological] symptoms" (Tone 2009, 229).

If, by the second decade of the twenty-first century, rates of anxiety and depression were soaring, nowhere was this trend more evident than in schools and on campuses around Canada and the United States. Students as well as faculty and staff complain of how anxiety plagues their day-to-day lives. As early as 2010, researchers in Canada and the United States found that college students of that time period suffered from anxiety and depression more than any generation since the 1930s (Belluz 2010). Today's teens and young adults, reports the National Education Association, are the most anxious ever. In 2016, nearly two-thirds of college students told pollsters that they felt "overwhelming anxiety," up from 50 percent just five years earlier. A school counsellor from southern Maryland claimed that "there's just so much going on in this day and age, the pressure to fit in, the pressure to achieve. . . .

And then you couple that with the fact that kids can't even feel safe in their schools—they worry genuinely about getting shot" (Flannery 2018).

Studies of faculty and librarians during the pandemic similarly reveal rising rates of anxiety and depression. Pandemic anxiety was actually higher among the nation's teachers than among health care workers. Teachers cited stressors such as overwork due to staff shortages. One study of three US universities stated in 2021 that professors who found themselves isolated at home and teaching online were "prone to increased mental health issues and engaging in unhealthy behaviors" (The University of Rhode Island 2021).

But blaming high rates of anxiety among academics on the coronavirus overshadows the fact that Canadian university faculty, for example, were complaining about job-related anxiety even prior to the pandemic lockdowns of 2020. In 2018, the Canadian Association of University Teachers (CAUT) stated that "postsecondary education work settings contain unique stressors and environmental drivers that are taking their toll on the mental health of Canadian academics" (Canadian Association of Universtiy Teachers 2018). CAUT added that the trend toward hiring college teachers on short-term, poorly paid contracts similarly increases stress. A Canadian academic who complained of "underemployment" said in 2018: "I don't qualify for a mortgage. Having children hasn't been a possibility for me, because I've never had a permanent job and felt it was too risky to have kids without a stable income. It's definitely affected the life I lead." Numerous American academics have voiced similar complaints.

Comments about workplace stress such as these suggest that gender factors also account for the baneful impacts of an illness-breeding culture on public mental health. Two researchers noted in 2022 that America was "in the middle of a great social experiment" as the ratios between men and women were changing dramatically in many important institutions hitherto populated primarily by men (Clark and Wineguard 2022). Studies have shown that, since the 1970s, women have been making revolutionary inroads into the paid workforce. Women now outnumber men on college campuses. Between 1950 and 1970, only 3 percent of lawyers were women, but today that statistic is almost two of every five. According to the American Bar Association, women today "significantly outnumber" men in law schools, "and the gap is widening" (American Bar Association 2022). The American Association of Medical Colleges reports that from 2007 to 2020 the percentage of women physicians rose from 28.3 to 36.3. By 2019, women outnumbered men in medical schools. (Boyle 2019). Similar trends are evident in the nation's boardrooms and halls of power in Washington, DC, and in state capitals. Nothing remotely like this has ever happened in history.

Both biology and social pressures interact to account for the rising levels of anxiety among women. On the one hand, governments, media, the entertainment world, social scientists and paid lobbyists cheer on the mounting success of educated women in the corporate worlds. Women are told they can have it all, that they can balance family and professional career, when everyday life shows how hard it is for men to cope. But the ideal of the high-performing career supermom often clashes with what studies in evolutionary psychology reveal about the differences between men and women. This ideal also clashes with the reality that "girls" rarely "rule" in the "decision-making networks," as Patricia Pearson observes (Pearson 2007, 14). The inevitable frustrations at home and in the workplace take an emotional toll on women especially, as the data repeatedly tell us that more women than men seek relief for their anxiety-related psychological and physical symptoms.

Workplaces affect anxiety levels in men as well as women. According to a Labor Force Survey in 2022, rates of work-induced anxiety have been rising alarmingly in recent years. Hostile bosses, heavy workloads, unrealistic deadlines, unreasonably long hours, and coworkers who do not respect boundaries are just some of the factors that make a workplace "toxic" and breed low morale. The telltale signs of workplace anxiety include irritability, tiredness, abnormal sleep patterns, and reduced productivity. Job insecurity also haunts daily work lives. As Patricia Pearson writes, many corporations in the twenty-first century "have no loyalty; they engage in the relentless manufactured cheer of 'team building' and then drop you like a stone if you have to do something inconveniently human, like care for an ailing father. . . . Their brutal disregard for your personal life can be downright scary." Because the "core self-esteem" of men is often bound up in career accomplishment, men who get fired in today's economy "feel a distress that's profound," writes Pearson (Pearson 2007, 122–23).

Last, but not least, of the factors that seemingly contribute to rising rates of anxiety for millions of Americans is what some experts call "election stress disorder." The term was apparently first coined in 2016 by psychologist Steven Stosny, who wrote in the *Washington Post* that during the election cycle that year he had been "overwhelmed" with "distress calls" from patients. America's divided political climate, Stolsny argues, amplified by the twenty-four-hour news cycle, made people feel tense, "and the way that most people deal with anxiety is to blame it on someone, and unfortunately the law of blame is it will eventually go to the closest person—your partner or children" (Elkind 2020).

More than two-thirds of Americans reported that the 2020 US presidential election was an important source of stress in their lives, according to the American Psychological Association, affecting people on both sides of the political divide. Large numbers of Americans claimed that as the election neared they felt fearful or depressed (or both), resulting in headaches, gastrointestinal upset, or sleeplessness. In October 2020, a Black Lives

Matter–affiliated thirty-year-old remarked on Twitter that "my appetite is non-existent and I feel nauseas [sic] most of the time. This presidential election is literally killing me." Exposure to political messaging which demonized certain candidates and warned about the catastrophic consequences of others running for office escalated the political tension and deeply affected the emotions of many Americans (Howland 2020).

The bitter debates between Republicans and Democrats in recent years have combined with the COVID-19 pandemic and the racial unrest in the wake of the 2020 death of George Floyd at the hands of police to create a cultural atmosphere that keeps millions of Americans on edge. This cascade of events has helped to divide families, neighborhoods and communities while unleashing waves of anger and deep suspicion that poison public life. It is little wonder that with each successive election cycle anxiety levels rise.

ILLNESS-AFFIRMING CULTURE

Thus, it is understandable why so many Americans in the 2020s are jumpy, nervous, anxious and depressed. The question is: is it solely because of the numerous stressors in society, or is there something else that also accounts for today's soaring rates of reported emotional sickness?

Alongside the many effects of an illness-breeding culture are the impacts of a culture that tells people that all their feelings are perfectly genuine, must be validated as certifiable illnesses, and require professional, expert management. The illness-affirming culture has been unfolding for a long time, stretching back at least to the mid twentieth century, the heyday of mental healing and self-help books such as Dale Carnegie's *How to Win Friends and Influence People* (1937) and Norman Vincent Peale's *The Power of Positive Thinking* (1952). By the 1980s, other authors were gaining notoriety as self-appointed experts, notably *Doctor Phil* McGraw, Tony Robbins, Deepak Chopra, and Robert Fulghum. The popularity of daytime television programs with millions of viewers, including *The Oprah Winfrey Show* and *The Phil Donahue Show*, eclipsed that of TV soap operas. Daytime TV talk shows also provided forums for experts to spread their teachings that Americans can never talk too much about their feelings. In the words of historian Eva Moscowitz, "Oprah's popularity stemmed not only from her willingness to probe what others had previously considered private but also from her own admissions of deep-seated emotional problems. Oprah was personal in a way that no talk show host before her had been. . . . Single-handedly, she and [television] have revolutionized talk shows and rendered the notion of Mid-western reticence quaint and obsolete" (Moscowitz 2001, 265).

Mainstream magazines such as *Redbook* and *Ladies' Home Journal* ran countless stories about how to improve one's emotional life. In 2003 alone, between 3,500 and 4,000 new self-help books were published. The cumulative effect of these trends was to spread the message that millions of Americans were victims who paid a steep emotional price to live in a hostile world, but that an entire industry of therapists, counselors, workshoppers, and life coaches was standing by to teach them that their symptoms were not their fault, they suffered from traumatic events earlier in life, and that they could enjoy a higher sense of self-esteem and self-worth by seeking the help they deserved.

In other words, when once Americans would have been told to stop blaming others for their misery and get on with their lives, by the end of the twentieth century, if you felt unwell there were medical labels which explained your pain and made it acceptable for people to adopt sick roles rather than use individual willpower to overcome your symptoms, as human beings had previously done for generations. Where once self-reliance and emotional toughness were highly prized, the acceptance of a diagnosis of emotional sickness was fast becoming a badge of personal honor for millions of Americans by the early twenty-first century. The gospel of therapism, recovery, victimization, authenticity, and healing, in the words of one historian in 2005, "pervade[s] our culture—from our schools to our offices to our homes and even to our hospitals" (Salerno 2005, 39). A process known as "cultural scripting" provides people with socially approved rules about what feelings mean and what roles they can adopt to make sense of their sicknesses (Furedi 2007). Historian of medicine Edward Shorter has noted that the "post-modern patients" of the late twentieth century "cherish their diagnosis," whether it is an anxiety disorder or chronic fatigue syndrome. One American woman too fatigued to leave her bed in the 1990s remarked, "If I'm not sick, I've got nothing" (Shorter 1994, 197).

Nothing has done more to foster the illness-affirming culture than what one historian has called "America's turbulent affair with tranquilizers" (Tone 2009). A major breakthrough occurred in the 1950s when a wave of new minor and major tranquilizers were introduced to an American public receptive to the ethos of consumerism, which celebrated the purchasing of goods ranging from soap to automobiles, all in the pursuit of happiness.

The mounting consumption of medications by late-twentieth-century Americans coincided with—and was reinforced by—the growth of a cultural atmosphere that taught Americans they deserved treatment for whatever emotional struggles they encountered in their daily lives. Miltown, hailed as "emotional aspirin," was followed by Valium, by the 1970s the single most-prescribed brand-name medicine. When worries about rising rates of prescription drug dependence soared in the 1970s, the pharmaceutical industry began introducing a new series of medications, the selective serotonin reuptake inhibitors (SSRIs). The best known of the SSRIs was Prozac, which psychiatrist Peter Kramer lauded in his best-selling book *Listening to Prozac* (1993). Kramer not only argued that Prozac would cure depression, he also viewed it as a form of "cosmetic psychopharmacology," a way of making pill-takers feel "better than well." "Since you only live once, why not do it as a blonde? Why not as a peppy blond?" Kramer asked. He even called Prozac a "feminist" drug. In recognition of the psychological stress endured by women entering the workforce by the end of the century, he recommended Prozac as the perfect drug for "super moms" who balanced motherhood and high-powered careers. By the turn of the new millennium, Kramer was just one of numerous voices popularizing emotional diagnoses by advocating drug therapy. The notion that someone with the help of drugs could undergo a "redefinition of self," to use Kramer's own words, bolstered the concept of authenticity underlying therapism (Kramer 1993, 15; quoted in Dowbiggin 2011, 171).

By the dawn of the new millennium, SSRIs were being touted as antidotes for anxiety and obsessive-compulsive disorders as well. Following dramatic increases in SSRI use in the 1990s, America by the second decade of the new century led the world in antidepressant use. From 2015–2018, 13.2 percent of American adults over the age of eighteen used SSRIs, and use was higher among women (17.7 percent) than men (8.4 percent). SSRI consumption encouraged Americans to believe that their emotional lives were out of control and warranted immediate treatment.

The powerful consequences of social media in the twenty-first century include both illness-breeding and illness-affirming dimensions. Between 2006 and 2018, the percentage of Americans listing the Internet as their primary news source jumped from 14 to almost 50 percent. Therapist Stephen Stosny argues that social media fuel election stress disorder. Social media, he writes, "gives you a voice but not an individuality, so people are frustrated on it" (Stosny 2021). San Diego State University professor Jean Twenge argued back in 2017 that American teens are "on the brink of a mental health crisis," and it is largely due to the prevalent use of smartphones. (Twenge 2017). Thanks to the high rates of teens spending hours online every day, many young Americans report feeling anxious, depressed, or suicidal. A Bridgeport, Connecticut, school psychologist with nearly thirty years' experience agreed in 2019, saying anxiety has blossomed because of social media. Other psychologists warn about students who are addicted to social media and their phones. A student who was reportedly "completely addicted" to her phone was prevented from doing what she needed to do at school. Her phone was "like an appendage, like her right arm," a school counselor reported (Flannery 2018).

The mounting popularity of smartphones and similar electronic devices favors "the ecosystem of hucksters" described by Patricia Pearson. (Pearson 2007, 128) Studies show that people say things to their screens which they never would say face-to-face. "You should kill yourself" is a familiar refrain online, and naturally some people take such cyberbullying to heart. It is hardly surprising that suicide rates among young people have climbed in recent years as smartphone use has multiplied.

The same studies reveal that tech companies such as Facebook, Twitter, and Snapchat provide online spaces which also foster the "openness, emotional self-absorption, and the sharing of feelings" characteristic of the therapeutic mentality. As Eva Moscowitz predicted in 2000, the therapeutic gospel has flourished online. Today, the seven-days-a-week, twenty-four-hours-a-day online market enables consumers to "do electronic therapy, find virtual support groups, visit advice sites, and participate in therapeutic news groups and chat rooms," in Moscowitz's words. (Moscowitz 2001, 2007) According to Twenge, researchers have determined that a sense of independence and self-reliance holds less sway with today's America's teenagers who spend hours per day on their devices. There is reason to believe that this leaves them vulnerable to therapism's overall message that emotional sickness can be a form of personal identity. Online users encounter others who share their same feelings of loneliness, depression and anxiety. While this can be reassuring to some, many others are exposed to the notion that they can do little to change this state of affairs without consulting professionals. Social media do not just create stressful anxiety in the lives of users, they spread the gospel of therapism by creating online "communities" of people who tend to embrace a shared sickness diagnosis as a form of personal identity.

Perhaps the most disturbing aspect of the march of therapism is how by the 2020s it has become politicized, exacerbating the partisan divisions within American society. According to physician and political scientist Ronald W. Dworkin, more and more Americans are embracing therapeutic ideas such as "the ideology of caring"—the "view that total strangers can solve people's life problems to make them feel better, thereby substituting for the friends or relatives who no longer exist in people's lives"—which has spawned an enormous "caring industry," "a nation-spanning network of organizations, leaders, and cadres that have organized, energized, and come to dominate American society." This ideology of caring, Dworkin writes, is "a revolutionary way of life," and the "caring industry," he maintains, now operates like a revolutionary political party replacing traditional culture. Its "model moves easily between personal life and politics," in Dworkin's words (Dworkin 2022). Daily we read or see examples of how people undergo consciousness-raising experiences on campuses and in the corporate world reminiscent of Mao's Chinese Red Guards during the Cultural Revolution of the 1960s.

Americans swept up in the caring industry and its diversity seminars and "struggle sessions" quickly learn its vocabulary and its core ideas—that "low self-esteem" and the "feeling of being marginalized" are natural responses to a world in which mounting numbers of Americans report feeling depressed or anxious. Terminology such as "safe spaces," "micro-aggressions," and "crying rooms" reflect the inroads this caring ideology has made, notably on college campuses.

A recent example of how the vocabulary and principles of therapism have seeped into politics was the reaction of various House of Representatives members on January 6, 2021, who described the events that day on Capitol Hill as a "traumatic experience." A House member from Vermont called January 6 a "trauma to our democracy" (whatever that means). Rep. Rashida Tlaib, a Democrat from Michigan, though not present at the Capitol during the siege, said "This is so personal, this is so hard." Another subtle way in which therapism permeates partisan politics is psychologist Stosny's advice to those feeling anxiety about US elections. Do not focus on "policies," he urges, which divide people, and instead "focus on deeper values" like compassion, equality and justice which supposedly foster agreement. But since when should voters not "focus" on policies? Is not an interest in policies key to being an informed voter? Whose definitions of compassion, equality, and justice should voters accept? Who says everyone agrees with what equality and justice stand for? Stosny's attempt to defuse political passions that might erupt in violence may be well-intentioned, but he runs the distinct risk of shutting down any meaningful political debate in the interest of avoiding any disagreement whatsoever.

CONCLUSION

In any case, there is no evidence that Stosny's approach would do anything to bridge the political divide. How do we know that reducing politics to vague terms such as compassion and equality foster agreement? Indeed, there is reason to believe that the therapeutic mentality, by politicizing unhappiness, in Dworkin's words, only makes matters worse. Therapism encourages what author Mila Ghorayeb calls "trauma politics," "emotional performances" by prominent political figures such as Democrat congresswoman Alexandria Ocasio-Cortez. Such "performances" predispose voters to identify with their victimhood and imagine their unhappiness derives from their status as emotionally damaged survivors. As Ghorayeb writes: "[Trauma politics] favor those that are more comfortable sharing their personal history. . . . The personal nature of this form of political discourse makes contesting facts a matter of personal attack rather than genuine truth-seeking. It forces us to contend with one's personal and subjective narrative rather than material social and political circumstances." Practitioners of trauma politics use narratives such as these to insulate themselves from any criticism and demonize their opponents who are routinely accused of minimizing, discrediting or belittling the accounts of survivors (Wordsman 2021). How employing these tactics can foster understanding among Americans is anyone's guess.

By now, it should be clear that the combination of the illness-breeding and illness-affirming qualities of American society in the twenty-first century has produced a revolutionary milestone in everything from medicine to politics. In the words of Eva Moscowitz: "The therapeutic gospel is . . . a fixture in American life" (Moscowitz 2001, 279, 281). Even if Americans wanted to challenge the therapeutic gospel, how then could it be done? As Moscowitz writes, we likely cannot go back to a pre-therapeutic era (Moscowitz 2001, 284). But lawmakers can always undertake reforms to reduce homelessness, income inequality, and the various forms of discrimination that are associated with addictions and make Americans feel stressed, anxious, and depressed. At the same time, Americans need to heed the verdict of history which suggests that no matter how much medication, counseling, destigmatizing, or access to services the average American receives, or how much "mental health literacy" Americans enjoy, expert groups such as Mental Health America concede that the country continues to do a "poor job" protecting its citizens from mental sickness (Mental Health America 2023). Can spending more on the same policies improve public mental health in America? Instead, the time may have come to question the principles of therapism which seemingly enjoy consensual support across class, racial, and religious lines. The medicalization of everyday life has been going on for decades, so the calls for more and more "mental health literacy" increasingly ring hollow.

Another starting point for rolling back therapism is the pervasive use of social media. As we have seen, social media both breeds anxiety and sustains the illness-affirming nature of therapeutic culture. As Twenge has urged her readers, "Put down the phone, turn off the laptop, and do something—anything—that does not involve a screen." Curtailing screen time is a voluntary step that Americans can take, but parents should also regulate the hours each day their children spend online.

Another theme for reflection is the fact, noted by Moscowitz and others, that the cascading "devotion to the psyche" coincides with the decline in religion, at least as measured by rates of churchgoing (Moscowitz 2001, 280). In this day and age, it is hardly likely that governments will cheerlead voters into attending services at churches, synagogues, temples, or mosques. Yet, raising awareness about the dangers of therapism may lead some Americans to seek emotional solace from other institutions, notably organized religion.

As this glimpse at recent history indicates, America is in the grip of therapeutic culture, despite the warnings of scholars ranging from Christopher Lasch to Ronald Dworkin. The stakes for the nation are high. As Lasch argued over thirty years ago, therapism in its ongoing quest for authenticity through self-absorption merely exacerbates the alienation which helps to account for the ascending anxiety levels of today. As Americans have become more dependant on the dreams of gratification through consumerism either thanks to advertising or the reliance on professional services, they have become increasingly unhappy and anxious. As the twenty-first century continues to unfold, this vicious cycle needs to be broken.

REFERENCES

American Bar Association. 2022. "Law School Applicants and Enrollees." ABA Profile of the Legal Profession 2022.

Belluz, Julia. 2010. "High Anxiety." *Maclean's* (18 November 2010). https://macleans.ca/news/canada/high-anxiety/.

Boyle, Patrick. 2019. "More Women than Men are Enrolled in Medical School." *AAMC News* (9 December 2019). https://www.aamc.org/news/more-women-men-are-enrolled-medicalschool.

Canadian Association of University Teachers. 2018. "Academic Anxiety." *CAUT Bulletin* 65: 14–19.

Clark, Cory, and Bo Winegard. 2022. "Sex and the Academy." *Quillette* (8 October 2022). https://quillette.com/2022/10/08/sex-and-the-academy/.

Dowbiggin, Ian. 2011. *The Quest for Mental Health: A Tale of Science, Medicine, Scandal, Sorrow and Mass Society.* New York: Cambridge University Press.

Dworkin, Ronald W. 2022. "The Politicization of Unhappiness." *National Affairs* 23. https://www.nationalaffairs.com/publications/detail/the-politicization-of-unhappiness.

Elkind, Elizabeth. 2020. "What Is 'Election Stress Disorder,' and Do I Have It?" CBS News (29 September 2020). https://www.cbsnews.com/news/what-is-election-stress-disorder/

Flannery, Mary Ellen. 2018. "The Epidemic of Anxiety Among Today's Students." National Education Association (28 March 2018). https://www.nea.org/advocating-forchange/new-from-nea/epidemic-anxiety-among-todays-students.

Furedi, Frank. 2007. "The Only Thing we have to Fear is the 'Culture of Fear' itself." *Spiked* (4 April 2007). https://www.spiked-online.com/2007/04/04/the-only-thing-we-have-to-fearis-the-culture-of-fear-itself/.

Howland, Jason. 2020. "Is Election Stress Disorder Real?" *Mayo Clinic News* Network (23 October 2020). https://newsnetwork.mayoclinic.org/discussion/is-election-stressdisorder-real/.

Jeffay, Nathan. 2022. "'A Mental Health Pandemic': Israeli Therapist Warns of COVID's Lasting Effects." *Times of Israel* (13 Ocotber 2022). https://

www.timesofisrael.com/amental-health-pandemic-israeli-therapist-warns-of covids-lasting-effects/.

Kovach, Bill, and Rom Rosenstiel. 1999. *Warp Speed: America in the Age of Mixed Media*. New York: Century Foundation Press.

Kramer, Peter. 1993. *Listening to Prozac. A Psychiatrist Explores Antidepressant Drugs and the Remaking of the Self.* New York: Viking.

Mental Health America. 2023. "Policy Agenda: 2023." https://mhanational.org/policy-issues.

Moscowitz, Eva. 2001. *In Therapy We Trust: America's Obsession with Self-Fulfillment.* Baltimore: Johns Hopkins University Press.

Pearson, Patricia. 2007. *A Brief History of Anxiety (Yours and Mine)*. Toronto: Random House.

Salerno, Steve. 2005. *SHAM: How the Self-Help Movement Made America Helpless*. New York: Crown Publishers.

Self, John. 2022. "The Rise and Fall of Sad, White Men." *The Critic* (July 2022). https://thecritic.co.uk/issues/july-2022/the-rise-and-fall-of-sad-white-men/.

Shorter, Edward. 1994. *From the Mind into the Body: The Cultural Origins of Psychosomatic Symptoms*. New York: Free Press.

Sommers, Christina Hoff, and Sally Satel. 2005. *One Nation Under Therapy: How the Helping Culture Is Eroding Self-Reliance.* New York: St. Martin's Press.

Stosny, Steven. 2021. "How Social Media Differences Can Warp Relationships." *Psychology Today* (23 June 2021).

Tone, Andrea. 2009. *The Age of Anxiety: America's Turbulent Affair with Tranquilizers*. New York: Basic Books.

Twenge, Jean M. 2017. "Have Smartphones Destroyed a Generation?" *The Atlantic* (September 2017).

University of Rhode Island. 2021. "Researchers find Pandemic Exacerbates Anxiety, Depression, Impulsivity and lack of Mindfulness among Faculty." *Rhody Today* (29 January 2021). https://www.uri.edu/news/2021/01/researchers-find-pandemic-exacerbates-anxietydepression-impulsivity-and-lack-of-mindfulness-among-faculty/.

Wordsman, Scott. 2021. "Trump, AOC, and the Triumph of Trauma Politics." *Tablet* (11 March 2021). https://www.tabletmag.com/sections/news/articles/triumph-of-trauma-politics.

Zeldin, Theodore. 1981. *France, 1848–1945: Anxiety and Hypocrisy*. New York: Oxford University Press.

PART II

The Nature and Meaning of Anxiety

Chapter 6

Generalized Anxiety Disorder

Natural, Normative, or Neither?

Jesse Prinz

Philosophical debates about psychiatric conditions pivot around two poles: naturalistic approaches, which explain these conditions in biological terms, and normative approaches, which place emphasis on cultural values. There are also hybrid approaches, combining both of these elements. Here, I will attempt to adjudicate this debate with reference to generalized anxiety disorder, or GAD. I will argue that GAD is neither natural nor normative, as those terms are often understood, but rather socially constructed. Norms and nature contribute in important ways, but this dichotomous pair of options has constrained theory choice. Here I develop an approach to social constructionism informed by relationalist approaches within disability studies. The resulting proposal differs from normativist and naturalist alternatives.

Why focus on GAD? First, anxiety disorders are the most prevalent mental health diagnoses in the world, and GAD is the most diagnosed anxiety disorder. For this reason alone, it deserves scrutiny. It has received far less philosophical attention than other diagnoses, such as depression, psychopathy, dissociative identity, and delusional disorders. Among anxiety disorders, GAD receives appreciably less attention from philosophers than phobias. This neglect needs to be corrected.

In addition, GAD is an instructive condition to examine in light of the debate between naturalists and normativists. Anxiety is a form of fear, which is the paradigm case of an evolved emotional response. This invites the suggestion that anxiety disorders involve evolved mechanisms. There is also evidence that GAD is heritable, and there are genes associated with predispositions. There are, thus, reasons for thinking a biological account of GAD has much promise. At the same time, biological theories usually associate ill-health with premature death and low fertility. As we will see, GAD is not strongly associated with either. This raises the possibility that GAD is not biologically disadvantageous. If we adopt a normative view, however, it is, for reasons I will present, far from clear what norms are implicated. GAD is thus a challenging case for both sides of the naturalism/normativism divide.

In what follows, I will survey naturalist and normative theories, and raise difficulties for both approaches when applied to GAD. I will then turn to social constructionism. Constructionism is strongly associated with normative theories (Murphy 2012). Constructionism has also been described as a blend of naturalism and normativism (Kingma 2013). But all three, it turns out, are dissociable. I will argue that social construction differs in crucial ways from leading normativist approaches, and that it offers considerable promise for understanding GAD. Social forces contribute to GAD in a number of ways, impacting symptoms, prevalence, and status as a disorder. These create real, but nonnatural, conditions for individuals diagnosed with GAD. Both biology and social norms contribute as well, but neither do the kind of ontological work that they are presumed to do on leading naturalist and normative theories. In my conclusion, I willy briefly suggest that these lessons may extend to mental disorders more broadly. If so, GAD helps point toward an alternative to the usual naturalist and normative accounts of mental disorders—an alternative that could be easily missed if we started with a different psychiatric condition.

Before starting, it will help to put the current clinical definition of GAD on the table. The definition has changed over time, and much can be said about its (in)stability as a construct (Crocq 2017). I will assume for discussion that the current conceptualization captures a real, but culturally variable, syndrome. For this, I will rely on the definitions in the 11th revision of *The International Classification of Diseases* (ICD-11) and the fifth edition *of The Diagnostic and Statistical Manual of Mental Disorders* (DSM 5). Both begin with a general features followed by characteristic symptoms. For the ICD-11, the general features are either free-floating anxiety or excessive worry. The DSM-5 refers to excessive worry and anxiety that are difficult to control. The additional symptoms include: restlessness, difficulty concentrating, irritability, muscle tension, sleep disturbance, fatigue (DSM only), and autonomic overactivity (ICD only). Both say symptoms must last for several months (six months, in the DSM), and they specify a similar criterion for qualifying as a disorder: the symptoms must cause significant distress or impairment in important areas of functioning. This criterion is intended to be theory-neutral in that it can serve practitioners with very different views about the nature of disorders. I will revisit this criterion below, but first want to survey more theoretically committal accounts.

NATURALISM AND GAD

Naturalistic Approaches to Mental Disorders

With the advent of modernity, mental disorders increasingly came under the medical gaze (Foucault 1973). Madness was reconceptualized as mental illness, and medical institutions and subfields emerged for the treatment of the mentally ill. Within this paradigm, there has been a concerted effort to find definitions of mental disorders that align with theories of organic diseases. In both cases, the medical approach invites the idea that disease can be defined objectively, in biological terms, without reference to human values. Health and disease, some claim, are states of the natural world, which can be characterized independently of classification and cultural norms. This is the "naturalist" viewpoint. Against this picture, there are some who think that mental disorders—perhaps in contradistinction to organic diseases—depend on human values. The most extreme versions of this "constructionist" approach claim the boundary between mental health and pathology is entirely a function of our preferences, attitudes, and conceptual schemes. Between these extremes, there are hybrid views that assign a role to both biology and societal values in defining mental disorders. I will briefly describe versions of each, and some of the obstacles they face.

Among naturalist approaches proposed by philosophers, the most widely discussed is Boorse's biostatistical theory (BST). Boorse aims to define diseases in general, but he specifically designed his account to apply to both mental disorders and organic diseases. His definition has three parts (Boorse 1997, 7). First, diseases are relativized to natural "reference classes" of organisms within a species (e.g., age-groups and sexes). Second, some of the parts and processes possessed by members of these reference classes have "normal functions"; there are statistically typical contributions that those parts and processes make to biological fitness (i.e., survival and reproduction). Finally, a disease is an internal state that reduces those functional abilities below "typical efficiency."

The notion of "function" in Boorse's account is Darwinian insofar as it implicates survival and reproduction, but the account makes no reference to the evolutionary past. Other naturalists are more willing to invoke evolution. They deploy a concept of biological "dysfunction" to designate a part or process that is not doing what it evolved to do through natural selection. Wakefield (1992) develops an account of this type, though he also includes a normative condition, as we will see below.

There are also naturalists who move away from Darwinian constructs, abandoning talk of evolution and fitness. One strategy is to replace Darwinian concepts of function with a less teleological alternative. For example, Lange

(2007) relies on Cummins's (1975) theory of functional explanation. For Cummins, some capacities can be decomposed into simpler subcapacities, as when we explain circulation by the beating of the heart. The subcapacity helps explain the capacity. Lange defines diseases as incapacities in subcapacties that contribute to sustaining health.

Within psychiatry, a related approach is the Research Domain Criteria (RDoC) project. RDoC relates mental disorders to mechanisms that are independently motivated by behavioral and biological research. For instance, they posit a negative valence system, which decomposes into simpler subsystems, which cope with frustrated nonreward, loss, potential threat, sustained threat, and acute threat (Cultbert and Insel 2013). Each of these has associated biomechanisms. Disorders are understood as dysfunctions in one or more subsystems.

In contrast to these approaches that preserve the concept of dysfunction while downplaying Darwinian ideas, there are approaches that jettison dysfunction while embracing evolution. Here, what we call mental disorders are products of evolution, and would be beneficial in certain circumstances. For example, Mealey (1995) argues that psychopathy increases the reproductive potential of psychopaths. Likewise, Garson (2021) rejects theories that define disorders as dysfunctional, noting that some psychiatric conditions would have been advantageous in human prehistory. On this view, disorders arise when there is a mismatch between an evolved response and current living conditions.

This is not an exhaustive list of naturalistic approaches, but it reflects the range of views occupying current discussion. We can now ask whether any of these offers a promising account of why GAD is a mental disorder. (I will assume, for discussion, that GAD is a disorder, since most naturalists would classify it as such.)

Against Naturalist Approaches to GAD

Though instructive in many ways, I do not think prevailing naturalistic theories provide satisfying explanations of GAD's status as a disorder. I will look at each in turn. My aim is not to decisively refute each, but to present prima facie worries that motivate a search for alternatives.

Let's begin with Boorse's biostatistical theory (BST). Boorse places some emphasis on frequency as a measure of disorder; he might argue that GAD is statistically rare and thus likely to be an aberration. This would be a problematic inference. First, GAD is more frequent than red hair (3.7 percent globally, according to Ruscio et al. 2017 vs. under 2 percent). GAD is also more frequent in women than in men. If infrequency indicates ailment, it would follow that GAD is more of a disorder in men, which is absurd. It's hard to see how the statistical part of Boorse's theory can help here. It is an imperfect measure of whether a trait has a normal function. A more direct measure is fitness, which is really the crux of Boorse's account. Does GAD reduce survival and reproduction? Perhaps not. According to some studies, GAD is not associated with excess mortality (Holwerda et al. 2007) or lower fertility (Jacobson 2016). In fact, people with GAD have significantly higher marriage rates than those without psychiatric diagnoses (Yoon and Zinbarg 2007).

These observations about fitness also threaten Wakefield's evolutionary dysfunction condition. It should be noted at the outset that Wakefield has reservations about calling GAD a disorder (Horwitz and Wakefield 2012, 237–47), but his evolutionary approach to dysfunction has enough traction in psychiatry to deserve careful consideration. Efforts to assess GAD with respect to evolved functions face an immediate epistemic hurtle: it is difficult to establish facts about the evolutionary past, since no fossil records can reveal the fate of ancestors with elevated anxiety. The preservation of genes that dispose people to GAD suggests that people with such symptoms were perfectly fit. One gene that has been associated with anxiety (the short form of 5-HTTLPR) is found in nearly 40–50 percent of Americans (Odgerel et al. 2013). There is also reason to doubt whether GAD's symptoms would have posed a threat to fitness in hominid prehistory. It's easy to imagine that the lives of our ancestors were filled with hazards: predators, extreme weather, constant need for food accrual, high infant mortality, intergroup aggression, little medical knowledge, limited understanding of nature's vicissitudes, and frequent need to relocate. Generalized anxiety, which may seem excessive now, could have been apt under such conditions, and adaptive.

In any case, evolutionary conjectures are largely irrelevant to clinical practice. Clinicians and patients do not need to establish conjectures about evolution to determine that a person has a condition that might benefit from medical attention. This brings us to accounts that posit a dysfunction in mechanisms that sustain health (Lange) or fundamental domains of mental functioning (RDoC). Mortality and marriage indicate that GAD is not a major threat to life, but it can certainly cause distress and disability (that is a matter of definition on the ICD and DSM definitions). GAD can negatively impact personal and professional life and diminish life satisfaction. But this does not establish a dysfunction, in the technical sense. Here we might look to RDoC for guidance, since that framework postulates mental mechanisms. However, there is no neat mapping between GAD and mental mechanisms. Intuitively, anxiety might seem most closely related to the potential threat system on RDoC's functional decomposition of the mind. But there is also evidence linking anxiety to sustained threat (Patriquin and Mathew 2017), and there is also evidence from brain imaging that suggests hypoactivation in both reward and loss systems (Bashford-Largo et al. 2021). This raises a difficulty for any approach that tries to explain mental disorders with reference to isolated mechanisms, since prevailing diagnostic categories are multi-dimensional, and neural systems are highly interactive. Furthermore, correlating GAD with responses in neural systems does not establish dysfunction, especially when the corresponding behavioral measures find no significant increases in error rates or inability to perform assigned tasks (as in Bashford-Largo et al.).

The failure to establish strong evidence for dysfunction or reductions in fitness could be taken as supporting the final naturalist approach that I reviewed above: the evolutionary mismatch view. On this approach, GAD is an adaptive response, furnished by evolution to cope with threats. It becomes a disorder only when there is a mismatch between the conditions we live in and the conditions under which GAD is designed by natural selection to operate. In support of this, Garson (2021) reviews evidence that exposure to childhood stressors increases incidence of GAD later in life; GAD systems may serve such individuals well as juveniles, but they can seem excessive in adulthood if living conditions improve. To assess this proposal, we must distinguish two possibilities. One is that evolution selected for GAD genes in a subset of the population. This seems unlikely. Genetic research on GAD has largely focused on a short variant of the serotonin gene, 5-HTTLPR. But this polymorphism as also associated with depression, aggression, and working memory performance (Kostić et al. 2017). Likewise for other candidate genes, and there is also a strong genetic relationship between GAD and neuroticism (Gottschalk and Domschke 2017). There is, thus, little evidence that GAD itself is selected for. A second possibility is that we are all born with an evolved GAD potential, which kicks in when exposed to highly stressful environments. But this is difficult to reconcile with variation in genetic propensities. Moreover, it is hard to square with a striking finding that rates of GAD are lower in countries with higher stress and fewer resources (Ruscio et al. 2017).

One might try to save naturalism by appealing to heritability results. GAD has a heritability score a rating of 0.32, which is relatively high (Hettema et al. 2001). This indicates a biological susceptibility to GAD, but it doesn't establish that GAD itself is biological. By analogy, suppose that athletic talent is heritable. It would not follow that being an athlete is a biological trait. It would be implausible to claim that biology makes no contribution to GAD. Biology might dispose some people to worry more than others. But this would not entail that GAD's status as a disorder is a biological fact. Here, prevailing naturalist theories seem to come up short.

The foregoing considerations raise prima facie doubts about naturalistic answers to the question, what makes GAD a disorder? Let's now consider normative theories.

NORMATIVISM AND GAD

Normativist Approaches to Mental Disorders

Normativists claim that the concept of disorder, or even "illness," in the psychiatric domain is inextricably evaluative. This has been a common view among historians, sociologists, and critics of psychiatry, but, as we will see, it is also a position defended by some who have less skeptical views. Norms can reflect deep and widespread human interests, and working, with psychiatric support, to live in accordance with things we value is an important aspect of living well, or healthfully.

Beginning with the cynical end of the spectrum, consider Thomas Szasz, who draws a sharp distinction between physical and mental health:

> The concept of illness, whether bodily or mental, implies deviation from some clearly defined norm. In the case of physical illness, the norm is the structural and functional integrity of the human body. . . . The norm from which deviation is measured whenever one speaks of a mental illness is a psychosocial and ethical one. (Szasz 1960, 114)

To illustrate, Szasz (1974, 28) notes that "addiction, delinquency, divorce, homosexuality, homicide, [and] suicide" have been regarded as illnesses. He thinks we are unjustified in using medical terms when there is no known organic cause, and the range of behaviors we medicalize indicates a covert moral agenda. Szasz concludes that mental illness is a myth. Psychiatric syndromes are perfectly real, but they are moral problems, not medical problems.

Foucault (1965, 56) brings out moral dimensions as well in his history of madness. Foucault argues that, as Europe moved toward a new economy in the seventeenth century, sloth replaced avarice and pride as the cardinal sin. People deemed mad were regarded as idle, not just irrational or foolish, which had been prevailing ideas in antiquity and the Renaissance. This was also the dawn of the asylum, and those deemed mad were removed from public view and placed in institutions where they could be monitored and controlled. It was in this context that a new medical approach emerged, but in its early forms it was overtly moralistic. "Moral treatments" served to cure through disciplinary techniques that were often cruel and humiliating (Foucault 1965, 247). These include submersion in water and cold showers, which evoked the logic of purification (Foucault 1965, 166–72). Foucault quotes Pinel, a founding figure in medical psychiatry, as attributing insanity to moral failings, including laziness, apathy, drunkenness, promiscuity, and debauchery (Foucault 1965, 258–59).

The moral dimensions of psychiatric diagnosis has been emphasized by more recent authors as well. Charland (2004, 71) argues that personality disorders, such as antisocial personality disorder, borderline, and narcissism are moral conditions; he equates successful treatment with moral conversion. Pickard (2009) says these categories can be analyzed as failures of virtue and character.

For some, the blurred boundary between psychiatric diagnosis and moral disapprobation invites skepticism about psychiatry. Others see the blurring more positively. Criticizing Szasz, Margolis (1966, 73) grants that moral values guide therapeutic practice, but argues that the extension of medical terms to the moral sphere is "perfectly legitimate (even necessary)." He sees medicine as concerned with happiness and well-being, and psychiatry can contribute to that. Elsewhere Margolis emphasizes prudential values as worthy aims for medicine: "avoidance of death, prolongation of life, restriction of pain, gratification of desires, insuring security of person and body and property" (1976, 251). These are "enabling interests" for the moral, political, and economic integrity of a complex society (1976, 257). Against this background, mental illnesses can be understood as psychological traits that threaten these interests.

In a similar spirit, Engelhardt (1976, 275) identifies illness with symptoms that are "distressful, displeasing, painful, or dysfunctional." Engelhardt does not mean "dysfunctional" in an evolutionary sense, but in accord with ideas about what qualifies as a properly functioning person. That, in turn, depends on our values. But Engelhardt thinks many of these values will be widely shared and will often relate to natural capacities, such as freedom and rationality (Engelhardt 1976, 266). Notice that Engelhardt's view takes the patient's perspective into account. If "illness" is an evaluative concept, we can ask whose values are at work. On Foucault's account, it often seems to be the values of those in power. For Szasz, there are evaluative struggles between patient and practitioner. Margolis and Engelhadt emphasize values that are widely shared, and their use of terms such as "distress" and "well-being" remind us that a normative approach need not be an oppressive approach.

For a more recent view in the tradition of non-cynical normativism, we can consider Cooper's (2002) definition of disease. She argues that three conditions must be met: a disease is something bad, unlucky, and in need of medical treatment. She does not define badness in detail, but she regards it as a normative condition. One difference with Engelhardt is that Cooper explicitly disavows patients' perspectives. She warns that people can be uninformed, incompetent, or self-deceived (Cooper 2002, 273). Thus, her badness condition requires external measurement. The unluckiness condition is designed to exclude bad things endured by everyone, like teething, and the medical treatment condition distinguishes illness from, e.g., economic misfortunes.

In addition to these theories, there have been attempts to combine normativism with naturalism. The most influential example is Wakefield's (1992) harmful dysfunction account. Wakefield's account, we have seen, involves evolutionary dysfunction, but he denies that this is a sufficient condition. Homosexuality, for example, might reduce fitness but should not be regarded as a disorder. To address this problem, we should limit disorders to dysfunctions that are "socially disvalued" (Wakefield 1992, 384). Recently, he has clarified that social values are, "value claims that have been subjected to a dialectic that goes deeper than immediate reactions or consensus to explore which of a culture's many often-conflicting value commitments are its most basic values, which serve long-run interests of justice" (Wakefield 2021, 555). I will pass over this proposal, below, since it is hard to assess how a dialectic about basic values would turn out with respect to GAD, and, as noted above, Wakefield has reservations with calling GAD a disorder.

Against Normativist Approaches to GAD

With a number of normative accounts on the table, we can see how each might treat GAD. Naturalist accounts faced prima facie worries about applicability because they posit mechanisms that seem untestable or unlikely to apply. Normative accounts do better in this respect, but, we will see, they still leave much to be explained.

Let's begin with Szasz's thesis that mental illness is a myth. Szasz says virtually nothing about GAD in his many books, but we might extrapolate that he'd regard GAD as a moral problem in two senses. First, he'd say that those who suffer from GAD should be regarded as fully responsible agents. Second, he might propose that GAD is medicalized because it is held in negative moral regard. The views of Charland and Pickard invite such a conjecture as well. Let's consider these moral claims in turn.

As for responsibility, the philosophical issues are complex, but I think we can agree that people with GAD are highly agentic, and, given that some symptoms are treatable, one could hold a person responsible for failing to change their dispositions were those dispositions subject to legitimate censure. This brings us to the second conjecture. Is GAD regarded as a moral failing? Perhaps. GAD is characterized by "excessive worry." The term "excessive" can be read as a moral criticism. With Pickard, one might postulate that GAD is regarded as a character flaw, akin to cowardice. But "excessive" might also be a statistical claim (worrying more than the norm), a claim about aptness (worrying about things that are benign), or a claim about well-being (worrying in a way the interferes with important life activities). To evaluate a moral account of GAD we must ask, what kind of disapproval is expressed when we call worry excessive?

At this point, it is important to distinguish two kinds of projects. On the one hand, we might want to know why, as a matter of fact, people regard individuals diagnosed with GAD as excessive in their worry. Probably all of the candidates just listed are relevant. When someone tells us we are worrying too much, they may think we are being craven, peculiar, irrational, or self-destructive. If we want to explain why GAD has been considered a disorder historically, we cannot rule out moral factors. Foucault's chilling exposé of moral treatments in the early nineteenth century indicates that moral and medical categories are often intertwined. But suppose we are interested in a normative question: should GAD be considered a disorder on moral grounds? Here the answer may be more firmly negative. Aristotle makes this point in *The Nichomachean Ethics* (1149a). He says we can distinguish the vice of cowardice from the disease of being afraid of everything. Diseases, he thought, could be inborn or the result of trauma or habit (nail-biting is given as an example). Someone who is afraid of everything would be insulated against moral blame, though there might be a charge of irrationality because their fears would be arbitrary (fear of weasels, for example). If we want to decide when, if ever, GAD should be regarded as a disorder, we might want to bracket off moral attitudes. After all, moral attitudes have led to unjust medicalization, as in the case of homosexuality. This is just what Szasz is worried about. Rather than abandoning a psychiatric vocabulary, as he would advise, we might offer an ameliorative approach that aims to medicalize more justly.

This brings us to Margolis, Engelhardt, and Cooper. They can be interpreted as developing ameliorative theories. They aim to identify normative factors that can be legitimately used to demarcate disorders. Margolis and Engelhard emphasize widely accepted prudential and hedonic norms like longevity, security, and freedom from pain and distress. Some of these norms are compromised by GAD. GAD might not shorten life, and it could improve security because it increases vigilance and reduces risk-taking. GAD is not particularly painful, though it can cause some muscle discomfort and fatigue. It's debatable whether the impact on these (contingent) dimensions would earn GAD's designation as a disorder. The most applicable hedonic norm is distress. Anxiety and worry are distressful states, but, as Cooper would remind us, many distressful states would not qualify as mental disorders—economic hardships, bad relationships, concerns about the politicians in power, and so on. In other words, distress can be appropriate.

In response, one might argue that the problem with GAD is not distress as such, but irrational distress. Perhaps the norm that is violated is a norm of reason. This is a hard line to defend. Those who suffer from GAD are not wrong to think that bad outcomes are possible. Risks are a regular part of human life, and anything can go wrong. One might counter that the anxieties are disproportionate to the likelihood of bad outcomes, but this is difficult to measure. Fear tends to operate on a false alarm principle. Caution is often better than carelessness, and ruminating about bad outcomes can help prepare us for the inevitable cases where they do occur. If so, GAD is neither a violation of hedonic norms, though it is unpleasant, nor of rationality norms, though some people may prefer to live carefree.

Cooper's account doesn't help us identify an adequate normative condition because she does not offer a full account of badness. But I want to express some doubts about her unluckiness and medical treatment conditions. With respect to unluckiness, Cooper comes close to the view that mental disorders are rare or unexpected. This is a strong commitment. In the United States, the lifetime prevalence of GAD approaches eight percent, which is hardly rare (Ruscio 2017, Table 1), and it is easy to imagine a world where the majority of people were ill. Moreover, talk of luck implies that GAD strikes randomly, but it could well be associated with social conditions. As for medical treatment, there are many who distrust the field of psychiatry. Within the academic field of Mad Studies, it is common to refer to people with mental disorders as "survivors," referring to their bad experiences with medical treatment (Beresford and Russo 2022). It is contentious to claim that mental disorders should be understood and treated medically.

I also want to comment on Cooper's distrust of patients' perspectives. She rightly points out that people can be misinformed or self-deceived about their states of health. This suggests that, for some disorders, we lack first-person authority on how we are faring. Still, I think this point may be inapplicable to GAD. Those of us who experience a lot of anxiety usually know we are anxious. It may be hard, at times, to see how much this effects our lives. A friend might counsel us to relax or focus on something else, or reassure us that things will be okay. Such support is welcome, but it is part of a dialogical process in which we can reflect on our own level of worry and decide whether it is excessive. Those who decide that they are worrying too much may seek help. They cannot be accused of lacking insight into their condition. But, for those of us who decide, on reflection, that we are okay with our level of worry, it would be paternalistic to insist that we are mistaken. We may, ironically, feel comfort in our worry, and feel at home there. Anxiety can become an aspect of identity—akin to being neurotic—or a deep conviction—a grim outlook on the world.

I don't mean to suggest that there is no room for error when it comes to GAD. Indeed, I think there are ways in which we can easily be uninformed about its impact. One thing we cannot ascertain from the first-person perspective is how GAD impacts us relative to others. We might have occasion to make such observations, as when peers and colleagues outperform us, but we have limited direct insight into GAD's impact and costs. These can be high even for those who identify with GAD and feel little motivation to find a cure. This, it turns out, provides a very general reason for doubting whether prevailing normative accounts can explain what makes GAD a disorder. These accounts tend to focus on the individuals who have the diagnosis. Those with GAD are described as immoral, imprudent, or unhappy. These norms may be externally imposed, but the problems are, nevertheless, attributed to individuals. But there is another way to look at GAD, and at mental disorders more broadly. The problems may not lie with the individual, but with society. Ironically, prevailing normativist and naturalist approaches share this focus on individuals in common. They both tend to locate disorders in the people who have them. Naturalism does this all the more so in its search for broken mechanisms. One exception is the evolutionary mismatch account. I will revisit the notion of mismatching below, but without the evolutionary commitments.

There are other general reasons for resisting prevailing normativist theories. A second reason concerns the focus on norms as the main source of demarcation between the normal and the pathological. Norms are no doubt implicated in how we diagnose and classify, but divisions between people can be imposed and maintained in other ways as well. For example, divisions can be based on factual beliefs, on behavioral patterns, and on structural factors, such as institutions. One can regard each of these as normative in some sense, since norms impact each of them, but the emphasis on norms distracts from the ways these other factors may contribute. By analogy divisions between races may be impacted by norms, but segregation, economic disparity, and scientific racism can contribute as well. These may be normatively driven, but their mode of impact is material and conceptual. It would seem odd to propose a normative theory of race, even if one grants that norms play an essential role.

The third general concern about normativism is that it can too easily be read as a nominalist approach to disorder. That is, normativism may be taken to imply that having a disorder is a matter of how people are classified. On this reading, being mentally ill is a mere projection of moral or prudential attitudes. Disvaluing, that is, confers illness in and of itself. Foucault is a possible exception. He recognizes how profoundly people's lives can be impacted by psychiatric classification. For him, values guide the use of therapeutic instruments and techniques, which then get "inscribed on the body" (Foucault 2006, 106). Far from confirming normativism, however, that insight points in another direction.

SOCIAL CONSTRUCTION AND GAD

Varieties of Social Construction

Social constructionism can be broadly defined as the view that a given category or kind is shaped by social forces. To apply this definition, we need an account of social forces, and we need to unpack the metaphor of "shaping." Social forces include decisions, beliefs, attitudes, behaviors, and practices, as well as social arrangements (e.g., caste and class) and cultural products (e.g., artifacts, institutions, and discourses). The term "force" simply signals that each of these things can have an impact, but they key question concerns the nature of that impact. What is it to shape?

To answer this question, I want to consider a number of different ways that social forces can impact a category. These can be regarded as different varieties of social construction. They are dissociable but compatible, and I will ultimately argue that all of them are applicable to mental disorders. The first variety I'll call "generative":

> A category is a *generative construction* to the extent that social forces impact which individuals have characteristics sufficient for membership.

The aristocracy, for example, is generatively constructed, since social forces determine who falls into that class. Generative construction comes in degrees and can interact with biological factors. For example, being a professional basketball player depends largely on social factors, but height and other aspects of biology matter too. Even here, though, we need not think of biol ogy as an ingredient that can be separated from the social, since height is impacted by social factors such as diet. Being a basketball player is best described as a generative construction to which biology makes a contribution. This is typical for constructed categories.

Generative construction makes reference to the conditions of category membership. Many of our categories have a dimensional structure, with multiple characteristic features. A second variety of construction concerns these features:

> A category is a *formative construction* to the extent that social forces introduce or alter its characteristic features.

Formative constructions include professional categories like being a schoolteacher. Occupations are generative constructions, in that membership depends on training, opportunity and so forth, but also formative constructions in that professional roles and responsibilities are socially determined. Conducting classes, devising assignments, and grading are all characteristic schoolteacher activities. A more familiar example from the social constructionist literature is gender. Here, social forces contribute to the construction of tastes, roles, and behaviors that we identify as masculine, feminine, genderqueer and so on.

Within philosophy of psychiatry, there is a third variety of construction that has attracted most attention. It can be called "delineative":

> A category is a *delineative construction* to the extent that social forces play a role in demarcating its boundaries.

In asking whether mental illness is a social construction, we are most often asking whether social forces determine the boundary between illness and health. Delineative construction can be intimately related to formative construction, in that boundaries may depend on characteristic features. For some categories having the preponderance of characteristic features is deemed sufficient for membership. But this is not always the case. A twelve-year-old might act like a typical teenager, while failing to meet the age threshold. Conversely, there may be cases where a socially delineated category has features given by nature. The category of weeds is a popular example. We decide what counts, so, when taken together, weeds are not a biological category, but each kind of weed is.

A further distinction can be drawn between two kinds of delineative construction. In some cases, getting categorized in a particular way is merely nominal: entities so categorized are not thereby impacted, except in how we think about them. When Pluto was demoted from planet to dwarf planet, Pluto kept doing the same old thing. Contrast this with the class of precious metals. These get mined, cast, polished, and sold. In this case, the delineative construction can be described as impactive rather than nominal.

In cases where delineative and formative construction are both in play, the two may interact bidirectionally. Most obviously, as noted, having certain socially determined features can lead to being categorized in a certain way. But the converse is also true. Categorization can impact features. For example precious metals are characteristically shiny, but they are far less so when found in nature. Getting classified as precious increases the probability of ending up with a smooth and lustrous surface.

The last distinction I will draw concerns two kinds of impactful delineative constructions. In some cases, categorization leads to an intrinsic change in the items that get classified; a hunk of jade may get carved, for example. In other cases, the impact is more relational. Boxers who are classified as exceeding the weight threshold for their desired division get barred from bouts. This is not like the Pluto case, where there is no impact, but neither is it like the precious metal case, where there is a direct bodily impact. The impact is extrinsic, rather than intrinsic, but nevertheless real. In many cases, there will be both intrinsic and extrinsic effects. The boxer who fails to meet a target threshold at weigh-in may try to sweat off the extra pounds.

Social Construction, Normativism, and Naturalism

With this taxonomy in hand, I now want to suggest that social construction is a genuine alternative to both naturalism and normativism. After making this case I will compare my position to Kingma (2013) who says social construction is a "combination" of normativism and naturalism. I will take issue with this description, though I emphatically agree that both nature and norms can contribute to socially constructed kinds.

Let's begin by contrasting social constructionism and naturalism. More specifically, let's begin with formative constructions. Some formative constructions (being an aristocrat) are entirely non-natural, but generative construction is fully compatible with naturalism in other cases. Social forces can determine membership for natural categories, as when social interaction determines who contracts COVID-19. (Or, one might say, "relatively natural," in this case, because COVID-19 status may depend on social decisions about the requisite viral load; the cycle threshold for a positive PCR test is stipulated by us.)

Things are more complicated with formative constructions. If a kind has characteristic features that are socially determined, then it cannot be regarded as entirely natural. But there might be mixed cases, where some features arise naturally and others socially, or cases where naturally arising features get socially tuned or transformed. If membership conditions for such a category were natural, we might call it a biosocial kind. Imagine, in contrast, a category whose membership conditions are socially determined—a delineative construction. In that case, I think we'd want to say the kind is decidedly social, since its joints would be given by us, not by nature. If such a kind had entirely natural features—if it were not formatively constructed—it would still be a social kind. Consider maguro nigiri—a kind of sushi made by combining tuna and rice. Maguro nigiri has natural ingredients, but it is a social kind. I will return to this point when discussing Kingma below. If this is right, generative constructions can be natural, formative constructions can be partially natural, and delineative constructions are nonnatural, though they can have natural or partially natural features.

Let's turn now to the relationship between social constructionism and normativism. These are often equated, but they can come apart. Normative kinds qualify as delineatively constructionist; if category membership depends on values, then category membership is socially determined. But the converse is not true: not all social constructions are normative. One can see this by recalling the definition of social forces. Values can function as social forces (they are attitudes), but nonevaluative beliefs, decisions, and behaviors qualify as well, as do social arrangements, artifacts, and institutions. Some constructed kinds will have only indirect connections to values: being a lottery winner, being a legal drinker, and being a ballroom dancer are all examples. There will also be cases where values are among multiple routes to category membership: being an accomplished artist can be measured by Instagram likes (a measure of values), sales, output, mastery of technical skills, or posthumous recognition. Values ordinarily contribute to each of these dimensions, but it would be misleading to equate artistic accomplishment with positive regard. Being positively valued is neither a necessary nor a sufficient condition.

Likewise, it could turn out that being a mental disorder has indirect or non-necessary connections to values. If so, it would be misleading to call mental disorders normative kinds, even if values make a significant contribution to category membership. It's helpful, in this context, to consider the use of diagnostic criteria in classifying people as mentally ill. Some criteria may be overtly or covertly normative in nature, but some might be possible to apply without direct reference to norms. Insomnia, for example, can be defined relative to statistical averages, rather than convictions about how much sleep is good. Values and statistical beliefs are often co-instantiated, so this dissociation is somewhat hypothetical, but it serves to make the point. Diagnosis can occur, in some cases, without explicitly forming evaluative judgments. This does not mean norms are irrelevant or even unimportant. It simply means, from an ontological perspective, if membership in a category does not depend on normative judgments, the category is not essentially normative.

If the foregoing is right, social constructions are often neither natural nor normative. Kingma (2013) lobbies for a different view. She advances the hypothesis that social constructions are often both normative and natural, and she suggests that concepts of health and disease might be best understood in this way. To make the case, she builds on earlier work in which she criticizes Boorse's biostatistical model. Boorse, recall, says we can determine whether a trait is healthy by seeing how it statistically contributes to fitness when placed in the appropriate "reference class." Kingma (2007) argues that there is no value-free way to settle what reference classes to use in such calculations. For example, if we want to assess whether homosexuality is healthy, we could consider the relative fitness of gay and straight people, including them both in the same reference class. This would lead to a negative verdict. But suppose we treat homosexuality as a "normal polymorphism of human sexuality" to be considered in its own reference class rather than measured against heterosexuality (Kingma 2013, 53). Then we get a positive verdict.

Kingma says that our decision to treat homosexuality as a separate reference class depends on our values, so the verdict is normative. But, she implies, homosexuality is a natural kind, and the statistical calculations that we make once reference classes are decided are value-free. So there is also a sense in which the resulting account of health is perfectly natural. Norms and nature interact to arrive at our verdict. This is what Kingma has in mind when she says social constructions combine naturalism and normativism.

I am not persuaded by this example. For one thing, equating homosexuality with a natural polymorphism is implausible. Homosexuality is a multidimensional, culturally varied phenomenon. It can include patterns of sexual attraction, sexual activity, companionship preferences, and self-ascribed identity. Even if we focus exclusively on same-sex activity, genetic contributions are low (8–25 percent), polygenic (individual genes make minuscule contributions), and genetically linked to many other traits (such as openness to new experiences)(Ganna et al. 2019). For another thing, I think Boorse's statistical approach is unpromising. The health status of homosexuality should not be measured by Darwinian fitness, and it should not hang on getting the equivalence class right.

More to the point, even if the details of Kingma's example were defensible, it would be misleading to conclude that social constructionism is a combination of naturalism and normativism. Constructed kinds are not natural, because membership conditions depend on human classification, and norms may be just one of many factors that contribute, if at all. In the debate about mental disorders, naturalism and normativism are theories of kinds. They say that psychiatric kinds are natural or normative, respectively. Socially constructed kinds are often neither natural nor normative, even if norms and nature play a role in deciding category boundaries.

Social Construction, Disability, and GAD

We can now return to GAD. To determine whether GAD is socially constructed, we need to see whether it is shaped by social forces. One way to do this is to investigate group differences, such as differences in gender, ethnicity, and culture. If groups differ in GAD, that would indicate that social forces are at work. We can examine different dimensions of differences to investigate different varieties of social construction. Let's see how this works.

To support the conjecture that GAD is a generative construction, one can look at group differences in prevalence. The reasoning is simple: if some groups show higher rates, social forces probably contribute to who falls into the category. This is just what research indicates. As already noted, there is cross-national differences with affluent nations showing dramatically higher rates (Ruscio et al. 2017). For example, the lifetime prevalence in the United

States is about seven times higher than in Peru, Mexico, and Romania. Ruscio et al. also report cultural differences in course and age of onset. In addition to culture, there are well-established gender differences: woman are twice as likely to be diagnosed with GAD (Vesga-López et al. 2008). Ethnic differences have been measured as well. In the United States, white people show higher rates than Asian, African, and Latin American (Asnaani et al. 2010). The rate for white Americans is four times higher than for Asian Americans. All this suggests that social locations impacts susceptibility to GAD, white Americans, especially white American women, showing particularly high vulnerability.

Such variation in prevalence supports generative construction: it shows that social factors play a role in determining who ends up with GAD. Perhaps more striking, there is research indicating variation in symptoms across groups. Such work indicates that GAD is, to some degree, a formative construction. The most replicated finding shows that somatic symptoms are more commonly reported in countries outside the United States and Western Europe, including Nepal, Mexico, Hong Kong, and the United Arab Emirates (see Marques 2011, for review). There may also be some variation in these symptoms, with Mexican reporting brain-ache, and Nigerians reporting "heat in the head" and "crawling sensations of worms and ants" (see Xie 2020, for review). One study found that people diagnosed with GAD in Nepal were much likelier than Americans to report feelings of numbness, wobbliness, and choking, whereas American reported much more abdominal discomfort, nervousness, and an inability to relax (Hoge et al. 2006). In Cambodia, anxiety is associated with "a weak heart" and "wind attacks" (Hinton et al. 2009). A study in Turkey reports further somatic symptoms that are not included in the DSM or ICD criteria, including dizziness, tremors, and palpitations (Asoğlu et al. 2018). The same study found dramatic gender differences, with women far more likely than men to exhibit somatic symptoms, and men far more likely to report cognitive symptoms. Higher levels of somatic symptoms among women have been found in the United States as well (Vesga-López et al. 2008). Women find GAD more debilitating (ibid.) and are less likely to recover (Rodriguez et al. 2006). There may also be group difference in the content of worry. In a Cambodian sample, worries included the spiritual well-being of dead relatives (Hinton and Otto 2006). Research with a nonclinical sample in the United States indicates ethnic differences in what people worry about (Scott et al. 2002): white Americans worry most about their lack of confidence and relationships, African Americans worry most about finances and work competence, and Asian Americans worry most about work competence and having an aimless future.

We have seen now that demographic variables impact who gets GAD and how GAD presents. That indicates that GAD is, to some degree, both generatively and formatively constructed. Turning to the question of delineative construction, things get a bit more complicated, because there is no simple way to read an answer off of group differences studies. There are cultural differences in views about which worries are excessive (Xie 2020), and that shows that social forces can influence attitudes about what counts as pathological. Difference in where cultures draw the line between the normal and the pathological would not settle the main question under consideration in philosophical debates about mental disorder. Debates between normativists and naturalists are not just debates about how we happen to diagnose; they are debates about what, if anything, renders diagnoses true. Stated ontologically, they are debates about what disorders really are. To answer that question, we must ask whether those who meet the diagnostic criteria for GAD should be regarded as having a mental disorder, and, if so, why.

Recall that, for both the DSM-5 and ICD-11, presenting with GAD symptoms is not enough to qualify as disordered unless there is significant "distress" or "impairment." I already suggested that distress on its own is a non-starter. GAD certainly feels terrible, but so does childbirth, grief, and bad weather. "Impairment" sounds more promising. If GAD symptoms began to impair a person in major domains of life, we'd have grounds for thinking the person was unwell. The term "impairment" has been most thoroughly explored in disability studies. We'd profit, therefore, from a detour through that subfield.

Those familiar with the area are likely to think of the "social model" of disability when they read the word "impairment." This model emerged from the activism of a group in Great Britain called the Union of the Physically Impaired Against Segregation (UPIAS). They defined an impairment as a missing or defective bodily mechanism. Impairments are just physical facts that distinguish some bodies from others. Disabilities, in contrast, were defined as disadvantages or restrictions caused by social organization that takes no or little account of people with impairments (Oliver 1990, 11). This was a major breakthrough for disability rights since, rather than placing blame on individuals, it defined disabilities in relational terms, drawing attention to the fact that having an unusual body is problematic only when external conditions are unfavorable. Disability is not a state of persons, on this view, but a disadvantage externally imposed on persons. From this perspective, the treatment of disability shifts from fixing (or excluding) individuals to providing accommodation.

Against this background, impairment seems like the wrong word for mental disorders. In this prominent application, it is associated with bodily traits, and it is intended to designate something neutral (Tremain 2001; Penson 2015). The neutrality claim might be challenged. Tremain (2001) compares it to the contested sex/gender distinction, saying impairment is not a prediscursive, natural condition, but rather reflects prevailing attitudes about "human function and structure, competency, intelligence, and ability" which are used to justify, multiply and expand disabling practices (Tremain 2001, 632). In response to such concerns, Thomas (1999) suggests that "impairment" can be defined as a social construction but nevertheless distinguished from disability. This is important, she argues, because impairment provides a way to describe forms of distress that are linked to a disabled person's distinctive physical traits. On her definition, impairments are, "body-related variations which in Western culture have become markers of socially, or more precisely medically, defined 'significant deviations from the normal type' or 'abnormalities'" (Thomas 1999, 124). Were we to adapt this to psychiatry, we might define psychological impairments with reference to current diagnostic criteria (perhaps excluding the term "impairment" in those criteria to avoid circularity). On this approach, the impairment of GAD would be the symptoms of GAD, but this doesn't answer our question: what makes GAD a disorder? The answer that should now be obvious is that GAD is a disorder when it becomes a disability.

But what is a disability? The social model gives one helpful perspective. Disability is not an inherent state, but a disadvantage that arises when external conditions fail to accommodate diverse ways of being. Garland-Thomson (2011) deploys the useful term "misfit" to capture the idea that disability involves a disharmony between the traits of a person and the world they inhabit. We might think of this by analogy with the evolutionary mismatch theory. The idea is that a perfectly adaptive trait might be poorly matched with present environmental conditions. If we subtract the evolutionary aspect of this theory, we arrive at the useful idea that certain psychological traits—regardless of the origin—may be a poor match for the world they inhabit. GAD, on this approach, is not inherently bad, though it may be inherently distressful. Rather, it is a bad fit for a world where there are strict deadlines at school, fixed hours in the workplace, and social expectations to be relaxed and willing to accept conditions that may feel uncomfortable or unsafe. Consider, by analogy, the predicament of someone who wants to wear a face mask during the COVID-19 epidemic long after others in the community have tired of doing so. Being the only masked person in a room transforms an initial anxiety (the reason for wearing the mask) into a disability in that this person may be ridiculed, shunned, or socially excluded. Disablement is not a state of a person, but a relational process: something done to a person by those who refuse to accommodate.

Here we might also return to Foucault. Above I lumped Foucault together with evaluative theories because of his emphasis on moral norms in his early work on madness. His more mature work, however, moves in another direction, as Tremain (2017) brings out in her pioneering work on Foucault and disability. Foucault's lectures on madness from the 1970s shifted from an emphasis on confinement and punishment to a new conception of power (Foucault 2003; 2006). Those deemed mentally ill are subjected to regimes of "normalization." This is not a mere labeling as bad, as normativist theories might imply, but an active effort to regulate behavior. Foucault had initially emphasized repression as the primary approach to behavioral control, but he came to see power as productive. Power creates kinds of people and kinds of subjectivity. In addition, power is not centralized in the state or authority figures, but widely distributed. Power exists in institutions, laws, instruments, architecture, urban planning, textbooks, training guides, mortgage calculators, therapeutic methods, and diagnostic manuals. And power inscribes itself on us physically and psychologically. Someone who is diagnosed will also be acted on and against in a variety of ways: they might be tested, analyzed, medicated, institutionalized, and so on. Diagnostic categories are not nominal, in the language I introduced earlier, but impactive.

Tremain pursues this point using Foucault's concept of normalization, which refers largely to techniques used in medical contexts. I think we might introduce a more expansive concept of disabilitization to refer to the many, vastly distributed ways, a person with a psychiatric impairment might be disadvantaged. This includes medical treatment, but also social ostracism, stigma, relationship difficulties, educational barriers, workplace discrimination, housing insecurity, and the attendant distress associated with each of these.

With this we arrive at an account of what makes GAD count as a disorder. It is a disorder to the extent that it is disabilitized. Disabilitization is not merely a matter of attitudes. It refers to concrete limits imposed on a person. Those limits can include distress, but need not. A person with GAD symptoms may not mind having them, and may not be aware that they are disadvantaged. Some people with GAD symptoms may not face much disabilitization, and that will be especially likely when social conditions are accommodating (e.g., when allowances are made for lapses at work or school), but most of the time, there will be some ways in which individuals with GAD are disadvantaged, and, to that extent, disordered. If this approach is right, then we should eschew the term mental illness for GAD, since the problems are relational. Even "disorder" invites an overly internal understanding, and it might be best to call mental disorders mental disabilities.

The disabilitization account allows an answer to our ontological question. GAD, I submit, is delineatively constructed through disabilitization. Since disabilitization is not merely nominal, GAD is an impactive delineative construction. What's more, the impact is relational, so GAD is an extrinsically impactive delineative construction. As for the contrast with naturalism and normativism, the answers should be clear. GAD is not a natural kind.

Biological predispositions may contribute to its symptoms, but these are formatively constructed as well, and generatively constructed; social forces influence how and whether someone will present. And, as we have now seen, the presentation of symptoms is always already filtered through operative diagnostic standards, so the impairment underlying GAD is never a matter of biology alone. Neither is GAD a purely normative condition. Norms may contribute to diagnosis of the GAD impairment and to disabilitization, but there is much more at play. Beliefs, expectations, school and workplace demands, medical discourses, medical treatments, and other institutional factors can result in disadvantages. If an individual with GAD is passed up for promotion because they took some sick days and missed a deadline, the disadvantage is not simply a matter of the employer's negative attitudes, but of the principles guiding professional advancement within a market economy. It is the structure of society that makes an impairment turn into a disorder, not just norms and values.

CONCLUSION

I have argued that GAD's status as a disorder cannot be adequately explained on leading naturalist or normativist theories. At least I presented prima facie objections, which motivated the search for an alternative theory. I argued that GAD is best explained on a social constructionist account, and, in particular, I proposed that GAD involves a psychological impairment, specified by current diagnostic instruments, together with disabilitizing forces that put individuals who meet those diagnostic criteria at a disadvantage. This makes GAD a delineative construction, since status as disordered depends on social forces, though there need be no explicit norm or judgment at play in that delineation. In addition, I suggested that GAD is generatively and formatively constructed to some degree: its prevalence and symptoms are socially influenced.

In developing this proposal, a central question for future work is its applicability to mental disorders (or, I would say, psychiatric disabilities) more broadly. I provisionally submit that it does. It seems highly likely that the full range of psychiatric diagnoses face forms of disabilitization. Everything from psychosis to borderline personality disorder is associated with disadvantages because they are mismatched with social conditions. The account also allows for specific exceptions. In corporate contexts, psychopathy could be an advantage, some obsessive symptoms might contribute to successful academic performance, and mild depression can operate under the radar of social awareness. There may be distress in some of these cases without (much) disability.

One might worry that the account over generalizes. Take two common objections to normativism. First, is illiteracy a mental disorder? After all, it is disvalued (see Gaete 2008, 335, who bites the bullet). I think the disabilitization account can exclude illiteracy because it is not a psychiatric impairment. Current approaches to nosology focus on emotions and modes of information processing, not knowledge or learned skills. Second, is homosexuality a disorder? The same answer is available, since homosexuality is no longer a diagnostic category, but think back to when it was. In a homophobic society, people who are gay are subjected to considerable disabalitization. Under such conditions, I think we might accept the conclusion that homosexuality is a disorder. This result would be problematic if we called homosexuality a disease. On the present proposal, such language is eschewed. It would be more accurate to say homosexuality is a disability and that disability status is externally imposed. Far from medicalizing homosexuality, such an outcome is a call to arms. The present proposal defines disorders in a way that allows us to identify external sources of oppression, rather than trying to "normalize" the individuals we diagnose. In that sense, the current proposal may not descriptively capture our folk or professional concepts of mental disorders, but it tracks application of that term reasonably well, and does so in a way that can support activist efforts. The analysis is ameliorative, not in the sense that it provides us with a positive way to think about mental health, but in that it can serve those who fight against discrimination and oppression.

REFERENCES

Asnaani, Anu, Anthony J. Richey, Ruta Dimaite, Devon E. Hinton, and Stefan G. Hofmann. 2010. "A Cross-Ethnic Comparison of Lifetime Prevalence Rates of Anxiety Disorders." *Journal of Nervous and Mental Disease*, 198: 551–55.

Asoğlu, Mehmet, İsmail Karka, , Faruk Pirinççioğlu, Meltem Göbelek, Hakim ÇeliK, Hatice Takatak, and Şermin Bílgen Ulgar. 2018. "Cultural Reflections of the Expressions of the Anxiety of Patients with Generalized Anxiety Disorder." *Bezmialem Science* 4: 242–47.

Bashford-Largo, Johannah, Joseph Aloi, Ru Zhang, Sahil Bajaj, Erin Carollo, Jaimie Elowsky, Amanda Schwartz, Matthew Dobbertin, Robert James R. Blair, and Karina S. Blair. 2021. "Reduced Neural Differentiation of Rewards and Punishment During Passive Avoidance Learning in Adolescents with Generalized Anxiety Disorder." *Depression and Anxiety* 38: 794–803.

Beresford, Peter, and Jasna Russo, eds. 2022. *The Routledge International Handbook of Mad Studies*. New York: Routledge.

Boorse, Christopher. 1997. "A Rebuttal on Health." In *What Is Disease?* Edited by James M. Humber and Robert F. Almeder, 1–134. Totowa, NJ.: Humana Press.

Charland, Louis. C. 2004. "Moral Treatment and the Personality Disorders." In *The Philosophy of Psychiatry: A Companion*, edited by Jennifer Radden, 64–77. Oxford University Press.

Cooper, Rachel. 2002. "Disease." *Studies in History and Philosophy of Science Part C: Studies in History and Philosophy of Biological and Biomedical Sciences* 33: 263–82.

Crocq, Marc-Antoine. 2017. "The History of Generalized Anxiety Disorder as a Diagnostic Category." *Dialogues in Clinical Neuroscience* 19: 107–16. https://doi.org/10.31887/DCNS.2017.19.2/macrocq.

Cummins, Robert. 1975. "Functional Analysis." *The Journal of Philosophy* 72: 741–65.

Cuthbert, Bruce N., and Thomas R. Insel. 2013. "Toward the Future of Psychiatric Diagnosis: The Seven Pillars of RDoC." *BMC Medicine* 11: 126.

Engelhardt, H. Tristram. 1976. "Ideology and Etiology." *Journal of Medicine and Philosophy* 1: 256–68.

Foucault, Michel. 1965. *Madness and Civilization: A History of Insanity in the Age of Reason.* Translated by Richard Howard. New York: Pantheon Books.

———.1973. *The Birth of the Clinic: An Archeology of Medical Perception.* Translated by A. M. Sheridan. New York: Routledge.

———. 2003. *Abnormal: Lectures at the Collège de France, 1974–1975.* Edited by Valerio Marchetti and Antonella Fontana. New York: Palgrave Macmillan.

———. 2006. *Michel Foucault: Psychiatric Power: Lectures at the Collège de France, 1973–1974.* New York: Palgrave Macmillan.

Gaete, Alfredo. 2008. "The Concept of Mental Disorder: A Proposal." *Philosophy, Psychiatry, and Psychology* 15: 327–39.

Ganna, Andrea, Karin J. H. Verweij, Michel G. Nivard, Robert Maier, et al.. 2019. "Large-scale GWAS Reveals Insights into the Genetic Architecture of Same-Sex Sexual Behavior." *Science* 365(6456), eaat7693.

Garland-Thomson, R. 2011. "Misfits: A Feminist Materialist Disability Concept." *Hypatia* 26: 591–609.

Garson, Justin. 2021. "The Developmental Plasticity Challenge to Wakefield's View." In *Defining Mental Disorder: Jerome Wakefield and His Critics*, edited by Luc Faucher and Denis Forest, 335–52. Cambridge, MA.: MIT Press.

Gottschalk, Michael G., and Katharina Domschke. 2017. "Genetics of Generalized Anxiety Disorder and Related Traits." *Dialogues in Clinical Neuroscience* 19: 159–68.

Hettema, John M., Michael C. Neale, and Kenneth S. Kendler. 2001. "A Review and Meta Analysis of the Genetic Epidemiology of Anxiety Disorders." *American Journal of Psychiatry* 158: 1568–78.

Hinton, Devon E., Curtis Hsia, Lawrence Park, Andrew Rasmussen, and Mark H. Pollack. 2009. "Cultural Anthropology and Anxiety Diagnoses." In *Current Perspectives on the Anxiety Disorders: Implications for DSM-V and Beyond,* edited by Dean McKay, Jonathan S. Abramowitz, Steven Taylor, and Gordon J. G. Asmundson, 245–74. New York: Springer.

Hinton, Devon E., and Michael W. Otto. 2006. "Symptom Presentation and Symptom Meaning Among Traumatized Cambodian Refugees: Relevance to a

Somatically Focused Cognitive-Behavior Therapy." *Cognitive and Behavioral Practice* 13: 249–60.

Hoge, Elizabeth A., Sharad M. Tamrakar, Kelly M. Christian, Namrata Mahara, Mahendra K. Nepal, Mark H. Pollack, and Naomi M. Simon. 2006. "Cross-Cultural Differences in Somatic Presentation in Patients With Generalized Anxiety Disorder." *The Journal of Nervous and Mental Disease* 194: 962–66.

Holwerda, Tjalling J., Robert A. Schoevers, Jack Dekker, Dorly J. H. Deeg, Cees Jonker, and Aartjan T. F. Beekman. 2007. "The Relationship Between Generalized Anxiety Disorder, Depression and Mortality in Old Age." *International Journal of Geriatric Psychiatry* 22: 241–49.

Horwitz, Allan V., and Jerome C. Wakefield. 2012. *All We Have to Fear: Psychiatry's Transformation of Natural Anxieties into Mental Disorders*. New York: Oxford University Press.

Jacobson, Nicholas C. 2016. "Current Evolutionary Adaptiveness of Psychiatric Disorders: Fertility Rates, Parent–Child Relationship Quality, and Psychiatric Disorders Across the Lifespan." *Journal of Abnormal Psychology* 125: 824–39.

Kingma, Elselijn. 2007. "What Is It to Be Healthy?" *Analysis* 67: 128–33.

———. 2013. "Health and Disease: Social Constructivism as a Combination of Naturalism and Normativism." In *Health, Illness and Disease: Philosophical Essays*, edited by Havi Carel and Rachel Cooper, 37–56. New York: Routledge.

Kostić, Milutin, Anna Munjiza, Danilo Pesic, Amir Peljto, Ivana Novakovic, Valerija Dobricic, Dusica Lecic Tosevski, and Millija Mijajlovic. 2017. "A Pilot Study on Predictors of Brainstem Raphe Abnormality in Patients with Major Depressive Disorder." *Journal of Affective Disorders* 209: 66–70.

Lange, Marc. 2007. "The End of Diseases." *Philosophical Topics* 35: 265–92.

Margolis, Joseph. 1966. *Psychotherapy and Morality: A Study of Two Concepts*. New York: Random House.

. 1976. "The Concept of Disease." *Journal of Medicine and Philosophy* 1: 238–255.

Marques, Luana, Donald J. Robinaugh, Nicole J. LeBlanc, and Devon Hinton. 2011. "Cross Cultural Variations in the Prevalence and Presentation of Anxiety Disorders." *Expert Review of Neurotherapeutics* 11: 313–22.

Mealey, Linda. 1995. "The Sociobiology of Sociopathy: An Integrated Evolutionary Model." *Behavioral and Brain Sciences* 18: 523–41.

Murphy, Dominic. 2012. *Psychiatry in the Scientific Image*. Cambridge, MA.: MIT Press.

Odgerel, Z., A. Talati, S. P. Hamilton, D. F. Levinson, and M. M. Weissman. 2013. "Genotyping Serotonin Transporter Polymorphisms 5-HTTLPR and rs25531 in European- and African-American Subjects from the National Institute of Mental Health's Collaborative Center for Genomic Studies." *Translational Psychiatry* 3(9): e307.

Oliver, Michael. 1990. *The Politics of Disablement*. London: Palgrave Macmillan.

Patriquin, Michelle A., and Sanjay J. Mathew. 2017. "The Neurobiological Mechanisms of Generalized Anxiety Disorder and Chronic Stress." *Chronic Stress* 1: 1–10.

Penson, William J. 2015. "Unsettling Impairment: Mental Health and the Social Model of Disability." In *Madness, Distress, and the Politics of Disablement*, edited by Helen Spandler, Jill Anderson, Bob Sapey, 57–66. Bristol, UK.: Bristol University Press.

Pickard, Hannah. 2009. "Mental Illness Is Indeed a Myth." In *Psychiatry as Cognitive Neuroscience*, edited by Matthew R. Broome, and Lisa L. Bortolotti, 82–102. Oxford: Oxford University Press.

Rodriguez, Benjamin F., Risa B. Weisberg, Maria E. Pagano, Steven E. Bruce, Michael A. Spencer, Larry Culpepper, and Martin B. Keller. 2006. "Characteristics and Predictors of Full and Partial Recovery From Generalized Anxiety Disorder in Primary Care Patients." *Journal of Nervous and Mental Disease* 194: 91–97.

Ruscio, Ayelet Meron, Lauren S. Hallion, Carmen C. W. Lim, et al. 2017. "Cross-Sectional Comparison of the Epidemiology of *DSM-5* Generalized Anxiety Disorder Across the Globe." *JAMA Psychiatry* 74: 465–75.

Scott, Erin L., Winnie Eng, and Richard G. Heimberg. 2002. "Ethnic Differences in Worry in a Nonclinical Population." *Depression and Anxiety* 15: 79–82.

Szasz, Thomas. 1960. "The Myth of Mental Illness." *American Psychologist* 15: 113–18.

———. 1974. *The Myth of Mental Illness: Foundations of a Theory of Personal Conduct* (Revised edition). New York: Harper & Row.

Thomas, Carol. 1999. *Female Forms: Experiencing and Understanding Disability*. London: Open University Press.

Tremain, Shelley. 2001. "On the Government of Disability." *Social Theory and Practice* 27: 617–36.

———. 2017. *Foucault and Feminist Philosophy of Disability*. Ann Arbor: University of Michigan Press.

Vesga-López, Oriana, Franklin R. Schneier, Samuel Wang, Richard G. Heimberg, Shang Min Liu, Deborah S. Hasin, and Carlos Blanco. 2008. "Gender Differences in Generalized Anxiety Disorder: Results From the National Epidemiologic Survey on Alcohol and Related Conditions (NESARC)." *The Journal of Clinical Psychiatry* 69: 1606–16.

Wakefield, J. C. 1992. "The Concept of Mental Disorder: On the Boundary Between Biological Facts and Social Values." *American Psychologist* 47: 373–88.

———. 2021. "Must Social Values Play a Role in the Harm Component of the Harmful Dysfunction Analysis? Reply to Rachel Cooper." In *Defining Mental Disorder: Jerome Wakefield and His Critics*, edited by Luc Faucher and Denis Forest, 553–76. Cambridge, MA.: The MIT Press.

Xie, Dong. 2020. "Cultural Perspectives in Understanding, Treating, and Studying: Worry and Generalized Anxiety Disorder (GAD)." In *Generalized Anxiety Disorder and Worrying: A Comprehensive Handbook for Clinicians and Researchers*, edited by A. L. Gerlach and A. T. Gloster, 173–201. London: Wiley Blackwell.

Yoon, K. Lira, and Richard E. Zinbarg. 2007. "Generalized Anxiety Disorder and Entry into Marriage or a Marriage-like Relationship." *Journal of Anxiety Disorders* 21: 955–96.

Chapter 7

Social Anxiety, Affordances, and Habitual Trust

Michelle Maiese

INTRODUCTION

Social anxiety disorder (SAD) is a common psychiatric condition, with a lifetime prevalence of around 12 percent in the United States (Ruscio et al. 2008); and Jeffries and Ungar (2020) found that over a third of participants (aged 18–24, from seven different countries) met the threshold for SAD. The severity of social anxiety symptoms can range from mild unpleasant experiences and increased emotional arousal to debilitating panic and social withdrawal. Subjects experience high negative affect and low self-efficacy during interpersonal interactions, and at the cognitive level, they exhibit increased self-monitoring, rumination, and negative interpretation biases. These symptoms tend to be associated with poor social functioning and lower levels of academic and professional achievement. However, it is important to acknowledge that anxiety is not necessarily disruptive; in some cases, it helps agents to recognize possible threats or disruptions to sociality and respond appropriately to them. What distinguishes these "healthier" instances of anxiety, which bring about awareness and needed caution, from the kind of intense dread that disrupts agency and social functioning in cases of SAD?

To gain a deeper understanding of how these healthier and more disruptive forms of anxiety differentially manifest in human agency and social interaction, I look to the notions of *affordance* and *habitual trust*. Based on someone's affective condition and the way in which they appraise their environment based on their subjective concerns, some action-possibilities are disclosed as inviting and enticing, whereas others are disclosed as threatening or repelling. The affective states that modulate affordance disclosure include not just occurrent, object-directed emotions, but also more diffuse mood states and background existential feelings. I propose that healthier and more disruptive modes of anxiety differ in terms of the existential orientation that forms the backdrop for subjects' engagement with available interpersonal affordances; in particular, their degree of "habitual trust" impacts their sense of ability and the extent to which they rely on others to help them engage effectively with relevant action-possibilities.

In healthier cases, habitual trust remains largely intact, and agents look to others to help them regulate their attention; anxiety operates as a kind of alarm system that allows subjects to attend to relevant social factors and regulate their engagement to gain an "optimal grip" on the affordance field. In cases of SAD, in contrast, subjects encounter an erosion of habitual trust and exhibit a heightened attunement to negative social stimuli. Because their perception of other people's bodily orientation, gestures, and expressions is influenced by this negative bias, many available possibilities for interpersonal interaction are disclosed as threatening or dangerous rather than inviting. Thus, due to diminished "habitual trust," agents with SAD are cut off from valuable social resources that ordinarily would help them to regulate their attention and action, and their field of interpersonal affordances constricts. Self-monitoring and rumination function as attempts to compensate for their diminished social skills, but these tendencies only serve to exacerbate anxiety and further constrict the affordance field. This affordance-based account emphasizes that the disclosure of action-possibilities is fundamentally affective, and that the alterations to metacognition that are characteristic of SAD are rooted in alterations to a subject's background existential orientation.

AFFORDANCE DISCLOSURE AND AFFECTIVITY

The notion of affordance is a theoretical concept introduced by J.J. Gibson (1979) that emphasizes the complementarity of the animal and the environment and the link between perception and action. What the environment affords are "what it *offers* the animal, what it *provides* or *furnishes*, either for good or ill" (Gibson 1979, 237). These action-possibilities are specified *relationally*: the environment dynamically offers various possibilities for interaction and engagement, but only in relation to an organism with particular capacities.[1] For example, an object is graspable by virtue of its physical properties together with an animal's bodily structure and ability to grasp that object. Stairs of a suitable height and incline afford climbing for able-bodied adult human beings, but not for infants. What is more, actions are afforded not just by objects or physical spaces, but also by other people. The skill of being attuned to relevant affordances includes a sensitivity to the possibility that one can engage in a social interaction. Brancazio (2020) distinguishes between environmental affordances that offer opportunities for socializing (such as public spaces) and those offered by agents themselves. First, the layout or structure of an environment can be conducive to, or facilitate, social interaction; for example, having chairs set up in a circle in the classroom might be understood as a "sociability affordance." Sociability could be afforded anywhere people tend to have social interactions, such as coffee shops, parks, or the grocery store.

Second, "interpersonal affordances" are opportunities offered by other agents in direct agent-agent relationships. Along these lines, Rietveld and colleagues note that "the sight of a sad friend affords consoling him or her, a colleague at the coffee machine solicits small talk, and an extended hand immediately prepares the body for shaking it" (Rietveld et al. 2019, 305). The perception of interpersonal affordances often involves specifically looking for affordances provided by an agent (e.g., in the event that someone has an appointment to meet up with a friend). Brancazio (2020) rightly notes that the perception of interpersonal affordances is uniquely interactive and depends on the dynamics of the social encounter as it unfolds. In many cases, affordances are disclosed as available and accessible not only to oneself, but also "to us together because of our abilities to engage in shared activities and projects as participants in shared practices" (Kiverstein 2015, 537).

However, agents do not engage with *all* the action-possibilities that are available to them on the basis of their bodily structure and capacities. Whereas "the world is rich with affordances . . . only a subset of the possible actions the environment offers matter to a person enough to move them to action" (Kiverstein 2015, 536). To make sense of these invitations to act, Rietveld and Kiverstein (2014, 342) maintain that an affordance becomes a solicitation "when it is relevant to our dynamically changing concerns," takes on a "demand character" and becomes manifest at the bodily level in a state of "action readiness." Along similar lines, Gallagher describes a solicitation as "an affordance that draws an agent to action due to its relevance, or the way that it stands out in the perceptual field" (2018, 722). For an affordance to have relevance is for it to beckon certain forms of perceptual-emotional appraisal and bodily engagement (Ramstead et al. 2016, 4–5).

Whether available affordances solicit action is a thoroughly dynamic process, with different action-possibilities becoming more or less inviting at different times (Dings 2018, 683). In addition, there are possibilities that do not call out to an agent to act on them, but instead immediately repel that agent. Action possibilities offered by the environment "may be threatening and challenging to me to different degrees," some of them pointing to an imminent danger, and others presenting a less serious or immediate threat (Kiverstein 2015, 536). Still other affordances offered up by the environment will be unimportant to the agent because they seem to have no bearing on their current goals or interests (Rietveld and Kiverstein 2014). Thus, agents encounter an environment in which some forms of bodily engagement are possible or inviting, whereas others are foreclosed. Affordance disclosure is best understood in terms of selective attention and responsiveness, i.e., as a process that involves the prioritization of some action-possibilities and the suppression of others.

Building on these ideas, we can distinguish between the broader set of available action-possibilities, and the smaller subset of affordances that become relevant and inviting from the standpoint of a particular agent. The landscape (or "total ensemble") of available affordances is comprised of "the entire set of affordances that are available, in a given environment at a given time" to particular sorts of living organisms (Ramstead et al. 2016). The *field* of affordances, in contrast, consists of the relevant possibilities for action that a particular agent is responsive to in a concrete situation (Rietveld and Kiverstein 2014); it can be understood as the "situation-specific, individual 'excerpt' of the general landscape of affordances" (de Haan et al. 2013, 7). Which of the many affordances an agent is responsive to in a particular situation depends partly on their built-up bodily habits, skills, and past experiencs; it also depends significantly on their unique goals, concerns, needs, interests, and preferences (de Haan et al. 2013, 7), including their longer-term intentions, goals, projects, and commitments (Dings 2021). Thus, an agent's affordance field has a self-referential quality and a *personal* dimension (Meynen 2011, 185): action-possibilities always are framed in relation to that specific agent's desires, needs, and modes of *openness* to the world.

One of the important factors that shapes an agent's affordance field (and their sense of which action-possibilities are relevant) is their affective condition. This includes an agent's occurrent emotions, more diffuse mood, and general background affective orientation. Along these lines, Rietveld (2012, 213) maintains that "the phenomenon of being attracted or drawn by a solicitation can be understood as an emotional perturbation." A specific action-possibility "solicits action (i.e., calls me to act) only when I am responsive to act (i.e., concerned)" [Dings 2018, 687]. A book sometimes affords reading, and at other times affords throwing; which of these affordances solicits action depends partly on my cares and concerns, and whether I am feeling angry. Depending on an agent's overall mood, occurrent emotions, and enduring concerns, some action-possibilities have greater significance or matter more than others, or in different ways. Insofar as an agent's affective attunement to a particular situation helps to determine which available affordances solicit action, it guides their selective responsiveness and enables them to engage effectively with a world that is overflowing with affordances. This capacity for selective responsiveness frequently operates prior to conscious reflection and involves very fine-grained discriminations connected to what this agent *feels in their gut*. Along these lines, Kiverstein and Rietveld (2021, 182) maintain that it "is through the caring engagement of their bodies that subjects experience a meaningful world." It is an agent's concerns, and the way that they affectively appraise their environment based on these concerns, that render some affordances "inviting and enticing, and others threatening and repelling" (Kiverstein 2015, 536). An agent's pre-reflective affective attunement to a particular situation thereby helps to carve out their field of relevant affordances.

The idea that affective states play an integral role in shaping the affordance field builds on enactivist accounts that conceive of emotions in terms of a living organism's active orientation toward (and pursuit of) salient value features in the environment. An agent's mode of "being in the world" is both fundamentally action-oriented and fundamentally affective. The lived body operates as "a resonance field in which the successes or failures of one's active operations are registered immediately in the form of positive or negative feelings" (Slaby et al. 2013, 38). Insofar as these feelings modify an agent's activities and keep them oriented toward their goals, they are emotionally directed toward the world in terms of an "I can" or "I can't" schema (Slaby et al. 2013, 41). The upshot of this action-oriented approach is that emotions are closely linked to an agent's awareness of ability and sense of what they can do. Characteristic emotional episodes can be understood as modifications of the ways in which an agent pursues goals, positions themselves toward others, and interacts with their social environment. Whereas fear is a "reorientation of one's current pursuit in response to what is apprehended as dangerous," (Slaby et al. 2013, 40), anxiety is a reorientation of one's current pursuit in response to an object or situation that involves problematic uncertainty. Social anxiety occurs when a subject anticipates indeterminate social threats, encounters the social world as somehow unpredictable or dangerous, and dynamically interacts with the social environment (Glas 2020) as if it were threatening.

To see why social anxiety becomes so disruptive in cases of SAD, it will be important to consider the role that *existential feelings* play in shaping an agent's field of relevant affordances. I have suggested that affordance disclosure depends significantly on an agent's affective condition. This includes not just occurrent emotions such as anger or fear, but also more diffuse mood states and the agent's general existential orientation. An agent's engagement with the world is always taking place in some sort of mood, and this influences which options are disclosed as relevant for them. Someone in an anxious mood, for example, will perceive and appreciate all kinds of threats in their environment because their mood attunes them to dangerous possibilities. What I wish to highlight is that this mood (together with the agent's occurrent emotional states) arises against the backdrop of their existential orientation (Ratcliffe 2005; 2008; 2015). This orientation does not have a specific, localized object or target; instead, it can be understood as an agent's general sense of their relationship to the world, which operates as a backdrop for all their experiences, thoughts, and attitudes. That is, someone's existential orientation is more fundamental to how they experience and make sense of the world than an object-directed emotional state (e.g., being angry at a colleague) or even a more diffuse mood state. All intentional states, including occurrent emotions and mood states, presuppose an existential orientation and a background existential feeling. This general mode of being in the world, which is constituted partly by bodily feelings, shapes an agent's perceptions and their sense of what sorts of action-possibilities a situation offers.

Some of the existential orientations that Ratcliffe (2005, 2008) discusses include feelings of connectedness to the world, feelings of familiarity, and feelings of belonging. Subjects ordinarily have a sense of being generally "at home" in the world, and of possessing a habitual, practical confidence. This "habitual trust" ordinarily includes a tacit, unreflective, and skilled sense of what is possible in the interpersonal domain, which Roberts and Osler (2023) call "social certainty." Like other existential orientations, this sense of habitual trust is not itself an attitude toward anything specific, but instead a more general stance that functions as a backdrop for thought and experience. In many cases, it is against this backdrop that agents have more localized experiences of problematic uncertainty, anxiety, or doubt, and anticipate or judge that specific events will or will not occur (Ratcliffe, Ruddell, and Smith 2014, 5). If an agent feels disconnected or loses faith in their ability to engage smoothly in social interaction, they are likely to feel awkward or self-conscious, the world will take on a different look and feel, and their affordance field will be altered in notable ways. For example, the field of interpersonal affordances and possibilities for sociability may constrict, or perhaps these action-possibilities will repel (rather than invite) action.

It is to be expected, then, that feelings of anxiety will shape the way that subjects appraise their social environment and engage with action-possibilities. For one thing, anxiety likely has an important impact on whether an agent experiences a particular social setting as an "interaction conducive space" (Brancazio 2020, 3), and the extent to which a social space is perceived as welcoming. We will see that in cases of social anxiety disorder (SAD), there is a change in a subject's general existential orientation. That is, while subjects with SAD may be anxious about specific situations or events (e.g., an upcoming speech or social gathering), there also a more fundamental shift in their existential orientation that changes how they relate to and engage with the social world. An erosion of habitual trust alters their overall mode of being in the world and disrupts their sense of themselves as social actors.

"HEALTHY" ANXIETY AND OPTIMAL GRIP

Although anxiety often involves unpleasant bodily sensations and feelings, it is not necessarily maladaptive or detrimental to social functioning. In fact, some instances of anxiety help agents to gain an "optimal grip" on available action-possibilities and engage effectively with their social environments. This notion of "optimal grip" comes from the Skilled Intentionality Framework (Rietveld et al. 2018; van Dijk and Rietveld 2017), which emphasizes that effective agency depends on embodied know-how and skill: "acting appropriately requires that a complex and particular situational context is taken into account by the individual's motor intentional activity" (Rietveld 2012, 215). Taking into account their particular situation, capabilities, and interests, the agent regulates themself and coordinates their engagement with the environment so as to move toward "optimal grip on multiple relevant affordances simultaneously, that is, on a field of relevant affordances" (Rietveld et al. 2018, 45). This is a matter of being appropriately attuned and responsive to available affordances, being able to switch from one sort of activity to another as events unfold over time, being open to engagement with previously unexplored affordances, and being able to modify built-up patterns of engagement. A person who has acquired a particular skill has become attuned to relevant affordances available in a specific context (on the basis of their history and past engagements) and is now equipped for smooth and fluid engagement. This includes skilled social interaction, which can be understood as getting a grip on a rich landscape of affordances that includes possibilities for social interaction (Rietveld and Kiverstein 2014). These opportunities for social engagement are in continual flux, pulling an agent in different directions at different moments, and in unpredictable ways. To navigate these varied aspects of the social domain, agents need to be able to read the faces and expressions of others and to master the conventions, codes, and norms that govern interpersonal behavior in the context at hand (Roberts and Osler, 2023); for example, they need to gauge how to respond appropriately depending on whether they are in a crowd, at home, at work, or at a party. Many of the skills the help agents to navigate diverse settings and engage fluidly with relevant interpersonal affordances are embodied and pre-reflective (Rietveld et al. 2019, 305).

Because other people have a special salience, they solicit attention in a way that alters an agent's bodily comportment, gaze, and train of thought. Being in the presence of others provides important perceptual and informational advantages that expand and enrich an agent's attentional field (Bader 2020) and thereby help them to gain an optimal grip on available affordances. From the beginning of life, agents learn what sort of significance things have partly via practices of shared attention; they follow cues from other people in their immediate surroundings, and this information helps them to gauge which action-possibilities to take advantage of and which situations to avoid. For example, infants often pre-reflectively modify their own behavior in accordance with how their caregiver responds to and appraises an unfamiliar object in the surrounding world. Likewise, adults rely on social referencing as a means of reducing dependence on their own attention. Bader (2020) presents the example of crossing the street in an urban setting: in such cases, the movements, gestures, and expressions of other agents signal to someone when it's safe to walk. In my view, this can be understood in terms of gaining an optimal grip on relevant affordances. Because an agent follows others' attention, they can engage more effectively with available action-possibilities and perhaps become more aware of dangers, hazards, or threats that escaped their own focus of attention or are currently hidden from them. Which action-possibilities are relevant is inseparable from what an agent anticipates others will do, what they gauge is likely to happen next, and how it matters.

Other people also can orient an agent's attention toward relevant social cues. For example, suppose that Janet is attending a faculty senate meeting for the first time. As she enters the room, she is likely to rely on others for valuable information about how to comport herself and what sorts of social "rules" are at play. Should she raise her hand if she wishes to speak, is it ever okay to interrupt others, and is this meeting to have a more or less formal tone? Is it okay to have her laptop or cell phone out, and is it acceptable to eat lunch during the meeting? Janet will navigate this new sort of social situation depending on what others around her do, and many of the adjustments she makes to her own engagement will take place pre-reflectively, on the basis of these social cues. Suppose that at some point in the meeting, Janet wishes to raise a question or concern and feels nervous at the prospect of speaking up. As she speaks, she is likely to rely on others' facial expressions and head nods for information about whether they understand what she is saying and are open to her continuing to speak. All of this will occur against the backdrop of Janet's general sense of trust in both herself and others, which is central to her ability to engage smoothly and fluidly with her social surroundings.

In addition, social referencing allows agents to pick up social information that enables second-person engagement, the coordination of activities, and the sharing of experiences. This opens them up to a multiplicity of perspectives, objects, and situations, so that the scope of their attention broadens, and they don't have to depend exclusively on their own attentional resources. Attending with others (rather than simply on one's own) also has a completely different experiential feel, according to Bader (2020). This is because attending with others gives someone access to a broader perspective on the surrounding world, one which includes the embodied perspectives of others, their future behaviors and movements, and their relationship to a shared environment. The anticipation of engaging in specific kinds of interpersonal relations amounts to a sense that "this is not all the world has to offer" (Ratcliffe, Ruddell, and Smith 2014, 6). An agent's special sensitivity to others' bodily presence (which occurs partly by way of pre-reflective bodily resonance, synchronization, or mimicry) discloses how these other agents are related to the surrounding world and available action-possibilities. Becoming attuned to others' perspectives allows an agent to assess the other person's expectations and desires concerning how the social interaction unfolds or how to engage in coordinated activity. Others' emotions and actions offer specific affordances (Gallagher and Allen 2018, 2641) and invite an agent to respond in specific, complementary ways. This allows for a dynamic "we-space" (Kreuger 2011) to emerge, so that an agent can interlock and interlink their intentions and activities with those of others and engage in various forms of collaborative or joint activity. What is more, because an agent attends to objects and situations partly in relation to the possible uses of other agents, their surroundings can look different depending on whether they are interacting with others and what sort of interaction unfolds. This impacts the perceived relevance and salience of specific affordances and shapes how they engage with available action-possibilities.

Thus, being in the presence of others enables an agent attend to a wider set of objects and events, provides them with valuable information, and opens up new opportunities for action (Bader 2020). Such considerations suggest that social resources ordinarily help an agent to gain an optimal grip on affordances and to exhibit what some theorists have termed "online intelligence" (Wheeler 2005); this involves the ability to produce fluid and flexible real-time responses to constantly changing environmental contingencies. How, then, does anxiety help agents to make use of these social resources and gain optimal grip on available affordances in instances of what Kurth (2016, 5) terms "problematic uncertainty"? These are cases in which the subject lacks information about the situation they encounter or will encounter, and such uncertainty is problematic in the sense that it concerns a possible threat, challenge, or thwarting of their goals. Vazard and Kurth (2022) maintain that anxiety can help subjects to cope with potential threats by rendering risk and danger more salient and orienting decision-making accordingly. This is because "anxiety reactions are embodiments of an alarm system" (Glas 2020, 41), one which sometimes interrupts current behavior and prompts a subject to reassess what they are doing, which in turn can allow for a more targeted and focused response. Insofar as anxiety makes someone more alert, focuses their attention, and prepares them for action, it can promote skillful attunement and responsiveness to relevant affordances.

Suppose, for example, that Mark is a new teacher who is in the middle of giving a lecture and experiencing feelings of anxiety. After all, the classroom is an uncertain setting, one in which the possibility of conflict, behavioral issues, or misunderstandings is ever-present. Mark's anxiety may very well make him especially attuned to his students and especially likely to notice their bodily orientations and facial expressions. As a result, he may have a heightened sense of when they are bored, confused, entertained, or frustrated. This capacity for perspective-taking helps him to engage with available action-possibilities, so that he slows down to clarify a key point, skips over material that will make his presentation too long, or interjects with a joke to try to recapture their attention.

Consider another example from Kurth (2016), who asks us to consider a familiar episode of modern life: after making an inappropriate comment in an email to a group of colleagues, Jordan begins to feel anxious about how they will react. Anxiety results from Jordan's sense that they have done something wrong or inappropriate, but not knowing whether, how, or to what extent they will be reprimanded for it. This shapes Jordan's affordance field and may very well attune them to relevant action-possibilities. For example, action-possibilities associated with efforts to learn more about others' reaction, or to apologize or rephrase what they said in a follow-up email, may become especially salient and solicit action. This illustrates how anxiety can prove to be beneficial insofar as it warns agents of potentially dangerous situations, sensitizes and attunes them to relevant dangers and threats, and helps them to react more quickly to avoid unwanted consequences or protect what they care about (Vazard and Kurth 2022). In addition, as an agent tries to better understand the situation they are in, affordances associated with information gathering or perspective-taking may become salient. This helps them to gain optimal grip on interpersonal affordances and more effectively navigate social situations.

Both Mark and Jordan experience some anxiety, but in neither case does it impair their ability to engage with interpersonal affordances. Instead, their anxiety appears to make them more skillful at taking advantage of possibilities for social interaction, and more capable of gaining optimal grip. Note that in the case of Jordan, there is a greater degree of offline engagement in the sense that Jordan is imagining and trying to anticipate how others will react. Nonetheless, Jordan and Mark alike have a significant degree of habitual trust, both in themselves and in those with whom they are interacting. That is, they trust that they are capable of navigating uncertainty in their social surroundings and behaving in socially appropriate ways; and they have a sense that there are available action-possibilities that will allow them to alter the course of how future events unfold. In addition, they trust that other people will cooperate in the social interaction and help them to take advantage of relevant affordances. This habitual trust likely shows up in the tone of voice and vocabulary that they use, their facial expressions, and their overall bodily comportment. Thus, the backdrop for their engagement with social affordances is a general sense of being "at home" in the world, being capable of connecting with other people, and being confident that they can take steps to ameliorate potential conflict. As we will see, this sense of trust and confidence is diminished in cases of SAD.

ALTERATIONS TO THE AFFORDANCE FIELD IN SOCIAL ANXIETY DISORDER

Can these notions of affordance disclosure and optimal grip help us to make sense of the disruptions to self-experience and agency that occur in cases of social anxiety disorder (SAD)? Can they shed light on how disruptive forms of social anxiety differ from the sort of "healthier" anxiety described earlier? Some theorists have looked to the notions of affordance disclosure and the affordance field to make sense of the disruptions to functioning that occur in various sorts of mental disorder. For example, de Haan and colleagues (2013) point to a breakdown in the structure of the field of relevant affordances, which involves at least three key dimensions: (1) "Width" of the field refers to the broadness of the scope of affordances that an individual perceives, which relates to her having a choice or action options; (2) "Depth" of the field refers to the temporal aspect: the individual not only perceives affordances that are immediately present here and now, but also is pre-reflectively aware of future plans and action-possibilities, and (3) "Height" of the affordances in the field refers to the relevance or importance of the affordances that one is responsive to, i.e., "the experienced solicitation or affective allure" (de Haan et al. 2013, 7), and relates to salience and motivation. In cases of mental disorder, the width, depth, or height of an agent's affordance field becomes narrower, lacks depth, or flattens out. In depression, for example, many action possibilities are closed off, and in cases of obsessive compulsive disorder, "there is a serious constriction of the affordance space as the subject finds herself limited to one repetitive action, or one set of specific actions, and unable to move beyond that" (Gallagher 2018, 723). Many of the difficulties encountered by agents with mental disorder stem from their attenuated ability to gauge the relevance of available affordances and be solicited appropriately (Maiese 2021).

Few empirical studies have examined the role that anxiety plays in an agent's perception and realization of affordances. To fill this gap, Pijpers et al. (2006) sought to investigate how anxiety impacted overhead reaching and adequately perceiving overhead reachability. The researchers predicted that higher levels of anxiety would result in a decrease of actual reaching height due to associated changes in movement execution, such as higher muscle tension and jerkier, more rigid movements. Resulting errors in some of an agent's sub-movements would result in a culmination of errors along the entire bio-kinematic chain. The researchers also predicted that decreases in actual maximal reaching height would be accompanied by decreases in perceived maximal height (Pijpers et al 2006, 135). Cast in the terminology outlined in this chapter, the researchers hypothesized that anxiety would contribute to a constriction of both the affordance landscape (actual possibilities available to an agent, given their bodily capabilities) and the affordance field (possibilities that stand out as relevant to the agent given their interests and concerns). Experimental results confirmed these hypotheses: high anxiety levels prevented climbers from paying attention to information sources that were relevant to their central task and thereby contributed to a narrowing of both their affordance landscape and their affordance field.

Can anxiety also lead to a constriction of the landscape and field of interpersonal affordances? I hypothesize that just as anxiety resulted in a decrease of actual reaching height among the climbers, anxiety may sometimes impair subjects' bodily capacity to partake in certain kinds of social interaction. This is because pronounced anxiety (such as that which occurs in cases of SAD) involves changes in an agent's bodily comportment, gestures, facial expressions, and vocal intonations. Such changes might result, for example, in decreased emotional resonance with others' positive emotions and attenuated bodily synchronization. This could change the actual social affordances that are available to the agent (e.g., possibilities for social coordination or joint activity) and lead to a constriction of their landscape of affordances. Cases of high threat sensitivity or social withdrawal, in particular, might be instances in which subjects are incapable of various forms of social interaction, given their overall bodily condition.

What is more, because agents with SAD are especially attuned to negative social feedback and predisposed to interpret others' behavior as threatening, their field of relevant interpersonal affordances is likely to be altered in distinctive ways. This is partly because their heightened attunement to negative social stimuli (Lin et al. 2016) diminishes their capacity to attend to and integrate multiple social and environmental cues. In addition to reducing the scope of their attention in everyday social environments, this tendency to focus on negative cues can prevent them from gaining valuable information about their immediate surroundings from other agents. Along these lines, Bader (2020) maintains that SAD involves a loss of the attentional broadness and the expansion of affordances that the presence of other people ordinarily facilitates. Because agents with SAD do not trust others to help them orient their attention, they lose out on the crucial advantages associated with social referencing and find it more difficult to engage in coordinated joint activity. Rather than relying on others to help them attend to relevant considerations and coordinate "expectations about shared meanings that structure the interactive space" (Bader 2020), they tend to put distance between themselves and others. Opportunities to create meaning together with other agents (e.g., in cases of collaboration, brainstorming, or joint problem-solving) begin to disappear, and there is a disruption to their sense of what is possible for them to do within the interpersonal domain.

Such disruptions to agency can be understood as alterations in their field of *sociability affordances* and *interpersonal affordances*. First, the field of sociability affordances narrows, so that agents with SAD do not perceive their surrounding environment as an interactive conducive space. Instead, social settings tend to be perceived as intimidating or threatening. Likewise, the field of interpersonal affordances constricts, so that the agent perceives fewer possibilities for social interaction. Second, the field of interpersonal affordances also lacks depth insofar as the subject feels alienated from future plans and action-possibilities related to upcoming social interaction. For example, the prospect of interacting with others at an upcoming social event may seem especially dauting and likely to result in nothing but awkwardness or embarrassment. Third, aversive affordances thereby take on greater height in the field and become especially salient; available possibilities for social interaction don't simply fail to invite or solicit action, but instead actually repel the agent and solicit avoidance of social situations. Thus, agents with SAD are responsive to social affordances, but in a way that is ordinarily associated with dangerous objects and events.

This raises a question, however, about why anxiety has this sort of debilitating impact in cases of SAD, whereas in "healthier" cases it appears to help agents gain a grip on relevant affordances. One possibility is that the anxiety in cases of SAD simply is more acute or intense; however, in my view, this would not yet provide a full explanation as to why this form of anxiety proves to be so disruptive. I propose that the constriction of social affordances in cases of SAD is a direct result of agents' background existential orientation, which is characterized by attenuated habitual trust or confidence in both themselves and others. First, loss of trust in oneself (and one's own abilities or capacities) can be understood in terms of diminished self-esteem or self-efficacy. I have suggested, building upon the work of Slaby, that an agent's sense of ability helps to shape their affordance field and makes an important difference to what the surrounding world (and other people) afford in terms of concrete possibilities; their sense of ability manifests their practical point of view and their "standing in the world" (Slaby 2012, 154). These self-construals often are not a matter of conscious reflection, but instead enacted via someone's pre-reflective bodily engagements. Depending on someone's background sense of ability, the world may appear as a space full of inviting possibilities, "or as a something removed and unreachable, or as a site of impending disaster, of threat and danger" (Slaby 2012, 154). Along these lines, Bortolan (2022) maintains that self-esteem is a self-evaluative affective experience that deeply molds people's cognitive, emotional, and practical life. Someone's current standing in the world, their relationships to others, and their sense of their own abilities all modulate how they confront the world, shaping their subsequent activities and their sense of which tasks they are capable of performing (Slaby 2012, 153).

In cases of SAD, agents have a low pre-reflective sense of their own ability and achievements, i.e., low "self-esteem" (Bortolan 2022) and a diminished sense "self-efficacy," particularly with respect to social interaction. This sense of inability helps to comprise their general mode of being in the world and contributes to a modification of their affordance field. For example, an agent's sense that they lack social skills or abilities may attune them to possibilities to withdraw from social engagement:

> I just kind of like for me, I'm just like I just wanna get out of that situation so I'll just leave normally . . . so like . . . if I'm out with people and I'm like not really feeling it and I start to feel anxious I'll just go home . . . cause it's like I just don't wanna deal with this. (Lee et al. 2022, 909–10)

Agents with SAD also may simply opt out of social situations:

> I was anxious just completely shut myself off from real life and I just escape to movies and games and stuff. (Lee et al. 2022, 911)

Even if someone does not completely withdraw from social situations, they may deploy various escape tactics, e.g., going out for a smoke or fixating on their cell phone, or become slow to respond to the interpersonal affordances that other agents are offering. These tendencies have an impact on the agent's affordance field and what sort of possibilities for interpersonal engagement become available as the situation unfolds. In addition, a diminished sense of self-efficacy may render dangerous affordances especially salient; and if a social setting appears "daunting, oppressive, unpredictable, uncontrollable" (Ratcliffe, Ruddell, and Smith 2014, 4), and the subject experiences themselves as unable to engage in a habitual practical performance, their actions and words may begin to lack their usual fluidity and spontaneity. And because a subject's loss of confidence and diminished self-esteem operates pre-reflectively, as a background existential orientation, it may remain resistant to change even if they explicitly endorse propositions such as "other people like me" (Ratcliffe, Ruddell, and Smith 2014, 4).

These feelings of inability, which help to constitute the agent's with SAD's low self-esteem, are inextricable from significantly modified corporeal experiences (Slaby 2012, 154). Like depression, anxiety involves marked changes in bodily dynamics that can lead to changes to both the agent's sense of self as well as their embodied interactive capacities, reducing their ability "to actively 'be with'" (Slaby et al. 2013, 45–46) other people. Bodily experiences commonly associated with the "alarm reaction" of anxiety include increased heart rate, rapid breathing or hyperventilation, sweating, nausea and upset stomach, light headedness or dizziness, tight chest, numbness or tingling sensations, bright vision or sense of unreality, muscle tension, and tendencies to avert one's gaze or chew or one's fingernails or a pen. These bodily feelings of anxiety can induce a felt pressure or pull to move away from social encounters and may make it difficult for agents to gain a grip on interpersonal affordances.

However, it is not simply that subjects with SAD have begun to lose confidence in themselves and their own abilities; in addition, there is a loss of trust in other people. Ordinarily, people anticipate and navigate social interactions with some degree of "habitual confidence" (Ratcliffe, Ruddell, and Smith 2014, 4), and their default mode of relating to others involves habitual trust. In many cases, this sense of security is so engrained that agents are oblivious to it. Indeed, the more at home someone feels in a particular social setting, the less likely they are to realize that this sense of familiarity and habitual trust functions as a backdrop for their worldly engagements. However, if this habitual trust begins to dissipate an agent's confidence begins to dissolve, they may begin to view the social realm as intimidating or threatening. In cases of SAD, alterations in bodily experience and loss of resonance with others help to comprise what might be understood as a loss of "habitual trust" or confidence in others. Agents lack confidence that others will cooperate in social interaction, recognize them as social actors, and respond appropriately to their social advances.

In "healthier" cases of anxiety, feelings of uncertainty and loss of trust are more localized and directed toward a particular event or situation. This can prompt the individual to seek out social information or take advantage of affordances associated with re-establishing social cohesion or coordinating behavior. Although associated feelings of anxiety may very well be unpleasant, if an agent's habitual trust in themself and others remains largely intact, their anxiety may help them to gain an optimal grip on available affordances rather than disrupting their functioning. In cases of social anxiety disorder, in contrast, there is a more general loss of "habitual trust" and a corresponding loss of confidence in other people. This loss of interpersonal trust has broad effects. Because interactions with others are not anticipated with habitual confidence, but instead with uncertainty and hesitation, the interpersonal environment seems less safe (Ratcliffe, Ruddell, and Smith 2014, 6). This may result in in a fear of the unknown that renders the sharing of social space a threatening experience, one in which available interpersonal affordances repel action. What is more, because agents with SAD are not confident that others will help them in moments of need, they may feel highly reluctant to turn to others for reassurance and support. As I will discuss further in the next section, they are thereby cut off from social resources that ordinarily might scaffold their ability to make sense of what is unfolding in the social realm.

In addition, "when interpersonal trust is lost, the prospect of entering into an interpersonal process that might otherwise have enabled a shift in anticipatory style is lost along with it" (Ratcliffe, Ruddell, and Smith 2014, 7). Subjects with SAD become "stuck" in their anxious orientation to the world, which leads them to view even relatively safe social environments as highly intimidating or threatening. Whereas someone with intact habitual trust displays confident engagement with what is coming next, in cases of SAD, "the default style of anticipation becomes that of anxious uncertainty" (Ratcliffe, Ruddell, and Smith 2014, 5). Because the agent tends not to rely on interpersonal relations to regulate their experiences and attention, they are less receptive to any attempts that other people make to establish a friendly connection. Instead, the subject with SAD feels threatened or intimidated, socially withdrawn, and less able to relate to others. And since much of goal-directed activity implicates other people in some way, feeling alienated from others also results in a shrinking of a subject's projects: "where there is pervasive uncertainty, where others cease to be dependable, where the world is unsafe and one's own abilities are in doubt, projects collapse" (Ratcliffe, Ruddell, and Smith 2014, 7). The agent with SAD therefore may find it increasingly difficult to gain optimal grip on action-possibilities associated with joint activity. As I will discuss in the next section, this may prompt rumination as an attempted means of compensating for these disruptions to agency.

THE FEEDBACK LOOP OF ANXIETY AND RUMINATION

Recall that in healthier cases, agents allow others to regulate their attention; as result, relevant external and social information becomes more salient, and they are better able to engage appropriately with available motor and social affordances. However, individuals with SAD tend to avoid trusting their attention in the hands of others (Bader 2020). They selectively attend to negative information about themselves as a situation unfolds, are especially attuned to others' negative reactions and emotional expressions, and do not effectively rely on others to shape their own attention allocation. Feelings of anxiety and low self-esteem also pull them away from social resources that otherwise would help them to regulate their attention and gain an optimal grip on relevant affordances. Because they experience encounters with others as intimidating or threatening, they do not look to them as a resource that might help them to enlarge and enrich their affordance field. This is especially true in cases where an agent with SAD withdraws from or avoids social situations; but even in cases where they do engage directly with others, their attenuated habitual trust makes it difficult for them to share affect with others or gain access to their perspective on the world. Rather than feeling comfortably immersed in their interpersonal surroundings, agents with SAD feel acutely vulnerable and estranged from others.

Because these individuals have fewer opportunities to "experience the richness of their resources in actual online engagement" (Meynen 2011, 5) with other people, they may begin to rely more heavily on offline contemplation (rumination) to navigate social situations. For example, one university student with SAD described "overthinking" her verbal communication in a classroom setting:

> We kind of let the other groups go first and whilst they're talking I'll be rehearing the lines over and over again in my head so I won't even be paying attention to the other groups I'll just be reading my sheet and what I've written down for myself like ok well how can I say this. (Lee et al. 2022, 904)

Meynen (2011) proposes that agents with anxiety disorder tend to underestimate their coping skills in feared situations; rather than relying on their online abilities and bodily resources (whose richness goes well beyond what can be accessed via detached contemplation), they look to worrying as a means of dealing with problematic uncertainty. Those who tend to operate primarily in an offline mode may end up thinking all day about what it will be like to go to a supermarket and interact with a cashier rather than actually going there. Relying on detached knowledge about the social environment makes it difficult for them to navigate fluctuating social situations and interact smoothly with affordances. What is more, this worry strategy stimulates avoidance of actual social interactions and thereby deprives them of the opportunity to correct some of their negative beliefs about themselves. In the case of SAD, avoidance of social situations also further distances agents from social resources that might allow for the expansion and enrichment of their affordance field (including opportunities to engage in joint activities with others, engage in perspective-taking, and pursue shared goals).

Meynen (2011) rightly notes that offline contemplation is not necessarily bad; however, this strategy needs to be used selectively rather than becoming someone's default mode of engaging with the world. Continuously imagining the point of view of others and evaluating one's own performance via an offline, third-person perspective can become excessive and maladaptive and lead to social difficulties. In my view, however, the difficulty is not simply that subjects with SAD rely on offline contemplation and worrying too extensively or too frequently. What drives these metacognitions is the agent's embodied, pre-reflective orientation of diminished habitual trust (comprised of both diminished self-esteem and diminished confidence in others). This existential orientation leads them not only to underestimate their own coping skills and their capacity for navigating social situations, but also to have little confidence that others can help them to orient their attention toward relevant considerations. Thus, they come to view rumination (rather than their own online abilities, and the real-time feedback provided by others) as the best way to prepare for future social situations (anticipatory rumination) and make sense of what has occurred in past social situations (post-event rumination).

Meynen (2011) proposes that the rumination strategy stimulates avoidance of social situations and thereby deprives the subject of the opportunity to correct the metacognition by discovering that they can actually deal with the situation. In my view, however, it is not simply a subject's metacognitions that are strengthened and reinforced, but also their general existential orientation, characterized by a diminished degree of habitual trust or confidence. Because agents with SAD have a diminished sense of their own online abilities and do not trust others to regulate their attention, fluid, online engagement with interpersonal affordances begins to break down. This contributes to their retreat into reflective, offline forms of self-consciousness, such as heightened self-monitoring and rumination. The agent with SAD becomes "frequently and intensely conscious of herself as the object of other people's attention and observation" (Bortolan 2022, 309) and takes a spectatorial or third-person observational perspective on her own behaviors and experiences. Therefore, when an agent with SAD enters a feared social situation, they are likely to already be in a self-focused processing mode (Norton and Abbott 2016) rather than allowing others to regulate their attention and orient them toward relevant affordances. Anticipatory rumination and post-event rumination likewise are strategies that an agent with SAD appeals to in order to compensate for the loss of social attentional resources. However, this focus on the self and associated efforts to prepare for social situations usually do not actually improve the agent's responsiveness to relevant considerations, but instead compromise social performance even further, thereby making feared social consequences more likely. This, in turn, potentially exacerbates social anxiety and prevents agents with SAD from disconfirming their negative beliefs about themselves.

To see how this feedback loop might occur, consider the example of Taylor, a subject with SAD who attends a work-related social event (due to a sense of obligation). They arrive at the faculty reception and exhibit a closed posture (with arms crossed) and eyes directed downward. Their body is tense, their heart rate is elevated, their breathing is rapid, and their palms are sweaty. Because Taylor exhibits a heightened attunement to negative social cues and has a sense of inability, they encounter this social setting as intimidating and threatening. Taylor's body and its capacities (to talk, gesture, and breathe steadily) become objects of their focal attention, which contributes to feelings of self-consciousness. Their response is to avert their gaze, hide in the corner of the room, and take out their cell phone; thus, Taylor's social agency is prevented from unfolding smoothly and without effort. Even when somebody friendly comes over to talk to them, Taylor is not adequately receptive to these overtures. They exhibit attenuated bodily synchronization and decreased emotional resonance with others' positive emotions and begin to worry about the negative judgments their colleagues likely are making about them. Because other faculty members at the reception think Taylor doesn't like them and doesn't want to be there, they avoid Taylor; this, together with Taylor's own tendencies toward social withdrawal, reinforces their feelings of alienation; their anxiety intensifies, creating a kind of self-fulfilling cycle. After the event, Taylor continues to ruminate and becomes more likely to experience more acute anxiety at future social events.

It is interesting to consider how the rumination that occurs in SAD is similar, in an important respect, to the sort of hyperreflexivity that sometimes occurs in schizophrenia. Theorists working in phenomenological psychopathology have described how subjects with schizophrenia sometimes become hyper-reflexive in an attempt to compensate for diminished bodily attunement. That is, in an effort to gain a handle on themselves, individuals with schizophrenia regard themselves as an object of reflection, so that various aspects of self-experience (including bodily sensations that ordinarily would remain in the background) become targets of explicit awareness. Continual, repetitive preoccupation with the self, in turn, can contribute to and reinforce feelings of unreality and self-alienation, and "the split between the observing and the acting self can, at its most extreme, become an out-of-body experience" (Simeon and Abugel 2006, 63). The subject's immediate experience of thinking may be replaced by a second-order awareness of *perceiving that* they are perceiving, acting, or thinking (Stanghellini 2004, 19). Along these lines, some subjects report examining their experiences as objects and having a sense that they are mere *spectators* or *scanners* of their own mental states. This reflective self-focus exacerbates disruptions to self-experience and contributes to feelings of alienation.

In SAD, the problem is not that agents have lost contact with their own bodies or have a diminished sense of self. Instead, they have a diminished sense of their own online abilities, and a decreased sense of trust in others.

Rather than functioning as a resource that helps to protect them from uncertain environmental conditions, the presence of other people is viewed primarily as a source of problematic uncertainty. Instead of trusting others to help orient their attention to objects and events and provide them with valuable information, the agent with SAD focuses reflective attention on themselves and their awkward performance in the social situation. In addition, the agent lacks confidence in themselves and in their ability to navigate an unpredictable or indeterminately threatening social environment. This sense that they are lacking in "online intelligence" leads them to get "stuck in their heads." Aspects of self-experience (namely, the pre-reflective sense of themselves as social agents) may become the target of explicit awareness, and an agent's continual, repetitive preoccupation with their own bodily hesitancy and clumsiness results in rumination. As in the case of the hyperreflexivity in schizophrenia, this simply intensifies and reinforces the difficulties that the agent encounters[2]; in the case of SAD, excessive self-monitoring contributes to the agent's sense that the social environment is threatening and that they are inadequate. Their confidence in themselves and others erodes even further, exacerbating their anxiety and potentially causing increased withdrawal from the social world. Anxiety and rumination thereby form a destructive feedback loop.

CONCLUSION

In this chapter, I have used the notions of affordance and habitual trust to examine how an agent's existential orientation shapes their affordance field and impacts agency in either a beneficial and enabling way or a disruptive and disabling way. I have suggested that what we attend to is regulated by others, and that their mere presence modulates what we take to be salient and what sorts of action-possibilities are relevant and inviting. In cases of SAD, agents are oriented toward other people in terms of an "I can't" schema, and the social world appears as a site full of problematic uncertainties. Because they experience acute anxiety in the presence of others and anticipate some sort of social danger, their affordance field may constrict. In part, this is because they have become cut off from social resources that ordinarily would enlarge and enrich their affordance field and help them to orient their attention toward relevant possibilities for social interaction and joint activity. To compensate for this loss of social resources and establish a "grip" on available affordances, agents with SAD sometimes turn to rumination to help them navigate the social realm. However, this offline mode of engagement further contributes to social withdrawal and prevents them from cultivating their online abilities for social engagement.

It is important to note that the attenuation of habitual trust that occurs in cases of SAD is experienced by individuals situated in a particular sociopolitical realm (Roberts and Osler, 2023), and that toxic social environments may very well play a contributory role in both the onset and maintenance of SAD. Someone's confidence in their ability to engage in social interaction and their trust in others can be undermined, for example, in cases where they are not treated as social equals, or when they encounter antagonism, rudeness, unwelcoming attitudes, or outright hostility. Thus, subjects who encounter hostile environments due to their social identity (e.g., in cases of racism or homophobia), childhood abuse, or bullying may have good reason to view others as a source of threat. Given that such environments clearly can contribute to diminished habitual trust, it would be a mistake to suppose that SAD is simply a problem located in individuals.

However, because the very notion of affordances emphasizes that complementarily of the agent and their environment, it is well-positioned to make sense of how SAD represents a disruption to the relationship between an agent and their social world. My affordance-based account also offers a way to make sense of how anxiety (as an affective condition) relates to metacognition and the sort of rumination that commonly occurs in SAD. In addition, it emphasizes the link between affectivity and agency. How an agent affectively engages with a situation is a function of their embodied sense of ability (self-efficacy and self-esteem) together with the relevant features of the situation (what the situation affords in terms of potential actions). Together, these two aspects form "an active, operative orientation toward the world" (Slaby et al. 2013, 42). In cases of SAD, the social world appears as a site of impending threat or danger and agents experience a diminished sense of trust, both in themselves and in others. This attenuated habitual trust helps to comprise their overall existential orientation and mode of being in the world, one which contributes to a modification of their affordance field and disrupts their sense of what is possible for them to do within the interpersonal domain.

NOTES

1. There is ongoing debate about the ontological status of affordances: are they real, and do they exist apart from perceivers? While I do not aim to weigh in on this debate here, it is important to note that I utilize an enactivist conception of affordances.

2. Subjects with schizophrenia likewise encounter a loss of trust, a sense of losing contact with reality, and a sense of being cut off from the social world. In cases of SAD, some degree of trust likely remains intact when agents are interacting with close friends or family members. In cases of schizophrenia, in contrast, this loss of

trust together with an attenuated sense of self are more likely to shape and seriously disrupt all an agent's dealings with the world.

REFERENCES

Bader, Oren. 2020. "The Human Extended Socio-Attentional Field and its Impairment in Borderline Personality Disorder and in Social Anxiety Disorder." *Phenomenology and the Cognitive Sciences* 19: 169–89.

Bortolan, Anna. 2022. "Social Anxiety, Self-Consciousness, and Interpersonal Experience." In *Empathy, Intersubjectivity, and the Social World*, edited by Anna Bortolan and Elisa Magri, 303–22. Boston: De Gruyter.

Brancazio, Nick. 2020. "Being Perceived and Being 'Seen': Interpersonal Affordances, Agency, and Selfhood." *Frontiers in Psychology* 11: 1750.

de Haan, Sanneke, Erik Rietveld, Martin Stokhof, and Damiaan Denys. 2013. "The Phenomenology of Deep Brain Stimulation-induced Changes in Obsessive-Compulsive Disorder Patients: An Enactive Affordance-based Model." *Frontiers in Human Neuroscience* 7: 1–14.

Dings, Roy. 2018. "Understanding Phenomenological Differences in how Affordances Solicit Action. An exploration." *Phenomenology and the Cognitive Sciences* 17: 681–99.

———. 2021. "Meaningful Affordances." *Synthese* 199: 1855–75.

Gallagher, Shaun. 2018. "The Therapeutic Reconstruction of Affordances." *Res Philosophica* 95: 719–36

Gallagher, Shaun, and Micah Allen. 2018. "Active Inference, Enactivism and the Hermeneutics of Social Congition." *Synthese* 195: 2627–48.

Gibson, James J. 1979. *The Ecological Approach to Visual Perception*. New York: Houghton Mifflin.

Glas, Gerrit. 2020. "An Enactive Approach to Anxiety and Anxiety Disorders." *Philosophy, Psychiatry, and Psychology* 27: 35–50.

Jefferies, Phillip, and Michael Ungar. 2020. "Social Anxiety in Young People: A Prevalence Study in Seven Countries." *PLoS One* 15(9): e0239133.

Kiverstein, Julian. 2015. "Empathy and the Responsiveness to Social Affordances." *Consciousness and Cognition* 36: 532–42.

Kiverstein, Julian, and Erik Rietveld. 2021. "Scaling-up Skilled Intentionality to Linguistic Thought." *Synthese* 198: 175–94.

Kreuger, Joel. 2011. "Extended Cognition and the Space of Social Interaction." *Consciousness and Cognition* 20: 647–57.

Kurth, Charlie. 2016. "Anxiety, Normative Uncertainty, and Social Regulation." *Biology and Philosophy* 31: 1–21.

Lee, Jennifer, Daniel Waldeck, Andrew Holliman, Moitree Banerjee, and Ian Tyndall, Ian. 2022. "Feeling Socially Anxious at University: An Interpretative Phenomenological Analysis." *The Qualitative Report* 27: 897–919.

Lin, Muyu, Stefan G. Hofmann, Mingyi Qian, Shelley Kind, and Hongyu Yu. 2016. "Attention Allocation in Social Anxiety During a Speech." *Cognition and Emotion* 30: 1122–36.

Maiese, Michelle. 2021. "Enactivism, the Field of Affordances, and Mental Disorder." *Journal of Mind and Behavior* 42: 175–96.

Meynen, Gerben. 2011. "Generalized Anxiety Disorder and Online Intelligence: A Phenomenological Account of Why Worrying Is Unhelpful." *Philosophy, Ethics, and Humanities in Medicine* 6: 1–7.

Norton, Alice R., and Maree J. Abbott. 2016. "Self-Focused Cognition in Social Anxiety: A Review of the Theoretical and Empirical Literature." *Behaviour Change* 33: 44–64.

Pijpers, Jan Robert, Raoul R. D. Oudejans, Frank C. Bakker, and Peter J. Beek. 2006. "The Role of Anxiety in Perceiving and Realizing Affordances." *Ecological Psychology* 18: 131–61.

Ramstead, Maxwell J. D., Samuel P. L. Veissiere, and Laurence J. Kirmayer. 2016. "Cultural Affordances: Scaffolding Local Worlds Through Shared Intentionality and Regimes of Attention." *Frontiers in Psychology* 7 (1090), 1–21.

Ratcliffe, Matthew. 2005. "The Feeling of Being." *Journal of Consciousness Studies* 12: 43–60.

———. 2008. *Feelings of Being: Phenomenology, Psychiatry and the Sense of Reality*. Oxford: Oxford University Press.

———. 2015. "The Interpersonal World of Psychosis." *World Psychiatry* 14(2): 176.

Ratcliffe, Matthew, Mark Ruddell, and Benedict Smith. 2014. "What is a 'Sense of Foreshortened Future?' A Phenomenological Study of Trauma, Trust, and Time." *Frontiers in Psychology,* 1026.

Rietveld, Erik. 2012. "Bodily Intentionality and Social Affordances in Context." In *Consciousness in Interaction: The Role of the Natural and Social Context in Shaping Consciousness*, edited by Fabio Paglieri, 207–26. Amsterdam: John Benjamins Publishing.

Rietveld, Erik, and Julian Kiverstein. 2014. "A Rich Landscape of Affordances." *Ecological Psychology* 26: 325–52.

Rietveld, Erik, Damiaan Denys, and Maarten van Westen. 2018. "Ecological-Enactive Cognition as Engaging with a Field of Relevant Affordances: The Skilled Intentionality Framework (SIF)." In *The Oxford Handbook of 4E Cognition*, edited by Albert Newen, Leon de Bruin, and Shaun Gallagher, 41–70. Oxford: Oxford University Press.

Rietveld, Erik, Ronald Rietveld, and Janno Martens. 2019. "Trusted Strangers: Social Affordances for Social Cohesion." *Phenomenology and the Cognitive Sciences* 18: 299–316.

Roberts, Tom, and Lucy Osler. 2023. "Social Doubt." *Journal of the American Philosophical Association, 1–18.*

Ruscio, Ayelet Meron, Timothy A. Brown, Wai Tat Chiu, Jitender Sareen, Murray B. Stein, and Ronald C. Kessle. 2008. "Social Fears and Social Phobia in the USA: Results from the National Comorbidity Survey Replication." *Psychological Medicine* 38: 15–28.

Simeon, Daphne, and Jeffrey Abugel. 2006. *Feeling Unreal: Depersonalization Disorder and the Loss of the Self.* New York: Oxford University Press.

Slaby, Jan. 2012. "Affective Self-Construal and the Sense of Ability." *Emotion Review* 4: 151–56.

Slaby, Jan, Asena Paskaleva, and Achim Stephan. 2013. "Enactive Emotion and Impaired Agency in Depression." *Journal of Consciousness Studies* 20: 33–55.

Stanghellini, Giovanni. 2004. *Disembodied Spirits and Deanimated Bodies: The Psychopathology of Common Sense*. Oxford: Oxford University Press.

Van Dijk, Ludger, and Erik Rietveld. 2017. "Foregrounding Sociomaterial Practice in our Understanding of Affordances: The Skilled Intentionality Framework." *Frontiers in Psychology* 7–2016.

Vazard, Juliette, and Charlie Kurth. 2022. "Apprehending Anxiety: an Introduction to the Topical Collection on Worry and Wellbeing." *Synthese* 200 (4): 1–17.

Wheeler, Michael. 2005. *Reconstructing the Cognitive World: The Next Step.* Cambridge, MA.: The MIT Press.

Chapter 8

Moral Anxiety

A Kantian Perspective

Charlie Kurth

In the early 1960s, Martin Luther King Jr. recognized that he would need the support of President Lyndon Johnson if civil rights legislation was going to be passed.[1] As result, King chose not to say anything negative about the United States' involvement in Vietnam. But as time wore on, not only did the war in Vietnam escalate, but people started calling King out for being a hypocrite. In particular, they did not understand how King could be so vocal an opponent of the use of violence in his fight for civil rights, but be completely silent about the violence in Vietnam. As King details in his autobiography, these developments led him to become increasingly "uncertain" and uncomfortable about his initial decision not to speak out: "doubts gnawed at [his] conscience" and he did "a lot of thinking" about the problem he faced (King 1998, 322). The result of this uncertainty and unease—and the thinking they spurred—was King's decision to confront the Johnson administration on the war.

What should we make of King's experience? His talk of his gnawing conscience is suggestive—pointing to his awareness of the moral significance of the situation he faced. But pointing to the pangs of his conscience only gets us so far given that the term "conscience" is, at least in its folk usage, a catch-all label for a variety of distinct psychological phenomenon: shame, guilt, fear of punishment, and the like.[2] However, if we look at King's experience as a whole—his talk not just of his conscience, but also his unease, uncertainty, and reflection that brought about his decision to protest the war—it suggests an alternative description of what he was going through. It suggests that King's experience was undergirded by anxiety: he was *worried* that he was making an exception to his explicit rejection of violence as a means to political change, doing so on the dubious grounds of wanting to stay in the good graces of the Johnson administration (1998, 342; Kurth 2019 for review). We get some confirmation of this account of King's psychology from his remarks in a speech that he delivered in Chicago on March 25, 1967, one of his first public statements against the war. There he exclaimed, "I speak out against [the war] not in anger but with *anxiety* and sorrow in my heart" (King 1967, emphasis added).

However, if King's decision to start protesting the war was driven by anxiety, it was anxiety of a very distinctive and morally laced sort. To see this, consider the social anxiety that one might feel on a blind date or before giving a public presentation—in these cases, one's anxiety prompts efforts toward deference and caution as one tries to minimize the cost of negative evaluations from one's date or the audience. This is quite different from what King experienced. His anxiety, after all, motivated not deference, but engagement as he reflected on, and reassessed, his initial decision not to protest. King does not seem to have been concerned about a negative social evaluation; rather, he was trying to come the right decision about what he ought to do. Moreover, King's anxiety seems not just distinctive, but distinctly valuable. His anxiety was instrumentally valuable insofar as it piqued his awareness of the fraught decision he faced and prompted the reflection that led to his revised decision about protesting the war. But King's anxiety also seems noninstrumentally valuable insofar it reflects well on his character—in being worried about whether to reverse course and start protesting the war, he displays an admirable emotional attunement to what matters.

Bringing these observations together, the King case points us to something we might call "moral anxiety"—an unease that is experienced in the face of a new or complex moral situation and that prompts various forms of higher cognition (deliberation, reflection, reassessment, etc.) aimed at helping one come to morally justified decision about what to do. Not only does thinking about King's case as an instance of moral anxiety shed new light on the psychology of his decision, bringing clarity to his vague talk of conscience, but it also connects up with a growing body of scholarship examining the nature and moral value of anxiety (e.g., Fritz 2022; Harbin 2016; Kurth 2015, 2018a, 2018b, 2018c; Lacewing 2005; Maibom 2022; Munch-Jurisic 2020, 2022; Pihkala 2021).[3]

But the picture of "moral anxiety" that emerges from the King example also raises a trio of challenging questions:

(1) What, exactly, is moral anxiety and in what sense is it "moral"?
(2) Is moral anxiety plausibly understood as a genuine psychological phenomenon, or is it merely a loose way of talking about (say) the aversion we have to making difficult decisions?

(3) Given all the ways in which anxiety can go awry, how can we make sense of the idea that moral anxiety is a distinctly valuable emotion?

In what follows, I want to approach these questions through a Kantian lens. While this Kantian framework isn't essential to either the phenomenon of moral anxiety or our understanding of it, we will see that it's an approach that brings conceptual, empirical, and normative insights for our understanding of the nature and value of moral anxiety.

Here is how we will proceed. In the first section, I draw on discussions of "conscience" from Kant and Kantians to develop a Kantian model of moral anxiety. In the second section, I develop this model further, showing how—initial appearances to the contrary—it fits with, and gains empirical support from, recent work on dual-process theories and associated work in the social and cognitive sciences. Finally, in the third section, I turn a critical eye to the Kantian model, showing how its core insights can be retained even after some of the more controversial elements of the proposal have been trimmed. The payoff of all this is twofold. First, we will see how taking a Kantian lens allows us to better assess recent debates about the nature and value of moral anxiety. More provocatively, we will also see that Kant turns out to be an early—and particularly sophisticated—dual-process theorist.

A KANTIAN MODEL OF MORAL ANXIETY

Kant is typically viewed as the paradigm of a moral rationalist.[4] So it's worth noting that he also gives significant place to "non-rationalistic" mechanisms in his account of both human moral psychology and ethical education. For instance, in the *Doctrine of Virtue*, Kant discusses the four "moral endowments" that he takes to be *essential* to our ability to appreciate and be moved by the concept of duty. These are moral feeling, conscience, love, and self-esteem. As Kant explains, these are not rational capacities, but rather *affective* ones (1797/1996, 6:399, 528). So, for instance, moral feelings of pleasure and displeasure are essential in Kant's eyes because it is only through these feelings that we are able to be "aware that our actions are consistent with or contrary to the law of duty" (1797/1996, 6:399, 528). Similarly, in his discussion of moral education and pedagogy, Kant emphasizes the need for teachers to focus not just on developing students' rational capacities, but also their habits and non-cognitive drives (2007, 9:451, 445). In fact, Kant's writings on virtue reveal that he takes our need to develop our nonrational capacities to extend beyond adolescence—hence his discussion of, for instance, our duty to bolster feelings of sympathy by visiting hospitals and poor houses (e.g., 1797/1996, 6:457, 575).

Against this backdrop, I want to look at Kant's comments on the role of conscience in shaping moral thought and action—for, as with King, Kant's conception of conscience has much in common with contemporary discussions of the nature and value of moral anxiety. Not only will this allow us to better appreciate the affective dimensions of Kant's moral psychology, but it will also provide us with an entry way for developing a Kantian model of moral anxiety.

Kant's Account

We can see Kant's account of conscience as grounded in three claims. First, he takes conscience to be an innate mechanism that is central to our capacity for *moral self-regulation* (6:399, 528; 6:438, 560). As he explains, a person's conscience functions as an "internal judge," one that "follows him like a shadow when he plans to escape" from doing his duty (6:438–40, 560–61). Second, Kant sees conscience's ability to operate as a self-regulatory mechanism to be grounded in its *distinctive affectivity*. When one is inclined to act contrary to the moral law, one's conscience sounds an alarm, "warning him before he makes his decision" about what he ought to do. Moreover, this alarm signals moral danger and manifests itself as a feeling of "anxiety" (6: 440, 561–62).[5] Finally, given conscience's status as a core moral endowment, it is something that Kant maintains we have a duty to *cultivate*—specifically, one has a duty "to cultivate one's conscience, to sharpen one's attentiveness to the voice of [this] inner judge" (6:401, 530). Together, these three elements help us understand Kant's view of conscience as an emotionally grounded mechanism of moral restraint—an aversively experienced signal that flags the need to proceed cautiously.

But important questions remain. In particular, Kant's comments do little to help us understand either why he took conscience to be a *foundational* moral capacity or how the role that he assign to this noncognitive mechanism is compatible with his *rationalism*. Moreover, while we see that there is a place for anxiety in Kant's proposal, his discussion of it seems to lack the substance necessary to explain things like King's experience of moral anxiety—the gnawing conscience, the uncertainty, and the reflection and reconsideration it brought.

Enter the work of Barbara Herman. As part of a larger project of refining Kant's account of moral judgment, Herman takes up questions about the role that deliberative and non-deliberative capacities play in a Kantian moral psychology—a discussion that helps us fill in the above gaps in the remarks we get from Kant.

Herman's Elaborations

Kant is often understood—caricatured—as directing us to constantly be deliberating about what we ought to do (e.g., Hampshire 1978; Williams 1981). Against this, Herman takes Kant's discussion of moral reasoning to be aimed at highlighting the *limited* role that he sees for moral deliberation. On the picture she develops, deliberation is not something Kant thinks we are, or should always be, engaged in. Rather, it is something we need to do only when we face a novel or difficult moral situation (Herman 1993 76–78, 145–46, 157). So, for instance, the point of Kant's lying promise example from the *Groundwork* isn't merely to illustrate how we are to use the categorical Imperative (as is standardly presumed in the literature), but also to highlight the kinds of *novel* situations that demand deliberation. So understood, the questions that interest Herman are ones that concern *how* one comes to see that deliberation is needed and *why* one is motivated to engage in it.

It's here that conscience reenters the picture. According to Herman, in focusing on conscience as a core moral endowment, Kant isn't just circumscribing a mechanism of moral restraint. He is also identifying a more encompassing, emotion-driven alarm—one whose function is to "cause the agent to be aware of and attentive to the significance of 'moral danger'" (78; c.f., Eran 2021). In developing this idea, Herman provides important detail on two central aspects of how conscience works, detail that helps fill in some of the gaps we noted in Kant's own account.

The first elaboration concerns how conscience flags moral danger. Here Herman points to what she calls "rules of moral salience" (RMS)—distinctive pieces of content that "constitute the structure of [an individual's] moral sensitivity" and that "indicate when certain sorts of action should not be taken without moral justification" (Herman 1993, 78). As she presents them, RMS are "predeliberative" mechanisms (Herman 1993, 147)—heuristics or scripts, perhaps—that flag instances "of moral conflict (or uncertainty)" for which moral deliberation is needed (Herman 1993, 157). Importantly, since the role of RMS is merely to warn of moral danger—not resolve it—these rules needn't be very complicated. In fact, and in line with Kant's ideas about moral education needing to focus on the development of both reason *and* habit, Herman takes much of our learning of RMS to come passively during childhood "as part of socialization" (Herman 1993, 78). That said, and this is the second core feature of conscience, a person's RMS are connected up with a distinctive form of motivation—in Herman's words, a "higher-order (or regulative) concern for the permissibility of his actions and projects" (Herman 1993, 83). It's this motivation, then, that gets one to engage in *moral* deliberation to resolve the danger that one's conscience has flagged; it's a motivation that gets one to think through one's situation by way of the

Categorical Imperative and not, say, more self-serving egoistic principles (Herman 1993, 146–47, 157).[6]

To put all this together, let's return to our earlier example. What gets the individual in Kant's lying-promises example to engage in moral deliberation is "his feeling" that, if he were to make an insincere promise, he might be making himself an exception to the rule that one ought not lie for personal gain (Herman 1993, 77–78). Given the unease—the anxiety—that he feels about the possibility of acting in a way that's morally unjustified, he's moved to deliberate. Thus, he reflects on whether allowing lying-promises in situations like the one he faces is something that could be willed as a universal law. Determining that it is not, he pulls away from his initial inclination to lie.

Upshots and Open Issues

Combining what we get from Kant and Herman suggests a picture on which the moral endowment of conscience is best understood as a distinctive, anxiety-driven type of moral self-regulation: an affective mechanism that uses simple, learned scripts (the RMS) to identify moral danger, and that sounds a moral-deliberation-engaging, aversively experienced alarm when an apparent danger is found.

Moreover, this proposal is explanatorily fruitful. For starters, it helps us understand why Kant may have taken conscience to be a foundational part of human moral psychology. Given that we're not always deliberating, Kant saw the need to explain what gets an individual to start reasoning. Moreover, he understood that his explanation couldn't rely on one reasoning about when to reason—for that would just launch a vicious "regress of reasoning" (1797/1996, 6: 402–3, 531; also, Kurth 2018a, 149–51, Railton 2009). Conscience solves this problem. After all, it's a *pre*deliberative emotional capacity that alerts one to moral danger and prompts deliberation to help one avoid acting contrary to duty. Notice as well that if conscience/moral anxiety is a *pre*deliberative mechanism that one develops via socialization, then we also get some clarity on why Kant thought moral education requires one to develop *non*rational capacities like the RMS. Finally, our Kantian model is also rich enough to capture the role that moral anxiety appears to play in the King example from above.

But this progress aside, some of our original questions remain, especially those regarding the empirical plausibility of moral anxiety. To help draw out why we should be concerned about the empirical credentials of moral anxiety, notice that the role that the Kantian model gives to the emotion seems to fit poorly with the dual-process accounts of (moral) thought and action that dominate the social and cognitive sciences. More specifically, according to the standard dual-process model, cognition is driven by two distinct systems: a "System-1" that is fast, automatic, and often emotion-engaging and a "System-2" that is slow, deliberative, and often rule based. Moreover, on the standard proposals, the two systems are presumed to operate in a manner that is quite different than what's suggested by the Kantian model.

To see this, first notice that the leading account of System-1/System-2 interaction builds from a *default-interventionist* structure: while much of (moral) cognition is driven by System-1 mechanisms, System-2 processes monitor this System-1 activity in order to determine when System-2 processing needs to be ramped up (e.g., Kahneman 2011; Stanovich and West 2000). But on a plausible translation of the Kantian picture in to dual-process terminology, we get something different: while the Kantian model accepts the default-interventionist structure, it differs in its account of which mechanisms do the monitoring and engaging. More specifically, on the Kantian proposal, it's moral anxiety—a System-1 mechanism—that looks for trouble and calls in System-2 deliberation when an apparent danger is found. But it's not just that the Kantian model differs from the standard dual-process view in its account which system does the monitoring and engaging, but also that the standard proposal seems more plausible. After all, the default-interventionist structure presumes that a decision needs to be made about when System-2 cognition should be engaged; but if a *decision* needs to be made, functioning of that sort seems to be the domain of deliberative System-2 processing, not quick-and-dirty System-1 heuristics. In short, if the truth about moral cognition lies in something like the standard dual-process proposal, then the Kantian model is in trouble.

THE EMPIRICAL PLAUSIBILITY OF THE KANTIAN MODEL

First Steps

In light of the above challenge, the Kantian could respond by saying, "so much the worse for dual-process thinking." While I believe there's something to this response, there are important subtleties that we need to take care to develop. To preview, there are other ways of thinking about dual-process theory, and the empirical evidence for them fits better with the Kantian model. Moreover, we have independent reason to want an alternative to the standard dual-process account that we just looked at. To see this, first notice that while the standard account is based on empirical findings, much of that work is correlational (e.g., Rand et al. 2012; Stanovich and West 2000), thus limiting the support it can provide. Add to this that meta-studies of work testing the predictions of the standard dual-process proposal reveal, at best, thin confirmation (e.g., Rand 2019, Kvarven et al. 2020). Finally, there are also important theoretical problems that undermine the standard proposal. For instance, taking System-2 to play a monitoring role, as the standard account does, invites regress of reasoning worries—for we have System-2 being cognition being posited to say when System-2 cognition should begin. Making matters worse, if one maintains—as that standard model does—that System-2 cognition is always operating, then we lose one of the primary selling points of the default-interventionist proposal—namely, the computational efficacy that comes with only selectively using more costly System-2 processing. Together, these issues provide us with reason to look for alternative to the standard proposal, reasons that stand independently of our interest in building an empirical case for the Kantian model.[7]

In part because of problems of the sort just reviewed, and in part for reasons independent of them, philosophers and cognitive scientists have started to develop alternative ways of understanding System-1/System-2 interactions. To date, most of this work has focused on developing a better understanding of transitions from System-2 to System-1 cognition.[8] Moreover, the little work that has focused on the alternative—understanding when and how System-1 cognition might transition to System-2—tends to focus on making a conceptual, not empirical, case for these transitions (e.g., Thomson 2008; Botvinick et al. 2001; Wunderlich et al. 2012). Against this backdrop, thinking about the Kantian model of moral anxiety is interesting for several reasons. First, the lack of significant research on System-1 to System-2 transitions forces us to get creative in building an empirical case for the Kantian model. But doing this reveals two avenues of support—one indirect, one direct. As we will see, not only do these findings bolster the credentials of the Kantian model, but seeing the empirical plausibility of the Kantian model, in turn, provides dual-system theorists with a much needed, concrete example of these transitions and the mechanisms that undergird them.

Indirect Support for the Kantian Model

Though not always recognized as such, work on *meta-cognitive emotions* provides us with theoretical and empirical evidence of mechanisms that underwrite System-1 to System-2 transitions. Moreover, these mechanisms are functionally very similar to the Kantian model's account of moral anxiety, and so offer indirect support for the Kantian account. Turning to details, the tip-of-the-tongue phenomenon (TOT) provides what is perhaps the best studied instance of a meta-cognitive emotion (Arango-Muñoz 2011; Thompson 2008; Schwartz and Metcalfe 2014). The TOT experience is familiar: it's what one experiences when one cannot remember (say) someone's name, but nonetheless one has partial recall of the content (e.g., the first letter of the name). This combination not only leaves one feeling that the name is just at the tip of one's tongue, but also gets one working to jog one's memory of what one cannot recall.

Shifting to the science, the most worked-out account of TOT suggests that the phenomenon is the upshot of a distinctive, emotion-driven mechanism. More specifically, TOT is taken to be underwritten by a two-part mechanism. First, there is a set of heuristics that map combinations of failed memory and partial recall to the distinctive TOT feeling: the feeling of familiarity. Second, this feeling is, in turn, accompanied by the motivations characteristic of TOT: the prompting of higher cognitive processing that's geared toward facilitating remembering (e.g., working through a particular mnemonic strategy). Put differently, in TOT, we have an emotion—a System-1 process—that works to both identify occasions where System-2 processing is needed and engage the requisite higher cognition.

In the present context, this account of the mechanisms underlying TOT is interesting for a couple of reasons. First, TOT gives us an existence proof: a concrete, empirically vetted example of an alternative to the standard dual-process account of System-1 to System-2 transitions. But we also get indirect support for the Kantian model. To see this, recall that the TOT model is just an instance of a more general mechanism—namely, a meta-cognitive emotion (Arango-Muñoz 2011; Proust 2009). In line with the above, we can understand meta-cognitive emotions as mechanisms that (i) use heuristics to map occasions of positive/negative value to distinctive feelings, and that (ii) incorporate these feelings into an "affective alarm" that engages a distinctive suite of higher cognitive processing. But now notice that the Kantian model also fits this template: as we've seen, it takes moral anxiety to be a mechanism that engages instances of (i) and (ii) and is thought of as a form of meta-cognitive regulation (recall the Herman quote from above). Given these parallels, one could reasonably take the Kantian model to inherit some of the empirical plausibility enjoyed by the TOT account. More specifically, to the extent that we're comfortable with the empirical credentials of the TOT account, we should also be optimistic about the empirical plausibility of the Kantian proposal.[9]

Direct Support for the Kantian Model

While indirect support is good, we should hope to do better. And we can. If the Kantian model is correct, then we should expect to find empirical work that affirms its distinct functional profile. To see that this is the case, consider the following three examples.

First, given the Kantian understanding of moral anxiety as a sensitivity to moral danger, we should expect to see connections between moral uncertainty and anxiety. And we do. For instance, there is research indicating that self-reported uncertainty about moral issues like the harm of climate change or the legitimacy of the Iraq War correlates with self-reported anxiety about these issues (Haltinner et al. 2021, Jylhä et al. 2016, Huddy, Feldman, and Cassese 2007). Further support comes from work in abnormal psychology. In particular, clinician case reports reveal that individuals suffering from scrupulosity—a form of obsessive-compulsive anxiety disorder—become highly anxious about the correctness of their behavior when faced with moral uncertainty.[10]

Second, given the Kantian model, we should also expect to see connections between anxiety experienced in the face of new or complex moral issues and System-2 cognition (e.g., deliberation, information gathering, reflection). And again, we do. For instance, there is a wealth of correlational findings showing that self-reported anxiety about difficult moral issues (e.g., the legitimacy of liberal economic policy, how best to respond to climate change) are correlated with efforts to become more informed about these issues (Hmielowski et al. 2018; Yang and Kahlor 2013; Marcus, MacKuen, and Neuman 2011; Huddy, Feldman, and Cassese 2007; Brader 2006; Marcus, Neuman, and MacKuen 2000). More importantly, we also have experimental work showing that anxiety about novel or difficult moral questions brings cognitive engagement (information gathering, reflection, deliberation) that is aimed at helping one come to a better, more informed decision. One family of studies, for instance, contrasted the behavioral profiles of anxiety and anger. This work found that individuals who experience anxiety in the face of a news story challenging their views on contentious ethical issues (e.g., affirmative action, liberal economic policy) tend to engage in more—and more open-minded—efforts to learn about the issue. By contrast, those who feel anger after reading the news story tend to seek out less information and primarily look to sources likely to support their preexisting views (e.g., MacKuen et al. 2010; Valentino et al. 2008; Sweeny and Dooley 2017).

Finally, if moral anxiety is a distinct form of anxiety—different from things like social or performance anxiety—then we should see evidence of differences in, e.g., the functional profiles of these phenomena. On this front, work in psychology affirms the prediction. For instance, we have work confirming the basic behavioral patterns characteristic of both moral and social anxiety. More specifically, we have findings affirming that anxiety about what to do in a novel moral situation tends to bring reflection and information gathering efforts geared toward figuring out what to do. Other work indicates that anxiety about how one will be perceived by others (say, when on a date or while giving a public talk) tends to prompt caution and risk-minimization efforts as one tries to reduce the chance or severity of negative social evaluation (see, e.g., Endler and Kocovski 2001; Leary and Kowalski 1995, chap. 8).[11]

Summing Up

We have a range of findings—across a variety of disciplines (e.g., neuroscience, social and clinical psychology, political science, philosophy) and methodologies (e.g., correlational, clinical, experimental)—that bring converging theoretical and empirical support for the core elements of the Kantian model. This is cause for optimism about the model's credentials. But the discussion brings further insights. For starters, we noted above that current dual-processing research provides only very general working models of the mechanism that undergird System-1 to System-2 transitions. As Wim De Neys notes, this means that there is much need for "further fleshed out, fine-tuned, and developed" accounts (De Neys, forthcoming). The Kantian model of moral anxiety speaks to this need by providing empirically vetted detail on what at least one of these mechanisms plausibly looks like.

Pushing further, given that we now have evidence not just of moral anxiety as a mechanism driving System-1 to System-2 transitions, but that the System-2 cognition brings open-minded inquiry and (re)assessment, we also have a response to those skeptical of genuine moral deliberation (e.g., Haidt 2001, Greene 2008, Doris 2009). Of course these authors are correct in holding not just that much of moral cognition is automatic and intuitive, but also that some of what may seem like "deliberation" is really just post hoc rationalization. That said, they push these truths too far. The Kantian model, and the evidence for it, helps us see that we do engage in genuine, productive (i.e., non–post hoc) reasoning—and we do so when circumstances present us with challenges that System-1 processing alone cannot handle. The secret joke, then, is that Kant was on to something in his work on human moral cognition.

DEPARTING FROM KANT

With support for the Kantian model in hand, I now want to take a closer look at a few aspects of it that are particularly relevant to understanding moral anxiety as a *distinct* and *distinctly valuable* moral emotion. In doing this, we will see that there are reasons to be skeptical of parts of the Kantian model. But we will also see that we can purge these features while still retaining the core aspects of the account. As a further benefit, looking more closely at the Kantian proposal will allow us to engage with several issues that have come up in recent discussions of moral anxiety and its value.

What Makes This *Moral* Anxiety?

As we've seen, Kant takes conscience to be an *innate* moral predisposition, a claim that offers a straightforward account of why moral anxiety is a distinctly moral sensitivity. But we should be skeptical of this proposal. While there may be some evidence of a distinct, genetic basis to *moral* anxiety (see, e.g., Martinez et al. 2020), the overall empirical case for the claim is scant. A more plausible alternative, I believe, is that moral anxiety is a "cognitive sharpening" of practical anxiety. To draw this out, some background will be helpful.

In other work (2018a, chapters 2–3), I've argued that research in emotion science suggests "anxiety" is best understood as the label for an umbrella category ranging over (at least) the following three distinct, biologically grounded subtypes of anxiety:

> Environmental. Environmental anxiety is anxiety about potential physical dangers. In the paradigmatic case, it is triggered by the possibility of something in one's environment that could bring physical harm (e.g., predators, cliff edges, conspecific aggression). It typically brings response behaviors that emphasize caution in one's movements (e.g., withdrawal, avoidance) and increased vigilance toward one's surroundings.
>
> Punishment (or social). Punishment anxiety is anxiety about the possibility of receiving negative evaluations or sanctions from others. The paradigmatic source of this type of anxiety is uncertainty about the outcome of a (public) performance, action, or social encounter—will one be viewed negatively and what consequences will occur if one is? As such, it tends to prompt socially oriented risk-minimization efforts (e.g., deference; efforts to ingratiate, flatter, or even appease).
>
> Practical. Practical anxiety is anxiety about what the correct or appropriate thing to do is. Its paradigmatic elicitors are situations where one is uncertain about what the (social, moral) norms prescribe or prohibit. It can also be prompted by uncertainty about how one might influence future, potentially threatening events. Anxiety of this sort tends to result in epistemic behaviors (e.g., inquiry, deliberation, reflection, (re)assessment) aimed at helping one better understand and so respond to the situation at hand.

If we assume that something like this picture of anxiety's subtypes is correct (and we saw that there is support for it in the above discussion), then we can see moral anxiety as a cognitive sharpening of practical anxiety.

Following Justin D'Arms and Daniel Jacobson (2003), consider fear of flying as the paradigmatic instance of a cognitive sharpening—in this case, a cognitive sharpening of fear. More specifically, fear of flying is a cognitive sharpening in the sense that the label picks out the combination of a noncognitive, biologically based emotion type (here the fear affect program) and some specific cognitive content that the fear is directed toward (namely, beliefs about air travel). Applying this model to moral anxiety, we can see that label as referring to tokens of practical anxiety that are focused on moral content (e.g., beliefs about right and wrong, praise and blame). The benefit of understanding moral anxiety in this manner is that it allows us to hold on to a biologically grounded account of *practical* anxiety without committing to the further, and more controversial, claim that there's a genetic basis for a distinctly *moral* form anxiety.[12]

But these gains may seem to come at a significant cost. If we jettison Kant's innateness claim, then moral anxiety becomes detached from genuine moral value. This would be bad—for, as the Kantian model suggests, moral anxiety is normatively significant in part because it acts as a bulwark to moral danger. To better see the issue here, consider the Duke of Wellington. When speaking before Parliament in 1833 about pending emancipation legislation, Wellington defended his opposition by pointing to his "anxiety" about freeing slaves before "they had become civilized" (Debates in Parliament 1833: 533–34). We want to say, of course, that Wellington's worries are badly misplaced. But if moral anxiety is a mere cognitive sharpening, then what reason do we have for thinking that moral anxiety will tend to be moral corrective and not a mechanism that perpetuates prejudice?[13]

The issue here is real, but its force should be tempered. First, we have seen—both anecdotally (the King example) and empirically (the experiments of, e.g., MacKuen et al. 2010 and Valentino et al. 2008 discussed earlier)—that moral anxiety is undergirded by a distinctive motivation. This motivation manifests in moral anxiety's concern to get it right, a motivation that promotes open-minded inquiry. And as we noted above, this distinctive motivation is part of what distinguishes moral anxiety from other forms of anxiety: moral anxiety brings an accuracy concern that contrasts with, for instance, the more ego-defensive motivations that are characteristic of social anxiety (Kurth 2016, 2018a, 67–84). Second, we shouldn't take moral anxiety to be some magical elixir—an all-powerful corrective to deviant moral thinking. Rather, it is one of many cognitive mechanisms that help us recognize, and think through, moral complexity. Taken together, I see this combination as going some distance toward deflating the worry of an unmoored moral anxiety.

How Is Moral Anxiety Valuable?

Famously, Kant maintains that the only thing that has moral value is action from duty. If that's right, then moral anxiety can only be instrumental valuable—only valuable insofar as it contributes to our ability to understand and do what the moral law commands. But one might challenge this in a couple of ways: one might deny that moral anxiety is even instrumentally valuable or, in the other direction, one might argue that it can also be noninstrumentally valuable. Let's look at each of these more closely.

In recent work, James Fritz (2022) provides the makings of a challenge to the claim of moral anxiety's instrumental value on the grounds of overwhelming trumping. The basic idea is this. A moment's reflection on all the world's ills (COVID-19, war, crime, etc.) reveals not only that we have nearly limitless occasion to feel morally anxious, but that such anxiety would be a fitting response to the moral danger we're surrounded by. But to feel all the moral anxiety that we have reason to feel would have devastating consequences for our well-being—we'd be in something like a perpetual episode of a general anxiety disorder. So whatever instrumental value moral anxiety might have gets massively outweighed by the costs that feeling it would bring.

But it's unclear how forceful this worry is. To see this, notice that the Fritz-inspired argument seems to generalize in ways that undermine its plausibility. Consider: A moment's reflection on all the world's wonders (the Grand Canyon, all the babies born today, acts of selfless giving, etc.) reveals not only that we have nearly limitless occasion to feel happy, but that such happiness would be a fitting response to the moral good we're surrounded by. But to feel all the happiness that we have reason to feel would have devastating consequences for our well-being—we'd be in something like a perpetual episode of mania. So whatever instrumental value happiness may have gets massively outweighed by the costs that feeling it would bring.

As this parity suggest, the conclusion to draw is not that moral anxiety (or, for that matter, happiness) lack instrumental value, but that there are complex normative questions about how we are to aggregate worries (joys). In fact, recognizing this reveals that the issue here is just part of a more general set of questions about how we're to determine what we have all-things-considered reason to do, think, and feel. So while there may be a problem here, it's not a problem that's specific to moral anxiety or our Kantian account of it.[14]

Let's now consider the idea that, contra Kant, moral anxiety is more than just instrumentally valuable. We can draw out the plausibility of this possibility by returning to the example of King from above. Part of what we admire about King in that example is that he was worried about something that really was worrisome. This suggests that moral anxiety of the sort that we see in King isn't merely instrumentally valuable—something that just leads to a better decision. It's also something that has noninstrumental value. More specifically, King's moral anxiety is aretaically valuable insofar as it reflects well on his character. In being anxious about his decision, he is *emotionally attuned to what matters*: the seriousness and moral complexity of the decision he faces. In fact, were King not worried in the ways that he was, our admiration for him as a moral exemplar would presumably diminish. If this is right, then looking to paradigmatic examples of moral anxiety in action reveal Kant's account of its value to be too narrow.[15]

What Role Should Moral Anxiety Play in Moral Development?

Not everyone is a moral exemplar. When we feel anxious about what we ought to do, those worries sometimes get the better of us. We may become overwhelmed or feel powerless and so shut down or try to evade the (moral) issue we face. Thus, there is much to be said of Kant's prescription for cultivation. But here two issues surface. First, Kant would likely qualify his call to cultivate moral anxiety given the concerns he had about the use of "external incentives" in moral education: without significant care, efforts to develop emotional capacities like anxiety risk inculcating bad motivations—doing good, not because it's what morality demands, but rather to avoid anxiety's unpleasantness.[16] These concerns feed into more recent skepticism about our ability to cultivate anxiety so that it is better able to track what's anxiety-worthy—especially nowadays, given that our social and physical environment is so "systematically, toxically anxiety inducing" (Kelly 2021, 254; Doris 2018, 784–85; 2009).

The best response to all this is, I think, to point to concrete examples of occasions where progress has been made in cultivating anxiety, and to examine the research that's been done to understand why the effective interventions were able to bring about the results that they did. On this front, "eco-anxiety" offers an informative case study. While the label "eco-anxiety" as it's used in both academic and popular contexts refers to a wide range of (at best) loosely related phenomena, a substantive core of this discussion seems to be referring to an ecologically oriented form of moral anxiety (see Kurth and Pihkala 2022 for an extended discussion). Moreover, debates about the value of this morally infused eco-anxiety are, in many ways, analogous to the issues we are discussing here: some maintain that eco-anxiety is valuable (Sims et al. 2020), while others see it as profoundly problematic (Clayton and Karazsia 2020).

But as with our discussion of moral anxiety, much of what's at issue in these disagreements turns on the question of what—if anything—can be done to shape eco-anxiety for the better. Briefly, here's what work examining the prospects for cultivating eco-anxiety suggests. First, it appears that we can make progress in addressing occasions where we feel either too much and too little eco-anxiety. For instance, various reappraisal strategies have been shown to be effective in countering tendencies to feel too much eco-anxiety or experience it on occasions that aren't actually worrisome (Ojala 2012; Grose 2020; Hamilton 2020). Additional work has identified ways to help individuals develop emotional sensitivities toward things that are worrisome, but that they aren't anxious about. The bulk of this work builds from research on "fear appeals," that is, advertisements and other communications aimed at arousing fear and anxiety in order to promote precautionary motivations. A range of studies suggest that these interventions can be an effective way to cultivate eco-anxiety in those who are not sufficiently eco-anxious (Moser 2019; Nabi et al. 2018; Witte and Allen 2000). Moreover, recent efforts by the psychologist Maria Ojala and others have helped shed light on why these techniques work. For instance, Ojala's research has not only found that interventions that engage combinations of eco-anxiety and hope are particularly effective, but also points to why. In short, the experience of anxiety elicits an aversive signal about the need for greater attention to environmental considerations; hope then brings positive affect that works to sustain the inquiry that anxiety has engaged (Ojala 2012). All told, then, research like this sanctions cautious optimism that the skeptical worries can be addressed.

CONCLUSION: REASONS TO BE MORALLY ANXIOUS

The above discussion suggests that Kant was an early—and particularly insightful—dual-process theorist. But it also invites a couple of big picture questions that I want to briefly discuss by way of conclusion.

First, we've just seen that there's good reason to back away from some of Kant's more contentious claims about the nature and value of moral anxiety—that it's innate, that it's only instrumentally valuable. Yet we've also seen that we can do this while nonetheless retaining the core insights of the Kantian model. But might we take this further? In particular, what might the lessons that we've learned about the function and value of moral anxiety say about the plausibility of Kant's rationalism? On the model we've developed, Kant remains a rationalist: though there is a deep and important role for affect-based moral endowments like conscience, the contribution these emotional capacities make remains secondary—the real work in tracking and engaging moral value is still left to reason. But this picture may underplay the place of sentiments.[17] Moral anxiety, as an emotion that sensitizes us to occasions of moral danger and justification, is in the very business of tracking a *particularly important* form of moral value. It, of course, needs to be refined and restrained—as the case of the Duke of Wellington makes plain. Yet one might reasonably see all this as pointing—not to a milder, emotion-infused Kantian rationalism, but a rationally tempered sentimentalism.

Second, while the discussion here provides reason to be morally anxious, it also raises the thorny question of how we might responsibly cultivate moral anxiety (and emotions more generally). After all, to say that we want to cultivate moral anxiety is not to say that we want to experience it more often or more intensely. Rather, it's to say, in an Aristotelian spirit, that we want to feel morally anxious at the right time and in the right way. But how do we do that? The issue here is both empirical and normative. Empirically, we've seen that there is much we don't know about how to shape emotions like anxiety for the better. Normatively, recent work by feminists and disability scholars shows that in thinking about how best to cultivate moral anxiety (and emotions more generally), we must also be sensitive to how prescriptions to "correct your inappropriate anxiety" can work to further marginalize the already marginalized (Gotlib 2020, Calhoun 2004). Thus there's real work to do in developing *responsible* moral and emotional development programs.[18] But success on this front may well point to moral anxiety as the source of the moral law within us.

NOTES

1. Thanks to audiences at the Moral and Political Philosophy Research Seminar at the University of Helsinki and the Philosophy Department at Università Vita-Salute San Raffaele for their input on earlier versions of this chapter. Here special thanks is owed to Federico Bina, Jaakko Hirvelä, Antti Kauppinen, Max Lewis, Roberto Mordacci, Stefano Pinzan, Massimo Reichlin, and Sarah Songhorian.

2. This broad use of "conscience" also finds its way in to academic writing. See, for instance, Boehm 2012 and Songhorian 2022.

3. For additional examples, see the discussion of John Woolman, Elizabeth Cady Stanton, and Nelson Mandela in Kurth 2018a, 2019.

4. Here I'm understanding moral rationalism as the view that moral thought and action are the upshot of reason and principles, not (say) emotions or desires.

5. More carefully, Kant's discussion suggests that he saw conscience as concerned with two types of moral danger: one where one must make a decision in the face of moral conflict or uncertainty (6: 440, 561–62), and another where we are tempted by contrary inclinations to stray from our duty (6:399, 528). In what follows, I will focus on the first strand. But it's worth noting that the second strand—where Kant focuses on conscience's role in countering akratic inclinations—can also be seen as a further dimension of moral anxiety. For elaboration, see the discussion of how moral anxiety can bring restraint in face of temptation and the empirical work that supports in Kurth 2018a, 88–90.

6. For a more detailed articulation of what these higher-order regulative (or meta-cognitive) capacities likely involve, see Kurth 2015, especially 182–90. Moreover, the idea that moral cognition involves capacities of this sort is not unique to Kant(ians). It is, for instance, key to Peter Railton's (1986) accounts of moral and prudential judgment, Allan Gibbard (1990) and Philip Kitcher's (2011) accounts of the role of normative discussion in practical decision-making, and Valarie Tiberius's (2008) virtue theoretic account of practical reflection.

7. For an extensive and insightful critical discussion of the problems with standard dual-process accounts, see De Neys, forthcoming.

8. For instance, some of this work supports a hierarchical model on which System-2 processes function, at least under certain conditions, to select among of System-1 habitual routines (e.g., Dezfouli and Balleine 2013). Other work adds to this by specifying some of situational conditions—e.g., high uncertainty about reward values or probabilities, stability of reward probabilities—under which System-2 processes will give way to System-1 (e.g., Kool et al. 2016). Similar work has flagged how reliance on S1 processing increases with cognate load and stress.

9. Objection: The analogy is dubious: while TOT may be plausibly understood as using System-1 heuristics, the Kantian model explicitly appeals to something more cognitively robust: *rules* of moral salience. So the posited structural parallels aren't really there.

Reply: To see why we needn't be worried here, first recall that Herman takes the role of the RMS to be "*pre*deliberative" (Herman 1993, 147, emphasis added). So we shouldn't think of the RMS as akin to the Categorical Imperative—i.e., an explicit, ex ante rule that we have stored in memory and draw on in the course of deciding if we are in moral danger. Rather, we should understand the RMS as ex post rules—that is, things we posit retrospectively in order to explain when and why an individual's habitual moral response gave way to a deliberated decision about what to do. So, contra the objection, the structural parallels are in fact there.

10. The argument here presumes that we can use findings in clinical research to shed light on the functioning of (normal) psychological processes. Though one might object to appeals of this sort, there's reason to think such worries are misguided, especially in the present context. As the clinical psychologist Bunmi Olatunji explains, looking to disorders can illuminate our understanding of the nature of well-functioning cognitive systems: "A substantial body of empirical research supports theoretical propositions that clinical obsessive-compulsive symptoms [including those associated with scrupulosity] have their origins in normally occurring phenomena and that such symptoms occur on a continuum, with many individuals in the general population reporting subclinical obsessions and compulsions" (Olatunji et al. 2007, 774, emphasis added). For others who have adopted a similar "pathology-as-guide-to-normal-functioning" approach, see Doris 2015, Maibom 2005, Nichols 2004, and Roskies 2003. Also see Kurth 2018a and 2016.

11. This picture is also supported by research in abnormal psychology and neuroscience: this work suggests that the behavioral patterns characteristic of these types of anxiety are the upshot of distinctive underlying mechanisms (Kurth 2016, 2018a, 77–84).

12. This, of course, assumes that there is a plausible account of practical anxiety as a biologically grounded emotion. For a defense of that, see: Kurth 2016, 2018a: chapters 2–3, 2018b. For further discussion of cognitive sharpenings of anxiety, see the discussion of "practical eco-anxiety" in Kurth and Pihkala 2022.

13. Shepherd 2019 raises worries along these lines.

14. To be clear, Fritz is sensitive to these issues; he takes the case of anxiety to be a particularly instructive way of drawing them out.

15. I develop this argument more fully in Kurth 2015; 2018a, 126–34; 2018c.

16. The worry here seems well-founded: individuals with social anxiety disorders report lower life satisfaction than people infected with herpes (Wittchen and Beloch 1996)—no surprise then that some individuals are so averse to feeling anxious that they will opt for a larger shock now rather than enduring the anxiety associated with the anticipation of a milder shock in the near future (Berns et al. 2006).

17. There are also questions about how this Kantian account of moral anxiety might fit with Kant's claims about respect—e.g., if moral anxiety is developmentally prior to respect (a claim Kant seems committed to), then how does moral anxiety get its distinctly *moral* orientation? Thanks to Roberto Mordacci for a helpful discussion of this issue.

18. For work that starts to do this, see Kurth 2022, Archer and Mills 2019, and Liebow and Glazer 2019.

REFERENCES

Arango-Muñoz, S. 2010. "Two Levels of Metacognition." *Philosophia* 39: 71–82.

Archer, Alfred., and Georgina Mills. 2019. "Anger, Affective Injustice, and Emotion Regulation." *Philosophical Topics* 47: 75–94.

Berns, Gregory S., Jonathan Chappelow, et al. 2006. "Neurobiological Substrates of Dread." *Science* 312: 754–58.

Bloom, Paul. 2016. *Against Empathy*. New York: HarperCollins.

Boehm, Christopher. 2012. *Moral Origins*. New York: Basic Books.

Botvinick, M. M., T. S. Braver, D. M. Barch, C. S. Carter, and J. D. Cohen. 2001. "Conflict Monitoring and Cognitive Control." *Psychological Review* 108: 624–52.

Brader, Ted. 2006. *Campaigning for Hearts and Minds*. Chicago: University of Chicago Press.

Calhoun, Chesire. 2004. "An Apology for Moral Shame." *Journal of Political Philosophy* 12: 127–46.

Clayton, Susan, and Bryan T. Karazsia. 2020. "Development and Validation of a Measure of Climate Change Anxiety." *Journal of Environmental Psychology* 69: 101434

D'Arms, Justin, and Daniel Jacobson. 2003. "The Significance of Recalcitrant Emotions (or, antiquasijudgmentalism)." *Royal Institutes of Philosophy Supplements* 52: 127–45.

De Nays, Wim. (forthcoming). "Advancing Theorizing about Fast and Slow-Thinking." *Behavioral and Brain Sciences*.

Debates in Parliament: *Session 1833 On the Resolutions and Bill for the Abolition of Slavery in the British Colonies*. Retrieved from: https://books.google.td/books?id =9bANAAAAQAAJ.

Dezfouli, Amir, and Bernard W. Balleine. 2013. "Actions, Action Sequences and Habits." *PLOS Computational Biology* 9: e1003364–14.

Doris, John M. 2009. "Skepticism About Persons." *Philosophical Issues* 19: 57–91.

———. 2015. *Talking to Ourselves*. Oxford: Oxford University Press.

———. 2018. "Making do Without (Reflection)." *Philosophy and Phenomenological Research* 97: 771–90.

Endler, Norman, and Nancy L. Kocovski. 2001. "State and Trait Anxiety Revisited." *Journal of Anxiety Disorders* 15: 231–45.

Eran, Uri. 2021. "Which Emotions Should Kantians Cultivate (and Which Ones Should They Discipline)?" *Kantian Review* 25: 53–76.

Fritz, James. 2022. "Fitting Anxiety and Prudent Anxiety." *Synthese* 199: 8555–78.

Gibbard, Allan. 1990. *Wise Choices, Apt Feelings*. Cambridge, MA: Harvard University Press.

Gotlib, Anna. 2020. Commentary on Charlie Kurth's *The Anxious Mind*. Chicago, IL: Central Meeting of the American Philosophical Association.

Greene, Joshua. 2008. "The Secret Joke of Kant's Soul." In *Moral Psychology*, Vol. 3. The Neuroscience of Morality: Emotion, Brain Disorders, and Development, edited by Walter Sinnott-Armstrong, 35–79. Cambridge, MA.: MIT Press.

Grose, Anouchka. 2020. *A Guide to Eco-Anxiety*. London: Watkins.

Haidt, Jonathan. 2001. "The Emotional Dog and its Rational Tail: a Social Intuitionist Approach to Moral Judgment." *Psychological Review,* 108: 814–34.

Haltinner, Kristin, Jennifer Ladino, and Dilshani Sarachandra. 2021. "Feeling Skeptical." *Emotion, Space and Society*. 39: 100790

Hamilton, J. 2020. "Emotional Methodologies for Climate Change Engagement." Dissertation, Doctor of Philosophy, University of Reading.

Hampshire, Stuart. 1978. "Public and Private Morality." In *Public and Private Morality,* edited by Stuart Hampshire, 23–54. New York: Cambridge University Press.

Harbin, Ami. 2016. *Disorientation and Moral Life*. Oxford: Oxford University Press.

Herman, Barbara. 1993. *The Practice of Moral Judgment*. Cambridge, MA: Harvard University Press.

Hmielowski, Jay D., Rebecca Donaway, and Meredith Y. Wang. 2019. "Environmental Risk Information Seeking." *Environmental Communication* 13: 894–908.

Huddy, Leonie, Stanley Feldman, and Erin Cassese. 2007. "On the Distinct Political Effects of Anxiety and Anger." In *The Affect Effect,* edited by Russel W. Neuman, George E. Marcus, Ann N. Crigler, and Michael MacKuen, 202–30. Chicago: University of Chicago Press.

Jylhä, Kirsti M., Clara Cantal, Nazar Akrami, and Taciano L. Milfont. 2016. "Denial of Anthropogenic Climate Change." *Personality and Individual Difference* 98: 184–87.

Kahneman, Daniel. 2011. *Thinking, Fast and Slow*. New York: Farrar, Straus and Giroux.

Kant, Immanuel. 1797/1996. "Metaphysics of Morals." In *Practical Philosophy*, edited by Mary J. Gregorand Allen W. Wood, 353–604. Cambridge: Cambridge University Press.

———. 2007. *Anthropology, History, and Education*. Edited by Robert B. Louden and Günter Zöller. Cambridge: Cambridge University Press.

Kelly, Daniel. 2021. "Charlie Kurth, *The Anxious Mind*." *Ethics* 132: 249–55.

King, Martin Luther, Jr. 1967. "Beyond Vietnam: A Time to Break Silence." Riverside Church, New York City. American Rhetoric: Online Speech Bank. Accessed May 8, 2017. http://www.americanrhetoric.com/speeches/mlkatimetobreaksilence.htm.

———. 1998. *The Autobiography of Martin Luther King, Jr.* Edited by Clayborne Carson. New York: Warner Books.

Kitcher, Phillip. 2011. *The Ethical Project*. Cambridge, MA: Harvard University Press.

Kool, Wouter, Fiery A. Cushman, and Samual J. Gershman. 2016. "When Does Model-Based Control Pay Off?" *PLoS Computational Biology* 12: e1005090.

Kurth, Charlie. 2015. "Moral Anxiety and Moral Agency." In *Oxford Studies in Normative Ethics*, edited by Mark Timmons, 171–95. Oxford: Oxford University Press.

———. 2016. "Anxiety, Normative Uncertainty, and Social Regulation." *Biology and Philosophy* 31: 1–21.

———. 2018a. *The Anxious Mind: An Investigation into the Varieties and Virtues of Anxiety*. Cambridge, MA.: MIT Press

———. 2018b. "Emotion, Deliberation, and the Skill Model of Virtuous Agency." *Mind and Language* 33: 299–317.

———. 2018c. "Anxiety: A Case Study in the Value of Negative Emotion." In *Shadows of the Soul: Philosophical Perspectives on Negative Emotions*. Edited by Tappolet, Christine, Teroni, Fabrice and Konzelmann, Anita Ziv, 95–104. New York: Routledge.

———. 2019. "Politicians, Policy, and Anxiety." *Center for the Study of Ethics and Society Papers* 25: 1–19.

———. 2022. "Inappropriate Emotions, Marginalization, and Feeling Better." *Synthese* 200: 155.

Kurth, Charlie, and Panu Pihkala. 2022. "Eco-anxiety: What It Is and Why It Matters." *Frontiers in Psychology* 13: 981814.

Kvarven, Amanda, Erik Strømland, Conny Wollbrant, David Andersson, Magnus Johannesson, Gustav Tinghög, Daniel Västfjäll, and Kristian Ove R. Myrseth. 2020. "The Intuitive Cooperation Hypothesis Revisited." *Journal of the Economic Science Association* 6: 26–42.

Lacewing, Michael 2005. "Emotional Self-Awareness and Ethical Deliberation." *Ratio*, 18: 65–81.

Leary, Mark, and Robin Mark Kowalski. 1995. *Social Anxiety*. New York: Guilford Press.

Liebow, Nabina, and Trip Glaze. 2019. "White Tears: Emotion Regulation and White Fragility." *Inquiry* 66: 122–42.

MacKuen, Michael, Jennifer Wolak, Luke Keele, Luke, and George E. Marcus. 2010. "Civil Engagements: Resolute Partisanship or Reflective Deliberation." *American Journal of Political Science* 54: 440–58.

Maibom, Heidi. 2005. "Moral Unreason: The Case of Psychopathy." *Mind and Language* 20: 237–57.

———. 2022. "Don't Worry, Be Happy?" *Synthese* 200: 67.

Marcus, George E., Michael MacKuen, and Russell W. Neuman. 2011. "Parsimony and Complexity: Developing and Testing Theories of Affective Intelligence." *Political Psychology* 32: 323–36.

Marcus, George E., Russell W. Neuman, and Michael MacKuen. 2000. *Affective Intelligence and Political Judgment*. Chicago: University of Chicago Press.

Martínez, Róger Marcelo, Chin-Yau Chen, Tsai-Tsen Liao, , Yawei Cheng, Yang-Ten Fan, Shih-Han Chou, and Chenyi Chen. 2020. "The Multifaceted Effects of Serotonin Transporter Polymorphism (5-HTTLPR) on Anxiety, Implicit Moral Attitudes, and Harmful Behaviors." *Frontiers in Psychology* 11: 1521.

Moser, Susanne C. 2019. "Not for the Faint of Heart." In *Climate and Culture*, edited by Giuseppe Feola, Hilary Geoghegan, , and Alex Arnall. 141–67. Cambridge: Cambridge University Press.

Munch-Jurisic, Ditte Marie. 2020. "The Right to Feel Comfortable." *Ethical Theory and Moral Practice* 23: 237–50.

———. 2022. "Lost for Words Anxiety, Well-Being, and the Costs of Conceptual Deprivation." *Synthese* 199: 13583–600.

Nabi, Robin L., Abel Gustafson, and Risa Jensen, Risa. 2018. "Framing Climate Change: Exploring the Role of Emotion in Generating Advocacy Behavior." *Science Communication* 4: 442–68.

Nichols, Shaun. 2004. *Sentimental Rules*. Oxford: Oxford University Press.

Ojala, Maria. 2012. "Regulating Worry, Promoting Hope." *International Journal of Environmental Science Education* 7: 537–61.

Olatunji, Bunmi O, Jonathan S. Abramowitz, Nathan L. Williams, Kevin M. Connolly, and Jeffrey M. Lohr. 2007. "Scrupulosity and Obsessive-Compulsive Symptoms." *Journal of Anxiety Disorders* 21: 771–87.

Pihkala, Panu. 2021. "Eco-Anxiety." In *Situating Sustainability: A Handbook of Contexts and Concepts*, edited by Parker C. Krieg and R. Toivanen, 119–34. Helsinki: Helsinki University Press.

Proust, Joëlle. 2009. "Is there a Sense of Agency of Thought?" In *Mental Actions and Agency,* edited by Lucy O'Brien and Matthew Soteriou, 253–75. Oxford: Oxford University Press.

Railton, Peter. 1986. "Moral Realism." *Philosophical Review* 95: 163–97.

———. 2009. "Practical Competence and Fluent Agency." In *Reasons for Action*, edited by David Sobel and Steven Wall, 81–115. New York: Cambridge University Press.

Rand, David G. 2019. "Intuition, Deliberation, and Cooperation: Further Meta-Analytic Evidence from 91 Experiments on Pure Cooperation." Available at SSRN 3390018. Retrieved from http://dx.doi.org/10.2139/ssrn.3390018.

Rand, David G., Joshua D. Greene, and Martin A. Nowak. 2012. "Spontaneous Giving and Calculated Greed." *Nature* 489: 427–30.

Roskies, Adina. 2003. "Are Ethical Judgments Intrinsically Motivational? Lessons from 'Acquired Sociopathy.'" *Philosophical Psychology* 16: 51–66.

Schwartz, Bennet, and Janet Metcalfe. 2014. "Tip-of-the-Tongue (TOT) States: Mechanisms and Metacognitive Control." In *Tip-of-the-Tongue States and Related*

Phenomena, edited by Bennet L. Schwartz, and Alan S. Brown, 15–31. Cambridge: Cambridge University Press.

Shepherd, Joshua. 2019. "*The Anxious Mind: An Investigation into the Varieties and Virtues of Anxiety*, by Charlie Kurth." *Mind* 128: 1337–44.

Sims, Laura, Rhéa Rocque, and Marie-Élaine Desmarais. 2020. "Enabling Students to Face the Environmental Crisis and Climate Change with Resilience." *International Journal of Sustainability in Higher Education* 3: 112–31.

Songhorian, Sarah. 2022. "Adam Smith's Relevance for Contemporary Moral Cognition." *Philosophical Psychology* 35: 662–83.

Stanovich, Keith E., and Richard F. West. 2000. "Individual Differences in Reasoning: Implications for the Rationality Debate." *Behavioral and Brain Sciences* 23: 645–65.

Sweeny, Kate, and Michael D. Dooley. 2017. "The Surprising Upsides of Worry." *Social and Personality Psychology Compass* 11: e12311.

Thomson, Valerie. 2008. "Dual-Process Theories: a Metacognitive Perspective." In *In Two Minds: Dual Processes and Beyond*, edited by Jonathan Evans and Keith Frankish, 171–95. Oxford: Oxford University Press.

Tiberius, Valerie. 2008. *The Reflective Life: Living Wisely Within Our Limits*. New York: Oxford University Press.

Valentino, Nicholas, Vincent Hutchings, Antoine Banks, and Anne Davis. 2008. "Is a Worried Citizen a Good Citizen?" *Political Psychology* 29: 247–73.

Williams, Bernard. 1981. "Persons, Character, and Morality." In *Moral Luck*. New York: Cambridge University Press.

Wittchen, H., and E. Beloch. 1996. "The Impact of Social Phobia on Quality of Life." *International Clinical Psychopharmacology* 11(Suppl. 3): 15–23.

Witte, Kim, and Mike Allen. 2000. "A Meta-Analysis of Fear Appeals." *Health Education and Behavior* 27: 591–615.

Wunderlich, Klaus, Peter Smittenaar, and Raymond Dolan. 2012. "Dopamine Enhances Model-Based Over Model-Free Choice Behavior." *Neuron* 75: 418–24.

Yang, Janet Z., and LeeAnn Kahlo. 2013. "What, Me Worry?: The Role of Affect in Information Seeking and Avoidance." *Science Communication* 35: 189–212.

Chapter 9

The Epistemic Virtue of Anxiety

Juliette Vazard

The idea that emotions such as fear and anxiety are worth cultivating runs counter to many of our assumptions. We tend to see many of our fears and anxieties as crippling; as states which stand in the way of us achieving in our endeavors. We commonly hear about anxiety in particular as an emotion we should aim to suppress and even eradicate from our lives. This suggests that anxiety has no value; that there is no point in feeling it. I am going to try and show that this message, although pervasive, is deeply misleading.

In moral psychology, it has long been recognized that violating moral norms is emotionally taxing. What is less known is that violating epistemic norms (e.g., of justification and coherence) also generates discomfort, unease, and anxiety, and that epistemically virtuous individuals attend to and exploit these feelings in their search for the truth. In the same way as moral philosophers have argued that we have a "built-in moral sense that creates pleasurable feelings of approval toward benevolent acts and corresponding feelings of disapproval toward evil and vice" (Haidt 2001, 816), we plausibly have a built-in epistemic sense that creates positively valenced affective states toward epistemic soundness, and negatively valenced affective states toward epistemic threats and gaps.

In this chapter I am going to focus on the contribution of anxiety to our intellectual lives, and in particular to the virtuous guidance of our cognitive operations. In particular, I will argue that "worrying well" in the context of inquiry can equate to exercising different intellectual virtues. This is counterintuitive, since we more often tend to consider our episodes of anxiety as a hindrance to the virtuous deploying of our reasoning capacities. This is, I believe, because we tend to focus exclusively on those instances in which anxiety prevents us from "thinking straight." In the same way as we admit that there are well-cultivated, well-calibrated dispositions toward, say, curiosity, the detrimental effects of some anxious tendencies should not convince us to cross off anxiety from the "epistemic emotions." When poorly regulated, anxiety can systematically prevent us from performing cognitively, and the fact that such instances of anxiety are so ubiquitous is probably in part due to our poor understanding of anxiety's benefits, and how to harness those by cultivating and exploiting this emotion as a guide in our intellectual practices.

In this chapter I will focus on three epistemically virtuous upshots of a well-calibrated anxiety. I will firstly highlight the role of anxiety in the initial phase of inquiry, by showing that our everyday inquiries are often about questions motivated by anxiety (rather than, say, curiosity). Secondly, I will argue that anxiety also helps regulate the *guidance* of our inquiries, by signaling how much (or how little) cognitive effort should be invested in a question, given the level of epistemic risk and the magnitude of the threat involved. Finally, relying on Samuelson and Church's (2015) cognitive model of *intellectual humility*, I will propose that anxiety participates in our ability to recognize the instances in which we cannot simply rely on our own judgments, assumptions, and intuitions but instead need to incorporate external information and alternative models to maximize accuracy.

My hypotheses on the function of anxiety will be drawn from the philosophy of emotion but also from literature in cognitive science on the different types of cognitive processes we deploy depending on whether we are trying to maximize accuracy or efficiency in a cognitive task. Using this framework, I will show that a properly cultivated anxiety routinely contributes to the success of our inquiries.

EMOTION AND INTELLECTUAL VIRTUES

Before diving into the connection between the emotion of anxiety and the exercise of intellectual virtue, a word of introduction is in order concerning virtue epistemology (the branch of epistemology which focuses on the excellences of the agents), and the role of emotion in our epistemic lives.

Two main theses structure the literature in virtue epistemology. On the one hand, virtue reliabilists take intellectual virtue to consist of *cognitive faculties* such as deft reasoning and inference-making, keen eyesight, and good memory (Sosa 2007; Greco 2010). On the other hand, virtue responsibilists take intellectual virtues to consist in character traits of an individual for which he is at least to some degree responsible, including traits such as open-mindedness, intellectual humility, intellectual courage, etc. (Zagzebski 1996; Hookway 2007; Baehr 2011, 2021). While reliabilists are focused on whether one's cognitive faculties are functioning properly and reliably, responsibilits focus on an agent's epistemic character. They "stress that agents should not only exhibit reliable cognitive traits but that they should also be in a position to take . . . reflective responsibility for their true beliefs" (Pritchard 2005, 194–95). Because of this focus on the epistemic responsibility of agents, responsibilists admit of a closer correspondence between moral and epistemic virtue. After all, both epistemic and moral virtue, in this sense, are essentially connected to the sort of person one should be or the sort of character one should have (including one's epistemic character). As some researchers have remarked, it is not clear that virtue epistemologists should have to choose between character trait virtues and faculty virtues (Fleisher 2017). Both open-mindedness and good memory are plausibly needed to excel in intellectual matters. The debate about whether one is better qualified to act as a virtue seems beside the point (Battaly 2015).

I will here assume that emotions such as anxiety, when they are well-calibrated, can be virtuous insofar as they aid the success and proper guidance of our inquiries. Some might understand this as meaning that anxiety participates or contributes to certain virtuous character traits, but this is not essential to my argument. However, I will allow for the idea that one can be responsible for the way in which one regulates one's anxiety, and also for the way in which one responds to one's anxiety. There is thus room for epistemic responsibility, as one can fail to regulate or respond to one's anxiety in ways conducive to maximizing accuracy in the output of one's inquiry. In this sense, I believe that learning to "worry well" can make one a more responsible and effective epistemic agent.

Still, the idea that well-calibrated *emotions* might be part of what constitutes a virtuous epistemic agent can at first seem puzzling. Reflecting on the difficulty of individuating a definite list of intellectual virtues, Mark Alfano (2016) suggests that we focus instead on studying epistemic emotions, which are easier to identify. These, he suggests, include "such states as curiosity, fascination, intrigue, hope, trust, distrust, mistrust, surprise, doubt, skepticism, boredom, puzzlement, confusion, wonder, awe, faith, and epistemic angst." He proceeds with an invitation, by noting that: "many of the virtues related to the emotions mentioned in the previous paragraph are unexplored or underexplored. These virtues are ripe for the picking." Now, while it is largely admitted within virtue epistemology that emotional dispositions toward curiosity, interest, and wonder contribute positively to our ability to inquire successfully, some of the emotions on the list have suffered a long-standing neglect. Here I take Alfano up on his invitation, and propose to analyze the epistemic benefits of the anxiety that arises in our epistemic activities (our "epistemic angst," as he calls it). First I will say a few words in what follows on the reasons why such states as emotions can aid in our inquiries.

The ability to experience specific emotions (so-called "epistemic emotions") to the right degree and in the right context, is considered by some to be indispensable to the capacity to exercise intellectual virtue (Morton 2010; Hookway 2003). As Adam Morton claims: "in order to acquire beliefs successfully people need to be careful, curious, imaginative, and responsible, all at the right moments and to the right degree" (Morton 2010, 7). Developing this point further, Christopher Hookway explains:

> epistemic evaluation requires emotional or affective evaluations that present inferences, propositions and questions as immediately salient, and it requires patterns in these evaluations that enable us to inquire responsibly and effectively. It is these patterns that manifest traits of character that we can describe (loosely) as habits or virtues. (2003, 92)

Unpacking Hookway's claim, we can already identify several reasons why emotions might be relevant to the exercise of epistemic virtue. First, emotions play an important part in making objects, ideas, and more generally specific features of our environment *salient*, that is, in focusing our attention on them in an immediate manner. Without emotions, many aspects of our environment might stay under our radar, we would remain oblivious to their existence and fail to notice them. This is relevant since many intellectual virtues require that we have the disposition to pay attention to different lines of inquiry or sets of evidence, instead of ignoring them. Hookway for instance argues that it is constitutive of open-mindedness that one be able to experience a varied array of different intellectual positions as salient and consider them worthy of attention.

A second important reason for the role of emotions in exercising intellectual virtue is their nature as *evaluative* states. Emotions are commonly viewed as states which constitute forms of "appraisal" of their objects as possessing certain evaluative or "axiological" properties (Mulligan 1998; Deonna and Teroni 2012; Sander 2013; Tappolet 2015). Some of these properties are relevant to the epistemic domain, like when we evaluate a proposition or a set of propositions as true, certain, doubtful, incongruous, or when we apprehend a question as interesting, novel, or complex. This set of appraisals (complex, new, incongruent) is viewed as the typical evaluative properties which "epistemic emotions" track in objects (Pekrun and Linnenbrink-Garcia 2012). Accordingly, when they are well-tuned, the emotions which allow us to immediately make these evaluations—think of curiosity, confusion, doubt, surprise, wonder, puzzlement, feelings of knowing, feelings of certainty, etc.—contribute to successful inquiry. The most largely recognized example of an epistemic emotion is perhaps curiosity, which is conceptualized as an emotion that appraises a situation or object as new, complex, but comprehensible (which means that one evaluates one's "cognitive coping potential" as high). This set of appraisals can be contrasted with other epistemic emotions like for instance *confusion*, an affective state thought to appraise an object or situation as new, complex, and not (easily) comprehensible (Silvia 2010; Vazard and Audrin 2021).

Lastly, and importantly, emotions comprise a motivational dimension: they come with a set of flexible "action tendencies" that they prompt in response to the appraisals they make. For instance, it is suggested that "exploratory affects" such as curiosity and interest, given that they signal *opportunities* to learn or understand, motivate one to deploy the behaviors (coming closer, manipulating, looking) which are conducive to achieving these epistemic aims (Lauria, forthcoming). Conversely, it is proposed that *feelings of knowing* function to appraise that cognitive operations have been successful in producing an output or solution to the problem, and that inquiry can thus be closed. Accordingly, they immediately generate a motivation to block decisions about double-checking or further inquiry on the topic (Koriat 2000).

But what does it take for an emotion to effectively contribute to successful inquiry? Kristjansson, who provides one of the most comprehensive view of virtuous emotions (2018), follows an Aristotelian framework. Within this model, emotional dispositions (stable tendencies to feel a certain emotion type) can contribute to virtuous character traits when they incline us to feel emotions in a *medial* way: in a way that is neither too intense nor too slack, too wide or narrow (in terms of the occasions in which one feels the emotion, the objects toward which one feels it, the motives, and the way in which we feel the emotion). The focus is thus not on individual emotional episodes (over which we might lack control and thus responsibility), but more broadly on one's tendencies to experience a specific emotion—say, anger—in the right way.

In Kristjansson's version of the Aristotelian account, medial dispositions toward given emotions contribute to distinct virtues. For instance, a medial disposition toward curiosity contributes to an individual's ability to manifest the virtue of inquisitiveness (Watson 2018). In this chapter I will loosely apply Kristjansson's model, by focusing on the benefits for our epistemic lives of cultivating a well-attuned disposition toward anxiety, by learning to attend to it and exploit it in our inquiries. Following Kristjansson, I will frame the virtuous and vicious manifestations of anxiety that I will identify in terms of their intensity, their broadness (the range of objects and situations they respond to), and the motives or concerns that drive them.

In what follows I will consider the role of anxiety at various stages of inquiry: starting with the initial motivation to search for an answer into a question, then moving on to the ability to *sustain* (the right amount of) *focus* throughout inquiry, and finally maintaining *intellectual humility* with regards to our own formed judgments and assumptions. I hope to show that anxiety might be more central to our epistemic lives than we assume, and that it might be worth paying attention to the anxiety that rises while we are looking for the truth.

ANXIETY, QUESTIONING, AND DOUBT

In the psychological literature, anxiety has been defined as an emotion through which we evaluate an event or situation as implying *a possible and uncertain threat* (Miceli and Castelfranchi 2005, 2015). In a similar vein, philosopher Charlie Kurth argues that anxiety is an emotion which tracks and responds to cues of "problematic uncertainty" (2015, 5). This formulation captures the two essential evaluative components of anxiety: 1) the lack of information on the part of the subject (an uncertainty) concerning 2) a possible threat or thwarting of one's goals (which renders the lack of information "problematic"). Feeling anxiety is a way in which we affectively evaluate our situation as involving a potential threat which is unpredictable or uncontrollable. Generally speaking then, anxiety is thus a valuable emotion insofar as it makes us aware of a wide range of potential threats—threats which may or may not occur—and prepares us to face them in the event that they should arise. But how might this complex of appraisals, feelings, and motivational tendency toward threat intervene and aid in our *epistemic* activities?

Curiosity and Anxiety: Inquisitive Emotions

Successful inquiry first requires an *initial motivation* to answer a specific question. This is where we will start. Curiosity has often been presented as the paradigmatic "epistemic emotion" (Pekrun et al. 2017; Whitcomb 2010; Inan 2017). In fact curiosity is often equated with the *desire for knowledge*, and said to be at the source of many of our inquiries (Williamson 2000; Goldman 1991). While this might be true—perhaps especially in the context of scientific inquiry—our everyday desires or motivations to acquire knowledge are I believe triggered by a larger array of states. In particular, I believe the role of anxiety in prompting a lot of our daily inquiries has been largely overlooked. Curiosity and anxiety are very different affective states: one is negatively valenced and the other positively valenced, and while curiosity is akin to an invitation to explore, anxiety feels more like an urgency to know. Given their phenomenological and motivational properties, they thus play very distinct roles in our efforts to acquire knowledge.

Nonetheless, curiosity and anxiety have in common that they both centrally involve a motivation to know, a desire for some epistemic content fit to answer a specific question. Both emotions are satisfied when (complete) answers to these questions have been reached: once one has come to know *what is in the box, who has won the contest, whether one has failed the exam* (that is, the answers to the questions expressed by those embedded complements), one is no longer curious or anxious. As has previously been noted (albeit only applied to curiosity), this suggests an interesting relation between these emotions and questions (Friedman 2020; Carruthers 2018).

Indeed, if one were to try and translate the content of anxiety in ordinary language, a few different options would seem readily available. Given that anxiety targets a threat that is only appraised as *possible*, a first available option is to formulate the content of anxiety as a modal proposition expressing worrisome possibilities. David Barlow (2001, 64), for instance, suggests that: "If one were to put anxiety into words, one might say, 'That terrible event could happen again, and I might not be able to deal with it, but I've got to be ready to try'." Modal statements of the type "There might be a threat" or "It is possible that my goal is under threat of being thwarted" seem apt to express the content of anxiety, however there is something missing to them.

Another, perhaps more surprising and novel option, is to formulate the content of anxiety as a question, or a cluster of questions.[1] Since anxiety is about a threatening event or situation that is crucially appraised as *uncertain*, it focuses our attention on *the information we lack* regarding this possible threat, and centrally on the question of its occurrence. In spite of its revisionary outlook, it seems intuitively plausible to think of anxiety as a state in which some unanswered questions are made salient to one, and one is driven to try and answer them. After all, when we feel anxiety, our mind is filled with questions. Whether it is environmental, social, or practical anxiety, questions are what comes to the forefront of one's mind when anxiety arises: "Will I pass the exam?" "Is someone following me?" "Did I say something stupid at the party?" When we are anxious (about taking the exam, walking alone at night, making a good impression at the party, etc.), some matters feel unsettled, unresolved, in a way which motivates us to inquire into them.

Anxiety has indeed been viewed as "closely associated with future-oriented 'questioning' cognitions" (Kendall and Ingram 1989, 36). In fact, Miceli and Castelfranchi have argued that anxiety should be considered an "epistemic emotion" alongside with curiosity, in virtue of its close connection to uncertainty and questioning. In particular, they suggest that anxiety manifests a need for *epistemic control,* or the need to *predict* events and their consequences—to "foresee with the greatest possible degree of certainty what will happen, which causes will bring about which effect" (Miceli and Castelfranchi 2015, 135), or to "attain cognitive mastery of the causal structure of the environment" (Kelley 1967, 193, as cited by Miceli and Castelfranchi 2005, 296). The epistemic motivation, they argue, is far more central to anxiety than psychologists had previously assumed. The motivation to "know with the highest degree of certainty 'how things are' and, as far as the future is concerned, how things will be" (2005, 296) is a necessary and central component of anxiety. This is why, when this need is satisfied—even with a negative certainty: "the threat has occurred"—anxiety soon vanishes and is replaced by other states.

Moreover, it should be stressed that feeling anxious about a possible and uncertain threat is much more powerful in motivating inquiring behaviors than simply judging or believing that one should inquire further into a question. This is because, as an emotion, anxiety is phenomenologically compelling: it gives priority to the concern that it raises, and mobilizes our attentional resources to address it. While it now appears plausible that anxiety focuses our attention on a question while conveying the priority to address it, thereby motivating inquiry, are the questions that anxiety raise ever *epistemically* relevant or valuable?

Asking the Right Questions

We thus have some evidence that anxiety is well placed to aid the initiation of inquiry, by providing a motivation to initiate the search the information with the goal of answering some question that has been made salient to one. But successful inquiry does not merely require that we ask some question: it requires that we ask *the right* questions. As Michael Brady (2019, 55) has recently put it: "we might be curious about, and hence motivated to attain knowledge and understanding of, a topic or issue or question that does not, for one reason or another, merit interest or curiosity." Emotions, such as curiosity can motivate us to pursue epistemic ends that are not valuable (such as learning extensively about the lifestyles of celebrities).

As Christopher Hookway has also famously pointed out: "our inquiries may fail if we fail to raise relevant questions; they may be inefficient or even falter if we ask too many" (2003, 86). Hookway emphasizes the importance for virtuous inquiring of knowing which questions to raise. Can a well-attuned anxiety contribute to the initiation of inquiry into questions *worthy* of inquiry? In Hookway's account, anxiety indeed plays an important role in our ability to readily identify which questions merit inquiry. As we have begun to see, more often than not, certain questions are made *salient* to us and brought to our attention by certain affective signals (including anxiety). In particular, Hookway (2003, 2008) argues that emotions are vehicles of "epistemic immediacy": they convey to us in a compelling manner that a certain gap in our knowledge requires urgent attention. It is part of a virtuous disposition toward these emotions that they immediately signal *which* questions are connected to our goals and concerns, and are thus relevant for us to address:

> These are the questions that are real in a stronger sense: they are experienced as needing an answer (rather than just as possessing one). Such questions are relevant to our concerns, and we have standards (tacit as well as explicit) that govern entry into our scene of response: the question how many grains of sand there are on Blackpool beach, for example, does not belong there. (Hookway 2008, 19)

What makes anxiety special in its ability to raise the right questions to mind? Well, as we have said, anxiety is an emotion which functions to detect "problematic uncertainties" (Kurth 2015, 2018). It is sensitive to cues of potential threats of various kinds: social, practical, moral, and epistemic. In the same way as we have *social anxieties* concerning potential threats to our social status ("Am I acting in a socially appropriate manner?"), we have *moral anxieties* about potential threats to our moral status ("Am I making the right decision?"), and we have *epistemic anxieties* about potential threats to our epistemic status ("Are my beliefs justified?") (Hookway 2008; Nagel 2010; Vazard 2019, 2022).

The anxiety that concerns our epistemic status functions to alert us of potential *epistemic threats*, and render us vigilant to the risk of erring in our belief formation processes. In the same way as social anxiety functions to signal the risk of negative social evaluation and prompt us to proceed with caution in certain social contexts, epistemic anxiety functions to signal the risk of falsely believing and prompts us to apply extra caution in our reasoning, inference-making, and consideration of the evidence at hand. Getting anxious about a belief we hold motivates us to check the reliability of the relevant operations leading up to this belief, and to consider whether and where we could have erred. Anxiety is not so much an emotion which, like curiosity, will motivate to explore new objects and ideas in an open-ended fashion. It is rather an emotion which will signal the urgency to revise an assumption or belief we hold, or at least reassess its epistemic credentials, if we are to avoid making a costly mistake. It signals a "problematic uncertainty" in our current doxastic position and prompts us to scrutinize its justification. As Hookway puts it, epistemic anxiety "alerts us to salient problems, or salient weaknesses in our epistemic position" (Hookway 2011, 36).

The urge to examine whether our belief is justified can be assimilated to what we commonly refer to as *doubting*. In fact, Hookway views epistemic anxiety as one of the central psychological mechanisms at work behind our inclinations to doubt. Hookway first introduced the idea of epistemic anxiety as the affective state that brings us to question the validity of a proposition and motivates us to reopen or pursue the inquiry into whether *p*. He suggests:

> In coming to doubt some proposition, I evaluate that belief as 'epistemically unsafe' . . . when I become anxious about the uses I make of some item of information, then I am motivated to reassess its credentials and look for further support before relying upon it in future. I become anxious about my belief. (Hookway 2008, 61)

The epistemic questionability of our doxastic stance is thus evaluated through affective means: we come to scrutinize the epistemic credentials of a proposition as a result of experiencing a feeling of epistemic anxiety. Epistemic anxiety can therefore be said to contribute to the success of our inquiries by prompting us to question "Is this reasoning valid?," "Is this proposition true?," "Is this the only relevant set of evidence, or should I look further?" It is here to remind us, by means of a negatively valenced feeling, the risk of error. There are various ways of cashing out the specific epistemic properties that this anxiety tracks. Epistemic anxiety can be understood to appraise the presence of a lack of safety, and act as a signal that one's cognitive operations might easily have produced a false belief.[2] Alternatively. Newton (2022) has recently formulated an account of epistemic anxiety in terms of *epistemic risk*: the risk of believing in error. She argues that epistemic anxiety is a response to epistemic risk triggered by normic and probabilistic, but not modal risk.

Now, one might argue that having the *faculty* to experience anxiety does not guarantee one's proper sensitivity to epistemic risk during inquiry. Defending a responsibilist framework, Hookway remarks:

> that I possess good eyesight says nothing about how attentive I am to the things I see. Nor does it say anything about which things I notice: I could exercise my good eyesight by dwelling obsessively on distinguishing the shades of the different bricks in the wall or constantly checking on the presence of all my finger nails. (2003, 91)

A virtuous disposition with regard to epistemic anxiety is one which attracts our attention to potential risks of error in our cognitive operations and signals potential defeaters to our beliefs only when those errors are worthy of one's attention. Epistemic anxiety (when it is well-calibrated and reliable) enables us to be sensitive to those uncertainties which merit engaging in doubt. When epistemic anxiety is experienced in excess, or too little, such affective dispositions can conversely contribute to epistemic vices which are commonly referred to as "obsessiveness" on the one hand, and "rashness" on the other.

Vices Counterparts: Obsessiveness and Rashness

Many will be reluctant to accept the conclusion that our disposition to feel anxiety enables us to doubt reasonably about the epistemic soundness of our cognitive operations. In fact, what many of us seem to experience is rather a tendency of our anxieties to raise excessive doubts in our minds in a persistent manner, parasitizing our attention and impairing us in the pursuit of more constructive epistemic aims. This mildly "obsessive" tendency is indeed likely rooted in an ill-calibrated anxiety, an anxiety which appraises too many of our cognitive operations as epistemically "risky" or "unsafe," and prompts us to reassess and verify.

At any given time in the course of an inquiry, there is a countless number of things which *might* have gone wrong. What we call "worries" are nothing more than uncertainties which are taken seriously and consume our attention for a given period of time. They can take the form of "what if" questions: "What if I have made a mistake in my data analysis?," "What if I have overlooked some detail?" "What if there is some counterevidence I haven't considered?," of counterfactual possibilities, "If I had spent more time checking my results, I could be more serene about them" or simple recurring questions. Although some of these uncertainties might be worth inquiring into, norms of *prudence* require us to limit the time we spend dwelling on them.

As Fritz (2022) has highlighted, in the case of anxiety particularly there is a tension between what is *fitting* anxiety and what is *prudent* anxiety. Although we are arguably constantly at risk of performing an epistemic mistake (and it would therefore be *fitting* for one to experience epistemic anxiety about all these possible errors), feeling anxiety about all the epistemically risky moves we make would certainly not promote overall epistemic success. While it might contribute to maximizing accuracy in the outputs of our reasoning, it would disregard another important goal in the guidance of our epistemic strategies: efficiency. As humans, we are confronted with the need to strike a balance between accuracy and efficiency in reasoning due to our limited cognitive resources. Getting anxious about each and every step of our inquiring processes is not compatible with striking such a balance. On top of taking into account how likely one is to have made a mistake, one's criteria for what qualifies as "risky" or "unsafe" reasoning need to take into account the order of priority in one's epistemic goals, and consequently the time and energy that one is justified in deploying in order to ascertain epistemic soundness to a particular bout of one's belief-forming process.

On the flip side, there is another vicious disposition toward epistemic anxiety, which leads one to pay too little attention to potential epistemic risks, and to spend too little time questioning our reliance on unsafe premises or incomplete sets of evidence. As Hookway (2003, 93) notes: "Some kinds of epistemic rashness are vices because they encourage us to ask too few questions." Epistemic rashness, as Hookway suggests, is plausibly rooted in a deficient sensitivity to epistemic risk, a failure to react with anxiety to the unsafe moves we perform in the course of our inquiries.

The vices of obsessiveness and rashness have to do not only with our ability to doubt our premises and reasoning strategies or not, but also with our ability to gauge how much to inquire into a given question, how much time and cognitive resources to invest before we settle for an answer and close inquiry. As we will see in the next section, anxiety does not only aid our epistemic success by signaling the presence of certain risks, it also signals *how much* inquiring needs to be done for the risk to be rendered minimal, depending on how important it is that we prioritize accuracy in a given instance of belief formation. This loosely corresponds to Jason Baehr's second step for successful inquiry: that once inquiry is initiated, we are able to sustain our focus for a definite amount of time so as to appropriately complete the inquiry.

ANXIETY AND SUSTAINED FOCUS

Anxiety Guides Thoroughness and Scrutiny in Inquiry

Remaining properly focused on one's subject of inquiry is necessary for successful inquiry, and requires intellectual virtues such as attentiveness, thoroughness, and scrutiny. The virtuous inquirer needs to be able to have a good sense of how much inquiring a given question calls for, and to actually be motivated to persevere accordingly in such questioning.

Certain questions merit that we invest much time and cognitive effort into them, while others do not. It has been argued that our ability to feel "epistemic anxiety" contributes to our ability to gauge how much evidence needs to be gathered before forming a belief on a given question, by signaling how costly a false belief would be. Jennifer Nagel thinks of epistemic anxiety as signaling "the heightened need for greater evidence and more thorough processing that is characteristic of high-stakes situations" (2010, 414). Nagel argues that epistemic anxiety involves a motivational tendency, inclination, or desire to gather additional evidence and postpone the closure of inquiry when important interests are at stake.[3] When it raises with a certain degree of intensity and persistence, epistemic anxiety acts as a signal that the satisfactory completion of the current cognitive task will require significant evidence and processing. Epistemic anxiety, she suggests, is thus responsible for the variations in our motivational tendencies to invest cognitive efforts in resolving a question, depending on stakes.

Another way of reformulating the function of epistemic anxiety is in terms of the goals of accuracy and efficiency which we mentioned in the previous section. While both goals are active during our inquiries, striking a balance between the two requires the possession of mechanisms that quickly and reliably gauge and signal the threshold of evidence that a given question requires, given goals at stake.[4] Certain inquiring contexts call for tilting this balance on the side of accuracy. While feelings of knowing arguably function to maximize *efficiency* by signaling when inquiry can be closed, and block potential desires to double-check or keep gathering evidence, conversely feelings of epistemic anxiety function to maximize *accuracy* by signaling that inquiry needs to be pursued and additional cognitive effort is worth investing. The conditions which justify the goal of maximizing accuracy may pertain to purely epistemic factors (such as the importance of a given inference step on which one's whole reasoning relies), or also to pragmatic factors (such as the risk of thwarting important pragmatic goals by forming a false belief, e.g., about whether the sandwich one is feeding one's allergic child contains peanut).

In terms of the cognitive processes that this mechanism is associated with, it has been suggested that "occurrent feelings of epistemic anxiety propel us to gather more evidence or employ more cognitively sophisticated tools, motivating us to transition from quick, heuristic System-1 processing, to slower, more analytic System-2 processing" (Cabrera 2022, 12).[5] According to a dominant model of the cognitive architecture of the human mind, we can distinguish roughly two types of cognitive processes: System-1 processes which are automatic, do not involve working memory, and do not demand "controlled attention" (Evans and Stanovich 2013, 236), and System-2 processes which are deliberate and controlled. In this context it has been suggested that epistemic anxiety functions as a signal that the circumstances (of a "problematic uncertainty" having been detected) call for a deployment of more demanding (System-2) cognitive processes (Vazard 2022). One is prompted to move out of the "autopilot," intuitive, or habitual mode of cognition that applies to routine, familiar, and low-stakes tasks, to a more effortful mode where higher-level processes like reflection and conscious reasoning are applied to deal with unusual, surprising, or problematic stimuli (Evans and Stanovitch 2013; Carruthers 2015; Evans and Frankish 2009; Koriat 2000).

The deployment of such processes increases attention to detail and thoroughness in our cognitive operations. Intuitive "System-1" processes are surprisingly accurate when it comes to dealing with routine and familiar tasks, but they can also lead to gross error, as Tversky and Kahneman have famously brought to light (Tversky and Kahneman 1973; Kahneman 2011). System-2 processes are thought to more reliably lead to accurate judgments.

As Alfano (2014, 116) has put it, "If you input truths to *modus ponens*, [i.e., System-2 thinking], it outputs truths . . . If you input triggering conditions into a heuristic—well, it depends." While the systematic, serial, slower mode of thinking is more truth-conducive, deploying such costly cognitive resources just anytime would not be adaptive. As Alfano has also rightfully noted, adaptiveness in belief formation requires that we prioritize accuracy when it matters (2014, 119). Epistemic anxiety is one of the signals which contributes to our ability to switch to more demanding and reliable cognitive operations for those epistemic tasks where an error is likely to occur and would be costly.

When it is properly calibrated, anxiety about the accuracy of our doxastic attitudes will therefore contribute to our ability to put the right degree of time and effort in the resolution of a problem or question. At the end of this process, once we become confident about the output of our inquiry, the waning of epistemic anxiety signals that we have reached a satisfying answer and may close inquiry. When epistemic anxiety is satisfied, "we switch from an anxious phase of searching for evidence and weighing it to a satisfied or relieved phase of possessing a determinate representation" (Nagel 2010, 418). Epistemic anxiety is thus helpful, both by signaling the amount of cognitive resources to invest in a problem (when it arises with a certain level of intensity), and by indicating that the search is over (when it wanes and eventually vanishes).

Vice Counterparts: Scrupulosity and Carelessness

Once again, it is easy to come up with examples in which an imbalanced disposition toward anxiety leads one to inquire for too long, or invest too much cognitive effort in ruminating about questions which do not merit such levels of involvement. *Scrupulosity* is an excessive disposition to sustain too much focus on a subject of inquiry, and deploy too much attention to detail when answering a given question.

Scrupulosity, in other words, is one of the vice counterparts of proper intellectual caution (Roberts and Wood 2007, chapter 8). It corresponds to a tendency to misidentify and overestimate epistemic risks. This tendency is plausibly rooted in a dispositional anxiety that can be (1) too wide in its application (it appraises too many contexts and instances of inquiry as "risky" or "unsafe"), (2) too sensitive (it responds to even the slightest probability of error), or both. A paradigmatic type of scrupulosity is exemplified by the talented PhD student who, paralyzed by the fear of imperfection, is unable to finish a paper (Roberts and Wood 2007, chapter 8).

While excessive caution may be conducive to attaining truth, other factors (such as prudential factors) are also relevant to rational epistemic conduct. In the words of Roberts and Wood: "epistemic goods must be weighed against the value of moral and prudential goods" (Roberts and Wood 2007, 233). Not all epistemic perils are worth our attention, and the cost in time and energy of improving one's epistemic position on a matter must be calculated against the benefits of such an improvement with regard to our goals. In other words, scrupulosity reflects a *maladaptive* use of our cognitive resources in Alfano's sense: it manifests a failure to prioritize accuracy *when it matters*. As Brady puts it (2019, 55): "the wise person knows when to *stop* inquiring and investigating: she knows when the level of knowledge and understanding she has attained is enough, relative to the topic or question at hand."

On the other side of the spectrum, it is plausible to think of the epistemic vice of *carelessness* as being causally grounded in an incapacity to respond with anxiety in the face of genuine epistemic threats: in contexts where possibilities of error are numerous and likely, and accuracy would lead to the acquisition of valuable epistemic goods. Carelessness and scrupulosity may be seen as two excessive dispositions to misgauge the level of "epistemic risk" through anxiety, and thereby to misapprehend when accuracy should be maximized over efficiency.

A well-calibrated disposition toward anxiety—that is, a stable tendency to react with anxiety to certain epistemic threats—can contribute to virtuous character traits such as thoroughness and scrutiny. By allowing us to apprehend epistemic risk throughout our inquiries, anxiety contributes to our ability to evaluate how much cognitive effort a given epistemic task requires, before we can safely settle for a firm judgment. Conversely, an ill-calibrated anxiety is plausibly also responsible for the disposition of the PhD student who never finishes a paper, out of excessive sensitivity to the risk of erring. And when our anxious disposition is too slack, we become careless in our inquiries, incapable of noticing when to shift to "System-2" cognitive processes, failing to react to possible missteps, logical errors, and often stopping our inquiry too soon. The disposition to engage System-2 processes to correct and complement of one's immediate intuitions and judgments has also, as we will now see, been equated with the virtue of intellectual humility.

ANXIETY AND INTELLECTUAL HUMILITY

Humility in Cognitive Processing

We have established that epistemic anxiety can play a role in indicating that a more thorough and deliberate mode of processing of information is required.

If this is the case, then it seems we can go further in drawing the virtuous consequences of such an ability to detect when uncertainty merits a shift in one's mode of cognitive processing.

Such as shift in one's cognitive processing mode means that we start processing information not by simply *exploiting* a model based on our previous experiences (our judgments, assumptions, intuitions), but by *exploring*, deliberating to improve one's model by integrating new and external information to process the stimuli (Wilson et al. 2014). While exploiting an existing model just requires us to apply prior knowledge to a new context, *exploring* requires us to envisage new possibilities, entertain hypotheses, and run simulations of other models than the one readily delivered by our own intuitive judgments. Although exploiting is cheaper (cognitively speaking), as we have seen, it is not always (epistemically) safe. The ability to recognize that our own existing model might not be sufficient to properly process information in given instances, and that one might need to take in new, external input, has been equated to a form of intellectual humility.

Samuelson and Church (2015) have put forward a unique account of intellectual humility, inspired by dual-process theories of cognition. In particular, they see the ability to balance the use of System-1 and System-2 thinking as a central part of what constitutes intellectual humility. They in fact "argue that the epistemic virtue of intellectual humility is mostly found in the conscious exercise of Type 2 thinking." Conversely, they see an improper balance in the use of these two kinds of processes as an important source of *intellectual arrogance*. I am going to argue that insofar as our ability to respond to problematic uncertainties in our own cognitive operations with an epistemic anxiety helps us balance the use of heuristics and intuitive processes with slow and effortful deliberation, a well-calibrated epistemic anxiety is part of an intellectually humble character. After all, taking seriously the signal that our own cognitive model might be lacking in that it allows for some "problematically uncertainty," is recognizing one's own limitations in an epistemically relevant sense.

As we have already mentioned, our cognitive system is prone to biased thinking. We are biased toward the information that comes faster and most easily to mind (the so-called "availability" or representative heuristic) (Kahneman and Frederick 2002), we tend to discount the weight of evidence that counts against hypotheses we endorse (Nickerson 1998), we tend to favor evidence received early in our inquiries (Kruglanski, Dechesne, Orehek, and Pierro 2009). Although we rely on System-1 processes as a default in our everyday cognitive tasks, most biases are generally attributed to an overreliance on System-1 processing. Now, relying on our immediate assumptions and intuitions is not intrinsically vicious, and given the need for efficiency in cognitive processing it is adaptive that we in fact do so. But there is a trade-off between System-1's striking efficiency and its liability to error.

As Samuelson and Church (2015) propose, these heuristics and biases manifest a sort of *self-centered* thinking, in which we remain attached to the immediate representations of reality as presented by System- 1 processes. We cling to our own model (the immediate judgments and readily available assumptions that immediately come to mind when presented with new information) in order to make sense of the incoming reality. Switching to an effortful, deliberate, analytic Type-2 processing will effectively reduce the chances of biases and errors (Kahneman 2011; Sloman 2002; Stanovich and West 1997). Getting out of this self-centered view requires us to extract ourselves from our own immediate intuitions and start to take in different perspectives and envisage alternative possibilities. This requires "hypothetical thinking, something only System-2 processes can achieve" (Evans and Stanovich 2013). Hypothetical thinking is a type of thinking that "suppresses the automatic responses of Type 1 processing, decoupling from the current representation of the world, in order to compare it to some kind (or kinds) of secondary representation(s)" (Samuelson and Church 2015 1100).

Decoupling from the System-1 generated representation of reality, to entertain hypothetical alternatives requires a signal that deeper processing is needed. If what we have said in the previous sections is valid, epistemic anxiety can be counted among the signals which detect that a shift to a more careful and attentive processing is required. More precisely, it does so by introducing an "uncertainty"—which is nothing else than *the possibility of an error*. Epistemic anxiety signals that we are vulnerable to a possible costly error in the exercise of our cognitive faculties. It signals that our intuitive thinking in a given instance is likely to mislead us, likely enough to warrant the deployment of more effortful and deliberative thinking, so as to mitigate the risk of this costly error. If epistemic anxiety correctly tracks "problematic uncertainties" in our thinking, then it acts as a signal that urges one to think carefully in situations in which intuitive responses are liable to mislead. Epistemic anxiety is certainly not the only signal apt to prompt a shift from System-1 to System-2 processing: phenomena such as the "need for cognition" have been identified as motivational tendencies to promote deeper and sustained cognitive processing (Kruglanski 1990; Roets et al. 2015).

More work should be done to determine the various ways in which we feel motivated to invest or keep investing demanding cognitive resources into a problem. What is clear is that certain motivational states trigger a mode of thinking that can be largely described as "accuracy-driven" (Kunda 1990). Summarizing this idea, Kunda states that when "people are motivated to be accurate, they expend more cognitive effort on issue-related reasoning, attend to relevant information more carefully, and process it more deeply, often using more complex rules" (1990, 481). Connecting this motivational tendency to a form of epistemic humility, Samuelson and Church conclude that, when agents are motivated to focus on accuracy, this "invites the agent into a more 'humble' epistemic posture because (a) that agent may realize that he or she has a less than complete understanding and needs to seek more information" (Samuelson and Church 2015, 1103).

Vice Counterparts: Intellectual Arrogance and Intellectual Cowardice

However, as we have already hinted at, the processes which determine whether arriving at the truth or reaching accuracy in a given instance demands the deployment of System-2 processes need to be correctly attuned to detect which instances require such a switch. Two opposite excessive dispositions can accordingly be identified. On the one hand, there is, as we have said, a consistent failure to deploy System-2 processes to correct one's biases. Samuelson and Church (2015) claim that this consistent failure can be treated as a form of intellectual arrogance. When one systemically fails to recognize when "it is necessary to move beyond what one immediately knows/believes, and/or remembers to incorporate other information" (1107), one mistakenly takes one's own assumptions, intuitions, and judgments as sufficient. This is a vicious disposition given the biases and errors we are systemically prone to, and the fact that incorporating "external" information by engaging hypothetical thinking is likely to help correct these biases.

On the other hand, a slightly different tendency emerges when one is able to recognize the need for hypothetical processing but unable to *react* to these signals in the appropriate manner. Instead of reacting by running simulations of alternative models, one reacts by clinging on to the evidence we already possess, while denying the epistemic risk. In certain instances, accepting even the possibility that one might be at risk of erring seems intolerable. One, in a certain sense, has registered the signal of epistemic risk, and so one knows that one is particularly vulnerable to error in this instance, but one prefers not to incorporate additional external information. This tendency is akin to what we call "burying one's head in the sand."[6]

This form of denial can be due to a tendency to prioritize prudential over epistemic aims: one experiences the threat that is involved by recognizing the possibility of error as greater than the threat of erring itself. Instead of exploiting the detection of a "problematic uncertainty" as an opportunity to improve one's epistemic position, one sees it as a threat to one's non-epistemic goals (i.e., finishing the data analysis before the deadline, salvaging one's reputation, etc). As a result, one chooses to dismiss one's feelings of anxiety and inhibit the launching of System-2 hypothetical thinking. This can for instance happen to the scientist who, although aware that they should take into account an additional variable into their analysis, are too afraid that this might make their entire argument collapse. Although they are able to experience epistemic anxiety (they feel that there might be a risk that their interpretation of the data is biased and mistaken) they do not respond to this anxiety by actually putting in the cognitive effort to inquire further and deeper into alternative interpretations.

If one becomes crippled by anxiety at the consequences that a mistake could have on one's career, reputation (and on the load of extra work it would require to add this overlooked variable), then one might indeed chose to ignore the possibility of error. In these cases the trouble seems to be located at the level of the motive which guides one's inquiry. The guiding motive is not the love of knowledge or the seeking of truth. When we are guided by other motives than the love of knowledge experiencing anxiety can be a reason to cling on to our prior judgments and assumptions even tighter.

An intellectually virtuous disposition toward anxiety is a tendency to experience epistemic threats as more salient than the threats regarding one's reputation, or the loss of putting extra effort in reconsidering one's arguments, calculations, or data analysis. An intellectually virtuous anxiety presents the threat of erring as bigger and more significant, because it stems from the concern to attain knowledge and promote this motive. The epistemically virtuous person responds with malaise when she becomes aware of a set of evidence which seems to run counter her held assumptions. But this malaise does not lead her to deny the evidence, bury her head in the sand, and indefinitely postpone taking on the inquiry necessary to account for the newfound evidence. On the contrary, her unease is an urge to resolve the uncertainty.

CONCLUSION

There is a variety of ways in which our ability to experience anxiety aids in the success of our inquiries. Virtuous epistemic agents need to be sensitive to epistemic risks, know how to balance the goals of accuracy and efficiency, and appropriately react to the risk of error by applying more caution. As I have shown, when it is felt to the right degree, about the right matters, and informed by the right motives, anxiety is an emotion which contributes to such intellectual virtues as: inquisitiveness, scrutiny, thoroughness, and humility. When it correctly tracks an elevated epistemic risk, anxiety guards us off many costly mistakes. We are naturally prone to bias and error, but we are also endowed with readily available tools that can be sharpened to help us recognize and counterbalance these fallible tendencies. If we are able to register it, channel it, and mobilize it properly, anxiety can be a valuable and constructive way of being attuned to our own liability to error.

NOTES

1. Knowledge-precluding emotions (Gordon 1969) such as hope, fear, and anxiety inherently involve that one evaluates the presence of some axiological property as *uncertain*. If this is so, questions appear as good candidates to express the content of such emotions.

2. Ernest Sosa initially proposed the safety condition on knowledge as an alternative to the condition of sensitivity (1999). While sensitivity requires that: "If *p* were false, S would not believe that *p*," safety requires that: "If S were to believe *p*, *p* would not be false." The safety condition can be and is often understood in modal terms: "In all nearby worlds were S believes that *p*, *p* is not false."

3. Nagel applies the concept of epistemic anxiety to explain cases of "pragmatic encroachment" (Fantl and McGrath 2002; Stanley 2005), by arguing that the level of epistemic anxiety that we attribute to a subject can explain why we have different expectations for epistemic behavior (i.e., evidence collecting and processing) toward subjects who are in similar epistemic positions but different practical contexts. In this context, Nagel (2010, 414) proposes that what explains the differences in our intuitive knowledge ascriptions with respect to subjects in a high-stakes as compared to subjects in a low-stakes context is the level of epistemic anxiety that we attribute to these two subjects. She suggests that we expect the subject in a high-stakes context to spend more time inquiring and collecting evidence than her counterpart in a low-stakes context, because we expect her to experience more *epistemic anxiety*.

4. As Nagel mentions, there are two main competing views on the market as to how variations in cognitive effort accompany shifting stakes: the "adaptive toolbox" approach (Todd and Gigerenzer 2000) and the "evidence accrual" approach (Lee and Cummins 2004; Newell 2005). It is compatible with both models that higher stakes would result in increased epistemic anxiety: epistemic anxiety may be seen as an automatic process which functions to select a more demanding cognitive strategy from the toolbox to resolve high-stakes issues, or to set a higher evidence threshold for belief formation (Nagel 2010).

5. According to certain dual-process theories, we can consider that there are accordingly two broad modes of cognition: the *intuitive mode* and the *reflective mode* of cognition (Evans and Stanovich 2013).

6. The fact that one's head needs to be buried so as to prevent the risk of being exposed to some inconvenient information suggests that one in fact knows the risk is there.

REFERENCES

Alfano, Mark. 2014. "Expanding the Situationist Challenge to Reliabilism About Inference." In *Virtue Epistemology Naturalized*, edited by Abrol Fairweather, 103–22. Cham: Springer.

———. 2016. "Epistemic Emotions and Intellectual Virtues." https://www.alfanophilosophy.com/blog/2016/4/22/epistemic-emotions-andintellectual-virtues.

Baehr, Jason. 2011. *The Inquiring Mind: On Intellectual Virtues and Virtue Epistemology*. New York: Oxford University Press.

———. 2021. *Deep in Thought: A Practical Guide to Teaching for Intellectual Virtues*. Cambridge, MA: Harvard Education Press.

Barlow, David. 2001. *Anxiety and its Disorders*. 2nd edition. New York: Guilford Press.

Battaly, Heather. 2015. "A Pluralist Theory of Virtue." In *Current Controversies in Virtue Theory*, edited by Mark Alfano, 7–21. New York: Routledge.

Brady, Michael S. 2019. "The Role of Emotion in Intellectual Virtue." In *The Routledge Handbook of Virtue Epistemology*, edited by Heather Battaly, 47–57. New York: Routledge.

Cabrera, Frank. 2021. "Is Epistemic Anxiety an Intellectual Virtue?" *Synthese* 199: 13471–95.

Carruthers, Peter. 2015. *The Centered Mind: What the Science of Working Memory Shows us About the Nature of Human Thought*. Oxford: Oxford University Press.

———. 2018. "Basic Questions." *Mind and Language* 33: 130–47.

Deonna, Julien and Teroni, Fabrice. 2012. *The Emotions: A Philosophical Introduction*. New York: Routledge.

Deonna, Julien, Tappolet, Christine, and Teroni, Fabrice. 2015. "Emotion, Philosophical Issues About." *Wiley Interdisciplinary Reviews: Cognitive Science* 6: 193–207.

Evans, Jonathan and Frankish, Keith, eds. 2009. *In Two Minds: Dual Processes and Beyond.* Oxford: Oxford University Press.

Evans, Jonathan S. B. and Stanovich, Keith E. 2013. "Dual-process Theories of Higher Cognition: Advancing the Debate." *Perspectives on Psychological Science* 8: 223–41.

Fantl, Jeremy and McGrath, Matthew. 2002. "Evidence, Pragmatics, and Justification." *The Philosophical Review* 111: 67–94.

Fleisher, Will. 2017. "Virtuous Distinctions." *Synthese* 194: 2973–3003.

Friedman, Jane. 2020. "The Epistemic and the Zetetic." *Philosophical Review* 129: 501–36.

Fritz, James. 2022. "Fitting Anxiety and Prudent Anxiety." *Synthese* 199: 8555–78.

Goldman, Alan H. 1988. *Empirical Knowledge*. Los Angeles: University of California Press.

Greco, John. 2010. *Achieving Knowledge: A Virtue-Theoretic Account of Epistemic Normativity*. Cambridge: Cambridge University Press.

Haidt, Jonathan. 2001. "The Emotional Dog and its Rational Tail: a Social Intuitionist Approach to Moral Judgment." *Psychological Review,* 108: 814–34.

Hookway, Christopher. 2003. "Affective States and Epistemic Immediacy." *Metaphilosophy* 34:78–96.

———. 2007. "The Inaugural Address: Fallibilism and the Aim of Inquiry. *Aristotelian Society Supplementary Volume* 81: 1–22.

———. 2008. "Epistemic Immediacy, Doubt and Anxiety: On a Role for Affective States in Epistemic Evaluation." In *Epistemology and Emotions,* edited by Brun George, Doğuoğlu Ulvi, and Kuenzle Dominique, 51–65. New York: Routledge.

———. 2011. "James's Epistemology and the Will to Believe." *European Journal of Pragmatism and American Philosophy* 3(III-1).

Inan, Ilhan. 2013. *The Philosophy of Curiosity*. New York: Routledge.

Kahneman, Daniel. 2011. *Thinking, Fast and Slow*. New York, NY: Farrar, Straus, and Giroux.

Kahneman, Daniel, and Frederick, Shane. 2004. "Attribute Substitution in Intuitive Judgment." In *Models of a Man: Essays in memory of Herbert A. Simon*, edited by Augier, Mie and March, James G, 411–32. Cambridge, MA: MIT Press.

Kelley, H. H. 1967. "Attribution Theory in Social Psychology." *Nebraska Symposium on Motivation* 15: 192–38. University of Nebraska Press.

Kendall, Phillip C, and Ingram, Rick E. 1989. "Cognitive-Behavioral Perspectives: Theory and Research on Depression and Anxiety." In *Personality, Psychopathology, and Psychotherapy. Anxiety and Depression: Distinctive and Overlapping Features,* edited by Kendall, Phillip C and Watson D, 27–53. Academic Press.

Koriat, Asher. 2000. "The Feeling of Knowing: Some Metatheoretical Implications for Consciousness and Control." *Consciousness and cognition* 9: 149–71.

Kristjánsson, Kristjan. 2018. *Virtuous Emotions.* Oxford University Press.

Kruglanski, Arie W. 1990. "Lay Epistemic Theory in Social-Cognitive Psychology." *Psychological Inquiry* 1:181–97.

Kruglanski, Arie W., et al. 2009. "Three Decades of Lay Epistemics: The Why, How, and Who of Knowledge Formation." *European Review of Social Psychology* 20: 146–91.

Kunda, Ziva. 1990. "The Case for Motivated Reasoning." *Psychological Bulletin* 108(3), 480.

Kurth, Charlie. 2015. "Moral Anxiety and Moral Agency." In *Oxford Studies in Normative Ethics*, edited by Mark Timmons, 171–95. Oxford: Oxford University Press.

———. 2018. *The Anxious Mind: An Investigation into the Varieties and Virtues of Anxiety*. Cambridge, MA: MIT PressLauria,

Federico. (forthcoming). "Interest and the Affective Springs of Inquiry—The '*Chiaroscuro'* Epistemic Emotion."

Lee, Michael D., and Cummins, Tarrant D. 2004. "Evidence Accumulation in Decision Making: Unifying the 'take the best' and the 'rational' Models." *Psychonomic Bulletin and Review* 11: 343–52.

Miceli, Maria, and Castelfranchi, Cristiano. 2005. "Anxiety as an 'Epistemic' Emotion: An Uncertainty Theory of Anxiety." *Anxiety, Stress, and Coping* 18 : 291–319.

———. 2015. *Expectancy and Emotion*. Oxford: Oxford University Press.

Morton, Adam. 2010. "Epistemic Emotions." In *The Oxford Handbook of Philosophy of Emotion*, edited by Peter Goldie, 385–400. New York: Oxford University Press.
Mulligan, Kevin. 1998. "From Appropriate Emotions to Values." *The Monist* 81 : 161–88.
Nagel, Jennifer. 2010. "Epistemic Anxiety and Adaptive Invariantism." *Philosophical Perspectives* 24: 407–35.
Newell, Ben R. 2005. "Re-visions of Rationality?" *Trends in Cognitive Sciences* 9: 11–15.
Newton, Lillith. 2022. "Epistemic Anxiety and Epistemic Risk." *Synthese* 200: 1–23.
Nickerson, Raymond S. 1998. "Confirmation Bias: A Ubiquitous Phenomenon in Many Guises." *Review of General Psychology* 2.2: 175–220.
Pekrun, Reinhard, and Linnenbrink-Garcia, Lisa. 2012. "Academic Emotions and Student Engagement." In *Handbook of Research on Student Engagement*, edited by Christenson, Sandra L, Reschly, Amy L, and Wylie, Cathy, 259–82. Boston: Springer.
Pekrun, Reinhard, Vogl, Elizabeth, Muis, Krista R, and Sinatra, Gale M. 2017. "Measuring Emotions During Epistemic Activities: the Epistemically-Related Emotion Scales." *Cognition and Emotion* 31: 1268-1276.
Pritchard, Duncan. 2005. *Epistemic Luck*. Oxford: Clarendon Press.
Roberts, Robert C, and Wood, Jay W. 2007. *Intellectual Virtues: An Essay in Regulative Epistemology*. Oxford: Clarendon Press.
Roets, Arne, Kruglanski, Arie W, Kossowska, Malgorzata, Pierro, Antonio, and Hong, Ying Yi. 2015. "The Motivated Gatekeeper of our Minds: New Directions in Need for Closure Theory and Research." In *Advances in Experimental Social Psychology* (Vol. 52, pp. 221–83). Academic Press.
Samuelson, Peter L, and Church, Ian M. 2015. "When Cognition Turns Vicious: Heuristics and Biases in Light of Virtue Epistemology." *Philosophical Psychology* 28 : 1095–113.
Sander, David. 2013. "Models of Emotion: The Affective Neuroscience Approach." In *The Cambridge Handbook of Human Affective Neuroscience*, edited by Armony, Jorge and Vuilleumier, Patrik, 5–53. Cambridge: Cambridge University Press.
Silvia, Paul J. 2010. "Confusion and Interest: The role of Knowledge Emotions in Aesthetic Experience." *Psychology of Aesthetics, Creativity, and the Arts* 4 : 75–80.
Sloman, Steven A. 2002. "Two Systems of Reasoning." In *Heuristics and Biases: The Psychology of Intuitive Judgment*, edited by Gilovich, Thomas, Griffin, Dale, and Kahneman, Daniel, 379–96. Cambridge: Cambridge University Press.
Sosa, Ernest. 1999. "How to Defeat Opposition to Moore." *Philosophical Perspectives* 13: 141–53.
———. 2007. *A Virtue Epistemology: Apt Belief and Reflective Knowledge*, volume I. Oxford: Clarendon Press.
Stanovich, Keith E, and West, Richard F. 1997. "Reasoning Independently of Prior Belief and Individual Differences in Actively Open-Minded Thinking." *Journal of Educational Psychology* 89: 342–57.
Stanley, Jason. 2005. *Knowledge and Practical Interests*. Oxford: Clarendon Press.

Tappolet, Christine. 2015. "Value and Emotions." In *The Oxford Handbook of Value Theory*, edited by Iwao Hirose and Jonas Olson, 80–95. Oxford: Oxford University Press.

Todd, Peter M, and Gigerenzer, Gerd. 2000. "Précis of Simple Heuristics that Make us Smart." *Behavioral and Brain Sciences* 23: 727–41.

Tversky, Amos. and Kahneman, Daniel. 1973. "Availability: A Heuristic for Judging Frequency and Probability." *Cognitive psychology* 5: 207–32.

Vazard, Juliette. 2021. "(Un) reasonable Doubt as Affective Experience: Obsessive Compulsive Disorder, Epistemic Anxiety and the Feeling of Uncertainty." *Synthese* 198: 6917–34.

———. 2022. "Everyday Anxious Doubt." *Synthese* 200 (3): 1–19.

Vazard, Juliette, and Audrin, Catherine. 2022. "The Noetic Feeling of Confusion." *Philosophical Psychology* 35: 757–70.

Watson, Lani. 2018. "Curiosity and Inquisitiveness." In *The Routledge Handbook of Virtue Epistemology*, edited by Batally, Heather, 155–66. New York: Routledge.

Whitcomb, Dennis. 2010. "Curiosity was Framed." *Philosophy and Phenomenological Research* 81: 664–87.

Williamson, Timothy. 2002. *Knowledge and its Limits*. Oxford: Oxford University Press.

Wilson Robert C, Geana Andra, White John M, Ludvig Elliot A, Cohen Jonathan D. 2014. "Humans use Directed and Random Exploration to Solve the Explore-Exploit Dilemma." *Journal of Experimental Psychology, General*. 143: 2074–81.

Zagzebski, Linda Trinkaus. 1996. *Virtues of the Mind: An Inquiry into the Nature of Virtue and the Ethical Foundations of Knowledge*. New York: Cambridge University Press.

Chapter 10

Anxiety's Allure

Michael S. Brady

INTRODUCTION

Anxiety can be characterized as unpleasant, unwelcome, and negative, and is so along a number of dimensions. The first is *evaluative*. Anxiety has, in the parlance of philosophy of emotion, "a formal object"—namely, something that anxiety is *about*—and is best understood as an event or state of affairs that the subject does not want to come about, but which is nevertheless possible. As Robert C. Roberts puts it, we might understand anxiety about some object or event X in terms of the following "defining proposition," namely: "*X vaguely presents an aversive possibility of some degree of probability; may X or its aversive consequences, whatever they may be, be avoided*" (Roberts 2003, 110. Italics his). Many philosophers think that we can capture this dimension in terms of a subject's accepting or acknowledging this propositional content: that when a person is anxious, they think or see some object as aversive and as possible. A second dimension of negativity is *affective*. Anxiety presents the object or event via a negative affective experience, which explains why anxiety *feels bad*. A third dimension of negativity is behavioral: the subject is averse to the object or event in question, and acts, insofar as they can, to alleviate the negative affect or remove the uncertainty. Thus, as Charlie Kurth writes, "anxiety is typically provoked in situations where one faces a potential threat, danger, or challenge and it tends to bring behaviours aimed at helping one address the uncertainty at hand" (Kurth 2018, 7). Anxiety would therefore seem to involve three dimensions of negativity: it is directed toward or responsive to a negatively valued object or event; it is a negatively valenced affective state; and it promotes aversive or avoidance behavior.

It is hardly a surprise, then, that we tend to think badly of anxiety, and regard the state or trait as something to be avoided and alleviated. In many cases, we are clearly right to do so. For anxiety can be utterly miserable, debilitating, and undermining, of both one's day-to-day existence, and one's long-term life projects.[1] Even when anxiety is not extreme, and does not undermine our projects and plans, it tends to be a blight on our daily existence when it occurs. In many instances, therefore, we would be better off if we were not anxious.

In spite of these obvious points, anxiety is not always a blight on our lives. As others have pointed out—notably Kurth in *The Anxious Mind*—anxiety can have practical benefits, and so can be instrumentally or extrinsically valuable. What is more interesting, however, is the idea that anxiety can be *attractive* or *alluring* in certain circumstances. In this chapter I want to investigate and explain why anxiety can be attractive or alluring for us, and can be an object of desire. I want to argue, further, that the lives of people who represent our highest ideals of character, the lives of the most admirable and enviable people, will be admirable and enviable partly *as a result* of very high levels of anxiety. Anxiety can thus often be alluring in our own lives, but also alluring in the lives of others we most admire. Or so, at least, I want to maintain.

In the first section of this chapter, I'll make a case for the alluring or attractive nature of the most general kinds of negative affective experiences—of pain and suffering, broadly construed—and give an explanation of why they are so. In the second section, I'll provide many instances where we embrace and find attractive particular kinds or forms of anxiety, across a range of dimensions, and provide a related explanation for the alluringness of anxiety in these instances. In the third section, I'll broaden my focus to look at the lives of the most admirable people—the lives of those who are exemplary—and show how these typically involve high levels of anxiety. Throughout the paper, I'll be careful to distinguish what we might think of as problematic anxiety—anxiety which is beyond our control—and anxiety which is to a large extent freely chosen. It is the latter which is most alluring, and which has considerable value for us.

THE ALLURE OF PAIN AND SUFFERING

Anxiety, if suitably intense, can be a form of suffering. As such, it might be obvious that we ought to avoid it when we can, and ought to relieve it when we cannot. However, it is simply not true—as a matter of psychological fact—that people always avoid or shy away from pain and suffering. Indeed, for many of us, such things can be attractive, alluring, and intentionally pursued. This is not a point about people who might be described as masochistic, nor about others who are arguably self-hating and self-destructive. Many who are non-masochistic or non-self-destructive willingly and intentionally pursue things that they know full well involve significant amounts of pain and suffering.

The case is perhaps most easily made by considering the popularity of certain forms of physical pastimes or sports—for instance, mountaineering, boxing, endurance running, MMA, mountain biking, the triathlon, rugby, caving, and the like.[2] But we need not focus only on the physical. People engage in intellectual pursuits that are arduous, challenging, difficult, and a lot of the time pretty miserable—doing philosophy, for instance. Many voluntary projects involve hours of arduous work and practice—consider what it takes to learn a musical instrument, or to learn a language—and many other games or pastimes are welcomed because they promise to be challenging: think, for instance, of the obvious point that video gamers usually want games that are difficult to complete, that test their skill, patience, and fortitude, that require them to face up to and overcome negative affective experiences. Now clearly, we don't do these things solely *because* they involve difficulty and suffering; that really would be masochistic. Nevertheless, and equally clearly, it seems that negative affective experiences are welcomed as a *condition* on the value of such things: in short, we wouldn't intentionally pursue them *unless* they were painful, arduous, challenging. The endurance runner eschews the gentle one-mile jog; the mountain climber ignores the lowly hill; the serious musician wants to master the violin rather than the recorder; the committed gamer has no interest in *Animal Crossing*. After all, part of the *point* of things like endurance cycling is to test oneself, to see how much pain and suffering and discomfort one can endure and overcome. The fact that endurance cycling (for instance) involves a great deal of physical suffering is part of what makes it worthwhile for those who do it. If it didn't involve pain and suffering, it wouldn't be a challenge, and people wouldn't be attracted by it, or admire those who engage in it. To take another example: we admire and esteem ballet dancers not just for their grace and beauty, but—as a condition of our admiration—for what we know it has cost and is costing them.[3]

But it is not just a brute psychological fact that many of us are motivated to pursue activities that involve pain and suffering in this way. We can, instead, propose a closer link between such experiences and the value of certain achievements, and argue that many of us are *right* to view pain and suffering as a condition on the value of certain activities. To see this, consider Gwen Bradford's rich and convincing account of the nature of achievement, as described and defended in her excellent book of that name (Bradford 2015). Bradford's basic claim is that achievements have two essential components: they involve *difficult processes*, and result in a product that is *competently caused*. Now the latter element isn't important for the point I want to make here. With respect to the former, Bradford writes:

> One feature that appears to distinguish . . . achievement—and, I will contend, all achievements—is that it is *difficult*. If tying my shoes presented a particular difficulty for me to overcome . . . then my success might count as an achievement too. If writing a novel were so easy that anyone could do it, we wouldn't think of it as an achievement. Finding a cure for cancer is turning out to be difficult task. Writing a dissertation, running a marathon, or even smaller scale achievements, such as winning a game of chess, baking a soufflé, or cultivating a bonsai—all of these achievements are difficult to do. Were it the case that any of these activities were easy, we wouldn't think of them as achievements. . . . This suggests that difficulty is a necessary component for achievements. (Bradford 2015, 12)

What, however, is difficulty? Bradford writes:

> Something is difficult in virtue of requiring some sufficient degree of *effort*. Things require effort in virtue of having certain *features*. Different activities require effort in virtue of various features that they have. Some activities require effort because they are very physically demanding, others require effort because they make use of multiple skills, or a lot of diverse knowledge. (Bradford 2015, 28)

My proposal is that we can add pain and suffering to this list of features. That is, it requires intense effort to face up to, endure, and overcome such experiences, and so such things clearly count as things that are difficult to do. Suffering is thus the condition on the value of certain activities precisely because suffering *makes* those things difficult, and hence as things which are candidates for genuine achievements. So it is not merely a psychological quirk that we are motivated to pursue activities insofar as they involve pain and suffering. Instead, this psychological fact reflects the normative truth—that by facing up to, enduring, and overcoming pain and suffering, we seek to achieve something of value, and thus enhance our own lives.

In the following section, I'll explain how this general argument can help to explain the allure that anxiety can have, at least for situations that are, to a large extent, freely chosen and somewhat under our control.

THE ALLURE OF ANXIETY

As noted earlier, anxiety is an ostensibly negative state, one that involves a negative affective experience involving a perception or assessment of "problematic uncertainty," as Kurth puts things, with respect to some valued object or event (Kurth 2018, 6). Might anxiety be alluring, as a condition on the value of certain objects or things that we pursue? If so, how might this particular story go?

One way in which anxiety is alluring is as an *epistemic* condition on the value of certain projects, actions, objects, and events. This can happen because the experience of anxiety both signals that something important is at stake, and that it is threatened; and this kind of experience often functions to make the importance or value in question more vivid or apparent to us. Anxiety can thus heighten awareness of valuable or significant objects and events, and in so doing bring home to us both that and why they are important As a result, anxiety can function as an "affective" way of knowing, and can enhance our understanding and grasp of the value in question. My anxiety before the interview can bring home to me how important the job is, how much it means to me that I conduct myself well, and how wonderful it would be to be offered the position. My anxiety on meeting her again might well inform me of the depth of my feelings for her, how out of my league she is, how significant a relationship with her might be. And so on. Of course, anxiety often has very serious and debilitating epistemic effects, not least when biasing someone to see the world as more threatening and dangerous than it actually is. Nevertheless, this is compatible with the thought that we can welcome feeling anxious because of its informational and epistemic worth. Moreover, the *absence* of anxiety might well signal to us that some previously valued person or object or event apparently lacks the value or importance that we thought it had. In such cases, it is not implausible to think that anxiety functions as an epistemic condition on the value or significance that something has.[4]

This is not all. As we know, emotional experience and evaluative reality can diverge: my anger or shame or pride might not "fit" their targets, and these facts might well be apparent to me. The same thing can be said about anxiety. I might be anxious about situations or events that I know full well are not problematically uncertain. By the same token, I might not be anxious about situations or events that I know full well *are*. In the latter cases, we might bemoan or regret our lack of anxiety, as itself evidence that something is amiss in our evaluative-affective viewpoint. For example: should I no longer be anxious before presenting an academic paper or giving a lecture to a large class, this *might* be a sign that I am confident and skilled enough not to worry any more about how things will turn out. But equally, and especially given my long history of feeling anxious before talks and large lectures, this is more likely to be a sign that I am no longer appropriately affectively engaged with things that are important to me and at risk in the relevant settings, viz. my reputation as a researcher and as a teacher. Such an affective lack might itself be a signal of distress for me, since I still judge that my reputation very much matters and is something that I ought to be concerned about. Here I would welcome (back) feelings of anxiety, as evidence of affective engagement with the relevant value. Here feelings of anxiety would be wanted.

A second way in which anxiety can be alluring is through its enhancing the pleasure of relief when the problematic uncertainty is resolved. This suggests that anxiety might be a condition on value in two ways. We can, after all, understand a particular kind of pleasure simply in terms of relief from negative affect: as when one scratches an itch, or when the neighbour's loud music finally stops. Similarly, one might feel significant pleasure when anxiety is relieved: when it turns out that the audience is friendly, or that you didn't "reply all." Such experiences aren't obvious instances of the alluringness of anxiety, however—even if there might well be cases where we put ourselves in anxiety-inducing situations simply for the feelings of relief when they are resolved. But a second way in which anxiety can be a condition on value is much more promising for an account of when it is alluring. For it seems that anxiety can *intensify* some experience of value, and can be attractive or alluring in this way. Indeed, the intensification of pleasure by a prior negative experience is well-known. As Siri Leknes and Brock Bastian write, "Although introspection suggests to many people that relief and pleasure are easily dissociated, most primary rewards are intensified by relief. Food and drink taste better when providing relief from hunger or thirst. . . . And where would the pleasure in going to bed at night be if we were not so tired, or muscles weary and aching?" (Leknes and Bastian 2014, 65)

Cases where anxiety can intensify pleasure are a very common phenomenon. Think, for instance, of how the pleasures of watching sports are intensified by anxiety about the outcome. For many spectators, the experience of anxiety is integral to the very great pleasure one feels when one's team wins (and the very great disappointment one feels when one's team loses). Without problematic uncertainty, the experience of watching sports can often descend into mild interest at best, and boredom at worst. Problematic uncertainty is at the very heart of watching and supporting a team (or sportsperson, nation, etc.); it is part of the allure of following sports, and an attraction to problematic uncertainty is part of what it is to be a real sports fan, rather than a dabbler or hobbyist or (to use the common insult) a part-time supporter.

Or consider, to move to a different dimension, how feelings of anxious tension are integral to our experience and enjoyment of books and plays and films, or at least those with a strong narrative or storytelling element (which is to say: the vast majority of these works of art). This is because books and plays and films are, standardly, structured around the generation and resolution of some crisis or problem: good storytelling sets up problematic uncertainty in the mind of the reader or listener or viewer, and then moves to resolve this in such a way that the pleasures of finding out are much enhanced.

The reader or listener or viewer typically experiences such a narrative arc via feelings of anxious tension and pleasurable relief; and such work would lose its emotional grip on the subject if this were not the case. The viewer's attention is thus captured as a result of the problematic uncertainty generated by a crisis or a problem; the viewer becomes interested and engaged as a result of feeling anxious tension for or toward the protagonists and their situation; and the viewer's pleasure at the denouement of the work is greatly enhanced as a result. This is why "spoilers" tend to undermine appreciation and enjoyment of a work of art, and equally why "spoiler alerts" in reviews of and discussions about plays and films and books are increasingly common. The latter help to preserve the anxious tension experienced by the viewer or reader, as a result of not knowing how things will turn out; the experience of problematic uncertainty in turn facilitates the subject's pleasurable enjoyment when they do finally discover how things end and how the uncertainty is resolved. Merely finding out what happened, or discovering the resolution of some story or narrative, is far less satisfying to most readers and viewers, if dissociated from feelings of anxiety that such knowledge relieves. Such feelings are therefore a condition on the value of much of our aesthetic experience; they are part of what we want, when we read, view, and listen.

The generation of dramatic tension, the inculcation of feelings of anxiety about the problematic uncertainty, and the pleasures of relief that are subsequent upon its resolution are increasingly prevalent in the entertainment industry, and nowhere more so than in reality TV. Given that entertainment of this sort cannot rely upon the preexisting renown or fame of participants to attract the attention of viewing audiences, the shows in question need to do this in other ways, and most commonly do so by generating conflict, tension, and the staging of a resolution—often in the form of a vote by the public or a panel of judges—at the end of the show. When made skilfully, such shows succeed in generating a situation of problematic uncertainty over the length of the program, building up to a dramatic resolution, and—depending on how the vote goes—subsequent feelings of joy or disappointment on the part of the viewer, depending on whether their preferences about the contestants are satisfied. Indeed, given the lack of much in the way of narrative or other forms of content, it might be argued that most reality TV shows consist of not much more than this generation and resolution of feelings of anxious and dramatic tension. (Just as celebrity has been famously described as a "pseudo-event" [Boorstin 1962/1992], reality TV shows might be described as "pseudo-narratives," where skilful manipulation of feelings takes the place of plot development as a device for making and resolving anxieties.) Here too feelings of anxious tension are a condition on the value of the entertainment in question; without such feelings, viewers would not care (less) about who is voted off, who gets to stay.

Note that feelings of anxiety are alluring or attractive in these cases insofar as they are part of activities—like watching sports, films, reality TV—that are freely chosen and to a large extent under one's voluntary control. My claim about anxiety's allure is thus limited, at least for now, to such cases. As a result, it is no part of my remit here to suggest that feelings of anxiety that are outwith one's control, or that emerge from unwanted situations or circumstances, are usually alluring. Nor would I wish to claim that in these latter cases the very genuine pleasures that can be had when anxiety is resolved normally or typically outweigh the disvalue of the negative feelings of anxiety themselves. It is clearly not the case that there is always some kind of upside to feelings of anxiety, in the shape of enhanced or intensified pleasure that helps to make up for the misery of unwanted anxiety. For all I have shown thus far, anxiety is alluring only in the above kinds of cases where it is part and parcel of activities that are voluntarily chosen, and where it is plausibly viewed as a condition on the value of those activities by the participants. In the following section, however, I'll argue for a stronger claim: that anxiety is alluring or attractive as part of an ideal kind or form of life, where this includes anxiety that is both wanted and unwanted.

ANXIETY AND EXEMPLARS

In this section, I want to argue that the most admirable and alluring lives will be lives with very high levels of problematic uncertainty, and hence are lives with very high levels of anxiety. In order to make this argument, we need to look at what might be said about ideals of character, or those who are most *exemplary*. Recent philosophical theorizing, in particular, work by Linda Zagzebski, supports a particular view of exemplars. On Zagzebski's view, exemplars are to be understood as "paradigmatically excellent persons": not simply good people, but the very best people (Zagzebski 2017, 20). What makes them so is that they possess deep and reliable character traits—virtues or excellences, on a traditional understanding—to a very high degree. Common sense seems to line up with this idea of exemplars as people who are maximally good and virtuous, and who count as exemplary because of their inner traits, skills, and abilities. When asked to name an exemplar, people very often mention figures such as Jesus, or Gandhi, or Mother Teresa. On this view, exemplars appear to be saintly people. But the category of exemplars—of those who are paradigmatically excellent—need not be restricted to those who are paragons of spiritual and moral goodness. For we might identify as exemplary those who perform heroic tasks—such as Oskar Schindler—or those who embody exceptional wisdom—such as Gautama Buddha. So alongside the saint, Zagzebski proposes that we can think of exemplars as including the hero and the sage. This is not all. For we can expand the class further to include ideals of artistic excellence, people embodying artistic virtues such as creativity and inventiveness, alongside high levels of artistic talent and sensibility that enable them to express themselves in great works of art. The artistic genius deserves to sit alongside the other models for paragons of excellence.

The saint, the hero, the sage, and the artistic genius are not simply of theoretical or intellectual interest, as instances of the most excellent kinds of people. Exemplars are held to be valuable or important in the main because they inspire and motivate us to become better people, or insofar as they promote character development. Exemplars inspire people, in other words, to improve themselves and their characters, their skills and abilities, and as a result to do better in word and deed. To see how this is meant to work, note that Zagzebski, Jonathan Haidt, and others think that exemplars, as people who are paradigmatically excellent, are equally people who are most *admirable*. This has two important implications. The first is epistemic: we identify exemplars, come to gain knowledge of those who are most admirable, through the emotion of admiration. (Instead of asking who someone takes as a role model or finds exemplary, we might equally ask, on this view, who they admire.) The second is practical: feelings of admiration have motivational force, and so having someone as an exemplar should bring with it a motive to be more like them. As Zagzebski puts it, "a person who is admirable in some respect is imitable in that respect. The feeling of admiration is a kind of attraction that carries the impetus to imitate or emulate with it"[5] (Zagzebski 2017, 20). If so, then a central value that exemplars have is to motivate similar kinds of behaviour in those for whom they are exemplary, and hence in those who admire them. Jonathan Haidt makes a similar point, although he talks about feelings of "elevation" rather than admiration. He writes of such feelings that they are "elicited by acts of charity, gratitude, fidelity, generosity, or any other strong display of virtue . . . [and give] rise to a specific motivation or action tendency: emulation, or the desire to perform the same kind of acts oneself" (Haidt 2003, quoted in Zagzebski 2017, 41).

Exemplars are therefore valuable because they move others to be more like them—more excellent in various respects—and to do the kinds of things that excellent people do for the reasons that they do them.

Exemplars, then, are paragons of excellence, the most admirable kind of persons. As such, exemplars would seem to be alluring. We typically find the lives of these people highly attractive and seductive; insofar as we admire them, we will desire to be more like them, wish that we too could be as heroic, saintly, sagacious, or artistically talented as the exemplars are. But it also seems clear that the lives of such people are admirable and alluring in part *because* they are lives in which there is very significant levels of anxiety.

In particular, the hero, the saint, the sage and the artistic genius will face high levels of anxiety as a result of two conditions. First, they are prepared to face great dangers and great risks in order to achieve valuable aims or goals, and fear and anxiety are the normative emotional responses to danger and risk. Second, anxiety and fear will be exacerbated due to the fact that an exemplar's goals are typically very difficult to achieve, which enhances the uncertainty around their pursuit. Moreover, we can assume that the lives of exemplars are admirable and alluring in part because they face danger or risk all in order to achieve valuable goals, and because such goals are very difficult to achieve. On both counts, exemplars are prepared to do what other people are typically not; and this is part of the reason why we regard them as exemplary. Taken together, this suggests that we can expect the lives of exemplars to be ones which are both alluring and admirable, and to be ones filled with significant levels of anxiety. Anxiety would thus seem to be a central experiential element in exemplary or admirable lives. In order to see this, let us consider these different models of exemplar, and the way in which anxiety is central to these.

The Moral Saint

According to Susan Wolf, in her famous paper from 1992 entitled "Moral Saints," "the moral saint is someone whose every action is as morally good as possible, a person, that is, who is as morally worthy as can be" (Wolf 1992, 419). Now Wolf herself, again famously, doesn't think that the moral saint is a particularly compelling personal ideal, in the sense of someone we should strive to be. Nevertheless, others commonly cite instances of moral saintliness when asked to name exemplary figures—as noted, Jesus and Buddha and Mother Teresa feature in standard lists of exemplars. As a result, and in spite of Wolf's skepticism, many people really do think that those who are saintly live the very best kind of life.

It is clear that moral saints, whilst paragons of moral excellence, are also likely to experience very high levels of anxiety. Not only is the life of a moral saint characterized by high levels of compassionate suffering for the plight of others. In addition, the moral saint is someone who courageously and steadfastly faces up to the moral emergencies and impossible moral demands that the world throws her way. The moral saint is someone whose desire to alleviate the suffering of others leads her to take on significant responsibility, with all of the attendant dangers and risks that this brings. She is someone who dedicates her life to helping those in need, in spite of the very real dangers that her work will not reach everyone who needs help, and the risks that her efforts will come to naught. The moral saint counts as saintly precisely because she does not give in to or succumb to her fear and anxiety, does not drift into despair at the ongoing parlous state of the moral universe, but keeps her hopes and desires intact and behaves accordingly. Indeed, the moral saint seems saintly to us precisely because she faces up to the fear and anxiety she has about the welfare of others, and remains unflinchingly committed to this come what may. The capacity to experience and endure fear and anxiety on this kind of scale is part of what makes the saint exemplary and admirable. Anxiety thus seems part and parcel of this kind of idealized life.

The Hero

If the moral saint is characterizable by an exemplary commitment to the needs of others, and the moral courage to see this through, the hero is someone who faces extreme danger for some greater good, and the physical courage that such things require. As a result, the hero goes way beyond what might be practically required in such a situation, or beyond what could be *reasonably* asked of someone, and holds steadfast in the face of fear and anxiety when the good in question is under threat.

Given what the hero is prepared to risk for the sake of others, or for the sake of some valuable cause, moreover, they are properly characterized as being disposed to experience very high levels of anxiety and fear in the relevant circumstances. After all, if anxiety tracks problematic uncertainty with respect to some valuable good, we might well expect that the highest levels of personal anxiety will coincide with problematic uncertainty regarding threats to one's own life—which is, for many who are heroic, precisely what is at stake. Of course, it is also true that the hero is sometimes portrayed as one who risks all and does so in a calm, indeed stylish, and nonemotional manner. But just as we can doubt that facing up to danger without fear constitutes genuine courage, we can equally doubt that risking all when one is unconcerned about what there is to lose constitutes genuine heroism. (Note that it is normally the *anti*hero who is unconcerned with their own life, and who thinks of themselves as having nothing much to lose.) Genuine heroism seems better characterizable as a willingness to risk all, in the full knowledge and awareness and concern for what one is risking. If so, it is plausible to assume that the hero, like the saint, will live a life filled with high levels of anxiety and fear.

The Sage

Unlike the moral saint, and especially unlike the hero, the wise or sagacious person doesn't strike us as an obvious candidate for someone whose life is filled with anxiety. Exemplars of wisdom are often characterized by relatively old age, calmness, equanimity, and the like. (Fictional characters such as Yoda or Gandalf are often taken to be paragons of wisdom, and the above traits seem well fitted to them.) Nevertheless, there is a strong case to be made that the sage, as well as the saint and hero, does indeed experience high levels of anxiety, and that a calm demeanor might thus hide the negative affective life within. For the sage must be *intellectually courageous*, and so face up to and overcome the intellectual fears and anxieties that come with the territory of being wise.

To see this, note that the sage is dedicated not just to amassing knowledge and understanding facts about themselves and the world around them. Instead, they are better characterized as seeking knowledge and understanding of important truths, and for inquiring into areas where knowledge is difficult. After all, it is not the sheer amount of information that separates the sage from the rest of us; many people could know a lot more trivia than the sage, for instance, and yet fail to count as wise. This is because their attention and inquiries are directed toward trivial rather than the important truths, to easy rather than difficult knowledge and understanding.[6] What distinguishes the sage from most of the rest of humankind is the kind of motivation to inquire into, and attain, knowledge or understanding that does not come easily, that requires commitment, dedication, and patience. It is plausible to think that the kind of motivation needed to engage in inquiries of this sort—into the deepest mysteries, the most pressing, complex, intractable problems—is characteristic of intellectual courage, since the more difficult or more intractable the problem, the greater the risk of failure. The sage is thus someone who has the intellectual courage to face up to such risks, and to overcome the fear and anxiety that are central to an acknowledgment of them. The wisest or most sagacious lives will thus be characterized by high levels of fear and epistemic anxiety, and will be admirable and exemplary in part because of this.

The Great Artist

Perhaps the clearest example of the presence of anxiety—alongside other forms of negative affect—in the lives of exemplary people can be seen if we look at the artistic genius. Indeed, the idea that anxiety is bound up with artistic excellence is so prominent that it has given rise to the well-known trope of the *tortured artist*. (Rilke writes that "If my demons leave me, I am afraid that my angels may take flight as well"; whilst Munch replied, when informed that psychiatric treatment could cure him of his depression and anxiety, that "They are part of me and my art. They are indistinguishable from me, and it would destroy my art. I want to keep those sufferings.") There is, in the public consciousness at least, a correlation between being a great artist and living a particular kind of impoverished, miserable, lonely existence—in short, living a life that is full of anxiety and suffering. The idea of the tortured artist has a long history. As Andrew Robinson notes in his study of genius, "In ancient Greece, Aristotle (or his pupil Theophrastus) asked: 'Why is it that all men who are outstanding in philosophy, poetry, or the arts are melancholic?'" (Robinson 2011, 55). Even more prominent in the public consciousness are the names of great artists who have suffered serious forms of mental and emotional suffering, with anxiety at the fore. It is difficult to read or listen to discussions of the myth of the tortured artist without hearing about Vincent van Gogh, Billie Holiday, Sylvia Plath, Fyodor Dostoyevsky, Kurt Cobain, George Orwell, Amy Winehouse, Charles Dickens, Frida Kahlo, and others whose lives are marked both by significant artistic achievement and long periods of mental and emotional suffering, including severe anxiety, depression, schizophrenia, bipolar disorder, and addiction.

Not all artists are tortured artists, however. And not all of the tortured artists listed above are described as suffering from severe anxiety. As a result, it is not clear, from the trope itself, that high levels of anxiety characterize the life of great artists as such. Nevertheless, we can—on the lines of the previous subsections—make the claim that artistic exemplars will typically experience high levels of fear and anxiety, given the nature of their motivations and aims. Just as we can distinguish the sage from someone who is only interested in attaining trivial and easy truth and understanding, we can distinguish the great artist from the hobbyist craftsman or weekend painter or occasional musician. The great artist can be distinguished from the hobbyist in terms of a motivation to pursue the most valuable, important, difficult, and risky aesthetic goals—viz. to produce great art, art which succeeds in changing our ways of viewing and thinking about ourselves and our world, which enables us to see and hear anew, bringing novel perspectives and interpretations and standards into being. But great artists also possess the fortitude and courage to pursue their artistic goals in the face of difficulties, challenges, and significant risks. (Given the rarity of great art, the risks of failure are great indeed.) As a result, those who strive to produce great art are deeply engaged in an endeavour whose aim is both extremely valuable, and extremely unlikely to come about. It is no surprise, therefore, that great artists can be characterized in terms of exceptional courage—the courage to risk all in the pursuit of artistic excellence, to face fear and anxiety that one's efforts will come to naught, and to nevertheless persist and ultimately to succeed. The great artist, like the saint, hero, and sage discussed earlier, is best understood as being disposed to deal excellently with the fear and anxiety that are a necessary feature of such motivation and such ambition. The lives of the great artists will also be characterized by high levels of fear and anxiety, and will be admirable and exemplary in part because of this.

CONCLUSION

We are right to think that anxiety is, in very many instances, something to be shunned, alleviated, and avoided. Such responses are appropriate, given the very damaging effects that anxiety can have on a person's well-being, and on those around them. Nevertheless, it is also true that anxiety can be, for some people and in some circumstances, alluring or attractive as a condition on the value of their activities and their aims. Moreover, it is also true that the lives of people we regard as the most admirable or exemplary of human beings are lives that will have very high levels of anxiety. For those who are exemplary or most admirable are those who take on the biggest risks and dangers for the sake of the highest goods, and as a result are engaged in activities that require great courage, and that have a very high chance of failure. It might well turn out, then, that our ideals of living incorporate more, rather than less, problematic uncertainty. Or so, at least, I have argued.

NOTES

1. "In the United States, anxiety is the most common mental illness, affecting more than 40 million adults each year. Data from the National Institute of Mental Health has indicated that about 30 percent of Americans experience clinical anxiety at some point in their lives. Globally, according to the Institute for Health Metrics and Evaluation, an estimated 284 million people had an anxiety disorder as of 2017, making it the most prevalent mental disorder worldwide" (Aarons-Mele 2020).

2. This line of argument is developed in more detail in my paper, "Suffering in Sport" (Brady 2019).

3. It is important to emphasize that such activities are voluntary or freely chosen. Part of their appeal, as freely chosen, is that they give us the chance to test ourselves against challenging circumstances, in instances where our lives aren't challenging enough. (Witness the rise in the interest in mountain climbing in the eighteenth century, for the middle and upper classes.) Physical and mental adversity will be much less alluring to those people whose lives are already filled with them.

4. For a detailed account of how emotion, including negative emotion, can help to facilitate knowledge and understanding, see my *Emotional Insight* (Brady 2013), especially chapters 3 and 4.

5. Zagzebski writes: "When I speak of emulating X, then, I mean taking X as my model, attempting to become more like X. I do not think of emulation in such a way that whenever A emulates X, it is possible for A to become as good as X, nor does it include A's belief that she can do so" (Zagzebski 2017, 24).

6. It is no surprise, given this, that folk and academic accounts of wisdom both highlight the importance of lived experience, and in particular the central role that reflection on negative life experience plays in its inculcation.

REFERENCES

Aarons-Mele, Mora. 2020. "Leading Through Anxiety." *Harvard Business Review*. (May 11, 2020). *https://hbr.org/2020/05/leading-through-anxiety*.

Boorstin, Daniel J. 1962/1992. *The Image: A Guide to Pseudo-Events in America*. New York: Vintage Books.

Bradford, Gwen. 2015. *Achievement*. Oxford: Oxford University Press.

Brady, Michael S. 2013. *Emotional Insight: The Epistemic Role of Emotional Experience*. Oxford: Oxford University Press.

________. 2018. *Suffering and Virtue*. Oxford: Oxford University Press.

________. 2019. "Suffering in Sport." *Journal of the Philosophy of Sport* 46: 115–28.

Haidt, Jonathan. 2003. "Elevation and the Positive Psychology of Morality." In *Flourishing: Positive Psychology and the Life Well-Lived*, edited by Keyes, Corey L.M, Haidt Jonathan, 275–89. Washington, DC: American Psychological Association.

Kurth, Charlie. 2018. *The Anxious Mind: An Investigation into the Varieties and Virtues of Anxiety*. Cambridge, MA: MIT Press.

Leknes, Siri and Bastian, Brock. 2014. "The Benefits of Pain." *Review of Philosophy and Psychology* 5: 57–70.

Roberts, Robert C. 2003. *Emotions: An Essay in Aid of Moral Psychology*. Cambridge: Cambridge University Press.

Robinson, Andrew. 2011. *Genius: A Very Short Introduction*. Oxford: Oxford University Press.

Wolf, Susan. 1992. "Moral Saints." *Journal of Philosophy* 79: 419–39.

Zagzebski, Linda. 2017. *Exemplarist Moral Theory*. New York: Oxford University Press.

Bibliography

Aarons-Mele, Mora. 2020. “Leading Through Anxiety.” *Harvard Business Review*. (May 11, 2020). https://hbr.org/2020/05/leading-through-anxiety.

Adler, Joseph. 2004. “Varieties of Spiritual Experience: Shen in Neo-Confucian Discourse.” In *Confucian Spirituality*, Vol. 2, edited by Tu Wei Ming and M. E. Tucker. 120–48. New York: Crossroad.

Alanen, Lilli. 2004. “Descartes and Elisabeth: A Philosophical Dialogue?” In *Feminist Reflections on the History of Philosophy*, edited by Lilli Alanen and Charlotte Witt, 193–218. Dordrecht: Kluwer Academic Publishers.

Alessandri, Mariana. 2023. *Night Vision: Seeing Ourselves Through Dark Moods*. Princeton: Princeton University Press.

Alfano, Mark. 2014. “Expanding the Situationist Challenge to Reliabilism About Inference.” In *Virtue Epistemology Naturalized*, edited by Abrol Fairweather, 103–22. Cham: Springer.

———. 2016. “Epistemic Emotions and Intellectual Virtues.” https://www.alfanophilosophy.com/blog/2016/4/22/epistemic-emotions-and-intellectualvirtues.

American Bar Association. 2022. “Law School Applicants and Enrollees.” ABA Profile of the Legal Profession 2022.

American Psychiatric Association. 2013. *Diagnostic and Statistical Manual of Mental Disorders*. 5th ed. Arlington, VA: American Psychiatric Association.

Ames, Roger T., and Henry Rosemont, Jr., trans. 1998. *The Analects of Confucius: A Philosophical Translation*. New York: Random House.

Angle, Stephen C., and Justin Tiwald. 2017. *Neo-Confucianism: A Philosophical Introduction*. Cambridge: Polity Press.

Arango-Muñoz, S. 2010. “Two Levels of Metacognition.” *Philosophia* 39: 71–82.

Archer, Alfred, and Mills, Georgina. 2019. “Anger, Affective Injustice, and Emotion Regulation.” *Philosophical Topics* 47: 75–94.

Armon-Jones, Claire. 1991. *Varieties of Affect*. Toronto: University of Toronto Press.

Asnaani, Anu., Anthony J. Richey, Ruta Dimaite, Devon E. Hinton, and Stefan G. Hofmann. 2010. “A Cross-Ethnic Comparison of Lifetime Prevalence Rates of Anxiety Disorders.” *Journal of Nervous and Mental Disease*, 198: 551–55.

Asoğlu, Mehmet, İsmail Karka, Faruk Pirinççioğlu, MeltemGöbelek, Hakim ÇeliK, Hatice Takatak, and Şermin Bílgen Ulgar. 2018. “Cultural Reflections of the Expressions of the Anxiety of Patients with Generalized Anxiety Disorder." *Bezmialem Science* 4: 242–47.

Bader, Oren. 2020. "The Human Extended Socio-Attentional Field and Its Impairment in Borderline Personality Disorder and in Social Anxiety Disorder." *Phenomenology and the Cognitive Sciences* 19: 169–89.

Baehr, Jason. 2011. *The Inquiring Mind: On Intellectual Virtues and Virtue Epistemology*. New York: Oxford University Press.

———. 2021. *Deep in Thought: A Practical Guide to Teaching for Intellectual Virtues*. Cambridge, MA.: Harvard Education Press.

Barlow, David. 2001. *Anxiety and Its Disorders*. 2nd edition. New York: Guilford Press.

Bashford-Largo, Johannah, Joseph Aloi, Ru Zhang, Sahil Baja, Erin Carollo, Jaimie Elowsky, Amanda Schwartz, Matthew Dobbertin, Robert James R. Blair, and Karina S. Blair. 2021. "Reduced Neural Differentiation of Rewards and Punishment During Passive Avoidance Learning in Adolescents with Generalized Anxiety Disorder." *Depression and Anxiety* 38: 794–803.

Battaly, Heather. 2015. "A Pluralist Theory of Virtue." In *Current Controversies in Virtue Theory*, edited by Mark Alfano, 7–21. New York: Routledge.

Beck, Jacob. 2012. "The Generality Constraint and the Structure of Thought." *Mind* 121: 563–600.

Beck, Judith S. 2011. *Cognitive Behavior Therapy: Basics and Beyond*. New York: Guilford Press.

Beck, Ulrich. 1992. *Risk Society: Towards a New Modernity*. London: Sage.

Belluz, Julia. 2010. "High Anxiety." *Maclean's* (18 November 2010). https://macleans.ca/news/canada/high-anxiety/.

Beresford, Peter, and Jasna Russo, eds. 2022. *The Routledge International Handbook of Mad Studies*. New York: Routledge.

Berns, Gregory S., Jonathan Chappelow, et al. 2006. "Neurobiological Substrates of Dread." *Science* 312: 754–58.

Block, Ned. 1995. "On a Confusion About a Function of Consciousness." *Behavioral and Brain Sciences* 18: 227–87.

Bloom, Paul. 2016. *Against Empathy*. New York: HarperCollins.

Boehm, Christopher. 2012. *Moral Origins*. New York: Basic Books.

Boorse, Christopher. 1997. "A Rebuttal on Health." In *What is Disease?* Edited by James M. Humber and Robert F. Almeder, 1–134. Totowa, NJ.: Humana Press.

Boorstin, Daniel J. 1962/1992. *The Image: A Guide to Pseudo-Events in America*. New York: Vintage Books.

Bortolan, Anna. 2022. "Social Anxiety, Self-Consciousness, and Interpersonal Experience." In *Empathy, Intersubjectivity, and the Social World*, edited by Anna Bortolan and Elisa Magri, 303–22. Boston: De Gruyter.

Botvinick, M. M., T. S. Braver, D. M. Barch, C. S.Carter, and J. D. Cohen. 2001. "Conflict Monitoring and Cognitive Control." *Psychological Review* 108: 624–52.

Boyle, Patrick. 2019. "More Women than Men Are Enrolled in Medical School." *AAMC News* (9 December 2019). https://www.aamc.org/news/more-women-men-are-enrolled-medicalschool.

Brader, Ted. 2006. *Campaigning for Hearts and Minds*. Chicago: University of Chicago Press.

Bradford, Gwen. 2015. *Achievement*. Oxford: Oxford University Press.

Brady, Michael S. 2013. *Emotional Insight: The Epistemic Role of Emotional Experience*. Oxford: Oxford University Press.

———. 2018. *Suffering and Virtue*. Oxford: Oxford University Press.

———. 2019. "Suffering in Sport." *Journal of the Philosophy of Sport* 46: 115–28.

———. 2019. "The Role of Emotion in Intellectual Virtue." In *The Routledge Handbook of Virtue Epistemology*, edited by Heather Battaly, 47–57. New York: Routledge.

Brancazio, Nick. 2020. "Being Perceived and Being 'Seen': Interpersonal Affordances, Agency, and Selfhood." *Frontiers in Psychology* 11: 1750.

Brewer, Judson. 2021. *Unwinding Anxiety*. New York: Penguin Random House.

Broad, Jacqueline. 2002. *Women Philosophers of the Seventeenth Century*. Cambridge: Cambridge University Press.

Brouwer, René. 2014. *The Stoic Sage: The Early Stoics on Wisdom, Sagehood and Socrates*. Cambridge: Cambridge University Press.

Brown, Deborah J. 2006. *Descartes and the Passionate Mind*. Cambridge: Cambridge University Press.

Brown, Deborah J., and Calvin G. Normore. 2019. *Descartes and the Ontology of Everyday Life*. Oxford: Oxford University Press.

Brown, Deborah J., and Jacqueline Broad. 2022a. "The Social Dimension of Generosity in Descartes and Astell." *Journal of the History of Philosophy* 60: 409–27.

———. 2022b. "Petticoat Power? Mary Astell's Appropriation of Heroic Virtue for Women." *Journal of the American Philosophical Association*: 1–20.

Burton, Robert. *The Anatomy of Melancholy. 1621/1826*. Reprinted. London: Thomas McLean.

———. 1621/1927. *The Anatomy of Melancholy*. London: Thomas McLean.

Cabrera, Frank. 2021. "Is Epistemic Anxiety an Intellectual Virtue?" *Synthese* 199: 13471–95.

Calhoun, Chesire. 2004. "An Apology for Moral Shame." *Journal of Political Philosophy* 12: 127–46.

Canadian Association of University Teachers. 2018. "Academic Anxiety." *CAUT Bulletin* 65: 14–19.

Carruthers, Peter. 2015. *The Centered Mind: What the Science of Working Memory Shows Us About the Nature of Human Thought*. Oxford: Oxford University Press.

———. 2018. "Basic Questions." *Mind and Language* 33: 130–47.

Charland, Louis. C. 2004. "Moral Treatment and the Personality Disorders." In *The Philosophy of Psychiatry: A Companion*, edited by Jennifer Radden, 64–77. Oxford: Oxford University Press.

Chiew, Hui Ho. 2017. "Sinitic Buddhist Narratives of Wonders: Are There Miracles in Buddhism?" *Philosophy East and West* 67: 1118–42.

Clark, Cory, and Bo Winegard. 2022. "Sex and the Academy." *Quillette* (8 October 2022). https://quillette.com/2022/10/08/sex-and-the-academy/.

Clayton, Susan, and Bryan T. Karazsia. 2020. "Development and Validation of a Measure of Climate Change Anxiety." *Journal of Environmental Psychology* 69: 101434

Cooper, Rachel. 2002. "Disease." *Studies in History and Philosophy of Science Part C: Studies in History and Philosophy of Biological and Biomedical Sciences* 33: 263–82.

Crocq, Marc-Antoine. 2015. "A History of Anxiety: From Hippocrates to DSM." *Dialogues in Clinical Neuroscience* 17: 319–25.

———. 2017. "The History of Generalized Anxiety Disorder as a Diagnostic Category." *Dialogues in Clinical Neuroscience* 19: 107–16. https://doi.org/10.31887/DCNS.2017.19.2/macrocq.

Cummins, Robert. 1975. "Functional Analysis." *The Journal of Philosophy* 72: 741–65.

Cuthbert, Bruce N., and Thomas R. Inse. 2013. "Toward the Future of Psychiatric Diagnosis: The Seven Pillars of RDoC." *BMC Medicine* 11: 126.

D'Arms, Justin, and Daniel Jacobson. 2003. "The Significance of Recalcitrant Emotions (or, antiquasijudgmentalism)." *Royal Institutes of Philosophy Supplements* 52: 127–45.

de Haan, Sanneke, Erik Rietveld, Martin Stokhof, and Damiaan Denys. 2013. "The Phenomenology of Deep Brain Stimulation-induced Changes in Obsessive-Compulsive Disorder Patients: An Enactive Affordance-based Model." *Frontiers in Human Neuroscience* 7: 1–14.

De Nays, Wim. (forthcoming). "Advancing Theorizing about Fast and Slow-Thinking." *Behavioral and Brain Sciences*.

de Sousa, Ronald. 1987. *The Rationality of Emotion*. Cambridge, MA: MIT Press.

———. 2008. "Epistemic Feelings." In *Epistemology and Emotions*, edited by George Brun, Ulvi Doguoglu, and Dominique Kuenzle, 185–203. New York: Routledge.

De Vries, Eline L. E., Bob M. Fennis, Tammo H. A. Bijmolt, Gert J. T. Horstc, and Jan Bernard C. Marsman. 2018. "Friends with Benefits: Behavioral and fMRI Studies on the Effect of Friendship Reminders on Self-control for Compulsive and Non-Compulsive Buyers." *International Journal of Research in Marketing* 35: 336–58.

Debates in Parliament: *Session 1833 On the Resolutions and Bill for the Abolition of Slavery in the British Colonies*. Retrieved from: https://books.google.td/books?id=9bANAAAAQAAJ.

DeLancey, Stephen C. 2006. "Basic Moods." *Philosophical Psychology* 19: 527–38.

Deonna, Julien, and Fabrice Teroni. 2012. *The Emotions: A Philosophical Introduction*. New York: Routledge.

Deonna, Julien, Christine Tappolet, and Fabrice Teroni. 2015. "Emotion, Philosophical Issues About." *Wiley Interdisciplinary Reviews: Cognitive Science* 6: 193–207.

Descartes, René. 1909. *Oeuvres de Descartes*. Edited by Charles Adam and Paul Tannery, 12 vols. Paris: Léopold Cerf.

———. 1984–1985. *The Philosophical Writings of Descartes*, vols. 1 and 2. Edited and translated by John Cottingham, Robert Stoothoff, and Dugald Murdoch. Cambridge: Cambridge University Press.

Desmond, William D. 2006. *The Greek Praise of Poverty: The Origins of Ancient Cynicism*. Notre Dame, IN: University of Notre Dame Press.

Dezfouli, Amir, and Bernard W. Balleine. 2013. "Actions, Action Sequences and Habits." *PLOS Computational Biology* 9: e1003364–14.

DiMauro, Jennifer, Janine Domingues, Geraldine Fernandez, and David F. Tolin. 2013. "Long Term Effectiveness of CBT for Anxiety Disorders in an Adult Outpatient Clinic Sample: A Follow-up Study." *Behavior Research and Therapy* 51: 82–86.

Dings, Roy. 2018. "Understanding Phenomenological Differences in How Affordances Solicit Action. An Exploration." *Phenomenology and the Cognitive Sciences* 17: 681–99.

———. 2021. "Meaningful Affordances." *Synthese* 199: 1855–75.

Doris, John M. 2009. "Skepticism About Persons." *Philosophical Issues* 19: 57–91.

———. 2015. *Talking to Ourselves*. Oxford: Oxford University Press.

———. 2018. "Making Do Without (Reflection)." *Philosophy and Phenomenological Research 97*: 771–90.

Dostoevski, Fyodor. 1879–1880/1990. *The Brothers Karamazov*. Translated by Richard Pevear and Larissa Volokhonsky. New York: Farrar, Straus and Giroux.

Dowbiggin, Ian. 2011. *The Quest for Mental Health: A Tale of Science, Medicine, Scandal, Sorrow and Mass Society*. New York: Cambridge University Press.

Dworkin, Ronald W. 2022. "The Politicization of Unhappiness." *National Affairs* 23. https://www.nationalaffairs.com/publications/detail/the-politicization-of-unhappiness.

Dyson, Henry. 2010. "Pleasure and the Sapiens: *Seneca De vita Beata 11.1*." *Classical Philology* 105: 313–18.

Elkind, Elizabeth. 2020. "What Is 'Election Stress Disorder,' and Do I Have It?" CBS News (29 September 2020). https://www.cbsnews.com/news/what-is-election-stress-disorder/.

Engelhardt, H. Tristram. 1976. "Ideology and Etiology." *Journal of Medicine and Philosophy* 1: 256–68.

Endler, Norman, and Nancy L. Kocovski. 2001. "State and Trait Anxiety Revisited." *Journal of Anxiety Disorders* 15: 231–45.

Eran, Uri. 2021. "Which Emotions Should Kantians Cultivate (and Which Ones Should they Discipline)?" *Kantian Review* 25: 53–76.

Evans, Jonathan, and Keith Frankish, eds. 2009. *In Two Minds: Dual Processes and Beyond.* Oxford: Oxford University Press.

Evans, Jonathan S. B., and Keith E. Stanovich, Keith E. 2013. "Dual-process Theories of Higher Cognition: Advancing the Debate." *Perspectives on Psychological Science* 8: 223–41.

Fantl, Jeremy, and Matthew McGrath. 2002. "Evidence, Pragmatics, and Justification." *The Philosophical Review* 111: 67–94.

Field, Thomas A., Eric T. Beeson, and Laura K. Jones. 2015. "The New ABCs: A Practitioner's Guide to Neuroscience-Informed Cognitive-Behavior Therapy." *Journal of Mental Health Counseling* 37: 206–20.

Flannery, Mary Ellen. 2018. "The Epidemic of Anxiety Among Today's Students." National Education Association (28 March 2018). https://www.nea.org/advocating-for-change/new-from-nea/epidemic-anxiety-among-todays-students.

Fleisher, Will. 2017. "Virtuous Distinctions." *Synthese* 194: 2973–3003.

Foucault, Michel. 1965. *Madness and Civilization: A History of Insanity in the Age of Reason.* Translated by Richard Howard. New York: Pantheon Books.

———.1973. *The Birth of the Clinic: An Archeology of Medical Perception.* Translated by A. M. Sheridan. New York: Routledge.

———. 1983. "Hypomnemata." *Corps Ecrit* 5: 3–23.

———. 1988. *Madness and Civilization: A History of Insanity in the Age of Reason.* New York: Random House.

———. 2003. *Abnormal: Lectures at the Collège de France, 1974–1975.* Edited by Valerio Marchetti and Antonella Fontana. New York: Palgrave Macmillan.

———. 2006. *Michel Foucault: Psychiatric Power: Lectures at the Collège de France, 1973–1974.* New York: Palgrave Macmillan.

Foulkes, Lucy. 2021. *Losing Our Minds: What Mental Illness Really Is and What it Isn't.* London: Penguin.

Freeman, Daniel, and Jason Freeman. 2012. *Anxiety: A Very Short Introduction.* Oxford: Oxford University Press.

Freud, Sigmund. 1952. *A General Introduction to Psychoanalysis.* New York: Washington Square Press.

———. 1959. *Inhibitions, Symptoms and Anxiety.* Translated by Alix Strachey. New York: W.W. Norton.

Friedman, Jane. 2020. "The Epistemic and the Zetetic." *Philosophical Review* 129: 501–36.

Frijda, Nico H. 1994. "Varieties of Affect: Emotions and Episodes, Moods and Sentiments." In *The Nature of Emotion: Fundamental Questions*, edited by Paul Ekman and Richard J. Davidson, 59–67. Oxford: Oxford University Press.

Fritz, James. 2022. "Fitting Anxiety and Prudent Anxiety." *Synthese* 199: 8555–78.

Furedi, Frank. 2007. "The Only Thing We Have to Fear is the 'Culture of Fear' Itself." *Spiked* (4 April 2007). https://www.spiked-online.com/2007/04/04/the-only-thing-we-have-to-fear-is-the-culture-of-fear-itself/.

Gaete, Alfredo. 2008. "The Concept of Mental Disorder: A Proposal." *Philosophy, Psychiatry, and Psychology* 15: 327–39.

Galen, Claudius. 1963. *On the Passions and Errors of the Soul.* Translated by Paul. W. Harkins. Columbus: Ohio State University Press.

Gallagher, Shaun. 2018. "The Therapeutic Reconstruction of Affordances." *Res Philosophica* 95: 719–36

Gallagher, Shaun, and Micah Allen. 2018. "Active Inference, Enactivism and the Hermeneutics of Social Cognition." *Synthese* 195: 2627–48.

Ganna, Andrea, Karin J. H. Verweij, Michel G. Nivard, Robert Maier, Robbee Wedow, Alexander S. Busch, Abdel Abdellaoui, Shengru Guo, J. Fah Sathirapongsasuti, *23andMe* Research Team, Paul Lichtenstein, Sebastian Lundström, Niklas Långström, Adam Auton, Kathleen Mullan Harris, Gary W. Beecham, Eden R. Martin, Alan R. Sanders, John R. B. Perry, Benjamin M. Neale, and Brendan P. Zietsch. 2019. "Large-scale GWAS Reveals Insights into the Genetic Architecture of Same-Sex Sexual Behavior." *Science* 365(6456), eaat7693.

Gardner, Daniel K. (trans). 1990. *Learning to Be a Sage: Selection from the Conversations of Master Chu, Arranged Topically, by Chu Hsi*. Berkeley: University of California Press.

Garland-Thomson, R. 2011. "Misfits: A Feminist Materialist Disability Concept." *Hypatia* 26: 591–609.

Garson, Justin. 2021. "The Developmental Plasticity Challenge to Wakefield's View." In *Defining Mental Disorder: Jerome Wakefield and His Critics*, edited by Luc Faucher and Denis Forest, 335–52. Cambridge, MA.: MIT Press.

Gibbard, Allan. 1990. *Wise Choices, Apt Feelings*. Cambridge, MA: Harvard University Press.

Gibson, James J. 1979. *The Ecological Approach to Visual Perception*. New York: Houghton Mifflin.

Giddens, Anthony. 1991. *Modernity and Self-Identity: Self and Society in the Late Modern Age*. Cambridge: Polity.

Gifford, Edwin Hamilton. 2013. *The Euthydemus of Plato: With Revised Text, Introduction, Notes and Indices*. Cambridge: Cambridge University Press.

Glas, Gerrit. 2020. "An Enactive Approach to Anxiety and Anxiety Disorders." *Philosophy, Psychiatry, and Psychology* 27: 35–50.

Goldie, Peter. 2000. *The Emotions: A Philosophical Exploration*. Oxford: Oxford University Press.

———. 2004. "Emotion, Reason and Virtue." In *Emotion, Evolution, and Rationality*, edited by Dylan Evans and Pierre Cruse, 249–68. Oxford: Oxford University Press.

Goldman, Alan H. 1988. *Empirical Knowledge*. Los Angeles: University of California Press.

Gordon, Robert M. 1969. "Emotions and Knowledge." *The Journal of Philosophy* 66: 408–13.

Gotlib, Anna. 2020. Commentary on Charlie Kurth's *The Anxious Mind*. Chicago: Central Meeting of the American Philosophical Association.

Gottschalk, Michael G., and Katharina Domschke. 2017. "Genetics of Generalized Anxiety Disorder and Related Traits." *Dialogues in Clinical Neuroscience* 19: 159–68.

Graver, Margaret. 2009. *Stoicism and Emotion*. Chicago: University of Chicago Press.

Greco, John. 2010. *Achieving Knowledge: A Virtue-Theoretic Account of Epistemic Normativity*. Cambridge: Cambridge University Press.

Greene, Joshua. 2008. "The Secret Joke of Kant's Soul." In *Moral Psychology*, Vol. 3. The Neuroscience of Morality: Emotion, Brain Disorders, and Development, edited by Walter Sinnott-Armstrong, 35–79. Cambridge, MA.: MIT Press.

Griffiths, Paul E. 1997. *What Emotions Really Are: The Problem of Psychological Categories*. Chicago: University of Chicago Press.

Grose, Anouchka. 2020. *A Guide to Eco-Anxiety*. London: Watkins.

Guanzi 管子. 2011. "Nei Ye" 內業. In *Chinese Text Project*, edited by Donald Sturgeon. https://ctext.org/guanzi/nei-ye.

Hadot, Pierre. 2001. *The Inner Citadel: The Meditations of Marcus Aurelius*. Cambridge, MA: Harvard University Press.

Haidt, Jonathan. 2001. "The Emotional Dog and its Rational Tail: a Social Intuitionist Approach to Moral Judgment." *Psychological Review* 108: 814–34.

———. 2003. "Elevation and the Positive Psychology of Morality." In *Flourishing: Positive Psychology and the Life Well-Lived*, edited by Corey L. M. Keyes and JonathanHaidt, 275–89. Washington, DC: American Psychological Association.

Haltinner, Kristin, Jennifer Ladino, and Dilshani Sarachandra. 2021. "Feeling Skeptical." *Emotion, Space and Society*. 39:100790

Hamilton, J. 2020. "Emotional Methodologies for Climate Change Engagement." Dissertation, Doctor of Philosophy, University of Reading.

Hampshire, Stuart. 1978. "Public and Private Morality." In *Public and Private Morality,* edited by Stuart Hampshire, 23–54. New York: Cambridge University Press.

Harbin, Ami. 2016. *Disorientation and Moral Life*. Oxford: Oxford University Press.

Haybron, Daniel M. 2008. *The Pursuit of Unhappiness: The Elusive Psychology of Well-Being*. New York: Oxford University Press.

Heidegger, Martin. 1993. *Martin Heidegger: Basic Writings*. Edited by David Farrell Krell. New York: HarperCollins.

Herman, Barbara. 1993. *The Practice of Moral Judgment*. Cambridge, MA: Harvard University Press.

Hettema, John M., Michael C. Neale, and Kenneth S. Kendler. 2001. "A Review and Meta Analysis of the Genetic Epidemiology of Anxiety Disorders." *American Journal of Psychiatry* 158: 1568–78.

Hinton, Devon E., Curtis Hsia, Lawrence Park, Andrew Rasmussen, and Mark H. Pollack. 2009. "Cultural Anthropology and Anxiety Diagnoses." In *Current Perspectives on the Anxiety Disorders: Implications for DSM-V and Beyond,* edited by Dean McKay, Jonathan S. Abramowitz, Steven Taylor, and Gordon J. G. Asmundson, 245–74. New York: Springer.

Hinton, Devon E., and Michael W. Otto. 2006. "Symptom Presentation and Symptom Meaning Among Traumatized Cambodian Refugees: Relevance to a Somatically Focused Cognitive-Behavior Therapy." *Cognitive and Behavioral Practice* 13: 249–60.

Hmielowski, Jay D., Rebecca Donaway, and Meredith Y. Wang. 2019. "Environmental Risk Information Seeking." *Environmental Communication* 13: 894–908.

Hoch, Paul. 1949. *Anxiety*. New York: Grune & Stratton.

Hoge, Elizabeth A., Sharad M. Tamrakar, Kelly M. Christian, Namrata Mahara, Mahendra K. Nepal, Mark H. Pollack, and Naomi M. Simon. 2006. "Cross-Cultural Differences in Somatic Presentation in Patients With Generalized Anxiety Disorder." *The Journal of Nervous and Mental Disease* 194: 962–66.

Holwerda, Tjalling J., Robert A. Schoevers, Jack Dekker, Dorly J. H. Deeg, Cees Jonker, and Aartjan T. F. Beekman. 2007. "The Relationship Between Generalized Anxiety Disorder, Depression and Mortality in Old Age." *International Journal of Geriatric Psychiatry* 22: 241–49.

Hon, Tze-Ki. 2005. *The Yijing and Chinese Politics: Classical Commentary and Literati Activism in the Northern Song Period, 960–1127*. Abany: SUNY Press.

Hookway, Christopher. 1998. “Doubt Affective States and the Regulation of Inquiry.” *Canadian Journal of Philosophy* 24 (supplement): 203–25.

———. 2003. “Affective States and Epistemic Immediacy.” *Metaphilosophy* 34: 78–96.

———. 2007. “The Inaugural Address: Fallibilism and the Aim of Inquiry. *Aristotelian Society Supplementary Volume* 81: 1–22.

———. 2008. “Epistemic Immediacy, Doubt and Anxiety: On a Role for Affective States in Epistemic Evaluation.” In *Epistemology and Emotions,* edited by George Brun, Ulvi Doguoglu, and Dominique Kuenzle, 51–65. New York: Routledge.

———. 2011. “James’s Epistemology and the Will to Believe.” *European Journal of Pragmatism and American Philosophy* 3: III–1.

Horwitz, Allan V. 2013. *Anxiety: A Short History*. Baltimore: The Johns Hopkins University Press.

Horwitz, Allan V., and Jerome C. Wakefield. 2012. *All We Have to Fear: Psychiatry’s Transformation of Natural Anxieties into Mental Disorders*. New York: Oxford University Press.

Howland, Jason. 2020. “Is Election Stress Disorder Real?” *Mayo Clinic News Network* (23 October 2020). https://newsnetwork.mayoclinic.org/discussion/is-election-stress-disorder-real/.

Huang, Grace C., Daniel Soto, Kayo Fujimoto, and Thomas W. Valente. 2014. “The Interplay of Friendship Networks and Social Networking Sites: Longitudinal Analysis of Selection and Influence Effects on Adolescent smoking and Alcohol Use.” *American Journal of Public Health* 104: 51–59.

Huddy, Leonie, Stanley Feldman, and Erin Cassese. 2007. “On the Distinct Political Effects of Anxiety and Anger.” In *The Affect Effect,* edited by Russel W. Neuman, George E. Marcus, Ann N. Crigler, and Michael MacKuen, 202–30. Chicago: University of Chicago Press.

Inan, Ilhan. 2013. *The Philosophy of Curiosity*. New York: Routledge.

Ing, Michael David Kaulana. 2012. *The Dysfunction of Ritual in Early Confucianism*. New York: Oxford University Press.

Inwood, Brad, and Lloyd P. Gerson. 1997. *Hellenistic Philosophy: Introductory Readings*, 2nd ed. Indianapolis: Hackett.

Ivanhoe, Philip J. 2016. *Three Streams: Confucian Reflections on Learning and the Moral Heart-Mind in China, Korea, and Japan*. Oxford: Oxford University Press.

Jacobson, Nicholas C. 2016. “Current Evolutionary Adaptiveness of Psychiatric Disorders: Fertility Rates, Parent–Child Relationship Quality, and Psychiatric Disorders Across the Lifespan.” *Journal of Abnormal Psychology* 125: 824–39.

Jeffay, Nathan. 2022. “‘A Mental Health Pandemic’: Israeli Therapist Warns of COVID’s Lasting Effects.” *Times of Israel* (13 October 2022). https://www.timesofisrael.com/a-mental-health-pandemic-israeli-therapist-warns-of-covids-lasting-effects/.

Jefferies, Phillip, and Michael Ungarl. 2020. “Social Anxiety in Young People: A Prevalence Study in Seven Countries.” *PLoS One* 15(9): e0239133.

Jeffery, Renée. 2017. “The Origins of the Modern Emotions: Princess Elisabeth of Bohemia and the Embodied Mind.” *History of European Ideas* 43: 547–59.

Jones, Charles B. 2000. "Mentally Constructing What Already Exists: The Pure Land Thought of Chan Master Jixing Chewu 際醒徹悟 (1741–1810)." *Journal of the International Association of Buddhist Studies* 23: 43–70.

Jylhä, Kirsti M., Clara Cantal, Nazar Akrami, and Taciano L. Milfont. 2016. "Denial of Anthropogenic Climate Change." *Personality and Individual Difference* 98: 184–87.

Kahneman, Daniel. 2011. *Thinking, Fast and Slow*. New York: Farrar, Straus and Giroux.

Kahneman, Daniel, and Shane Frederick. 2004. "Attribute Substitution in Intuitive Judgment." In *Models of a Man: Essays in Memory of Herbert A. Simon*, edited by Mie Augier and James G. March, 411–32. Cambridge, MA.: MIT Press.

Kambouchner, Denis. 2014. "Le cas Élisabeth: Générosité et Mélancolie." In *Élisabeth de Bohême face à Descartes: Deux philosophes?,* edited by Delphine Kolesnik-Antoine and Marie-Frédérique Pellegrin, 1139–53. Paris: J. Vrin.

Kant, Immanuel. 1797/1996. "Metaphysics of Morals." In *Practical Philosophy*, edited by Mary J. Gregor, and Allen W. Wood, 353–604. Cambridge: Cambridge University Press.

———. 2007. *Anthropology, History, and Education*. Edited by Robert B. Louden, and Günter Zöller. Cambridge: Cambridge University Press.

Kelley, H. H. 1967. "Attribution Theory in Social Psychology." *Nebraska Symposium on Motivation* 15: 192–238. Lincoln: University of Nebraska Press.

Kelly, Daniel. 2021. "Charlie Kurth, *The Anxious Mind*." *Ethics* 132: 249–55.

Kendall, Phillip C., and Rick E. Ingram. 1989. "Cognitive-Behavioral Perspectives: Theory and Research on Depression and Anxiety." In *Personality, Psychopathology, and Psychotherapy. Anxiety and Depression: Distinctive and Overlapping Features,* edited by Phillip C. Kendall and D. Watson, 27–53. Cambridge, MA: Academic Press.

Kierkegaard, Søren. 1980. *The Concept of Anxiety*. Edited and Translated by Reidar Thomte. Princeton: Princeton University Press.

Kim Yung Sik. 2015. "Zhu Xi on Scientific and Occult Subjects: Defining and Extending the Boundaries of Confucian Learning." In *Returning to Zhu Xi: Emerging Patterns Within the Supreme Polarity*, edited by David Jones and Jinli He, 121–46. Albany: SUNY Press.

Kind, Amy. 2013. "The Case Against Representationalism About Moods." In *Current Controversies in Philosophy of Mind*, edited by Uriah Kriegel, 113–34. New York: Routledge.

King, Martin Luther, Jr. 1967. "Beyond Vietnam: A Time to Break Silence." Riverside Church, New York City. American Rhetoric: Online Speech Bank. Accessed May 8, 2017. http://www.americanrhetoric.com/speeches/mlkatimetobreaksilence.htm.

———. 1998. *The Autobiography of Martin Luther King, Jr.* Edited by Clayborne Carson. New York: Warner Books.

Kingma, Elselijn. 2007. "What Is It to Be Healthy?" *Analysis* 67: 128–33.

———. 2013. "Health and Disease: Social Constructivism as a Combination of Naturalism and Normativism." In *Health, Illness and Disease: Philosophical Essays*, edited by Havi Carel and Rachel Cooper, 37–56. New York: Routledge.

Kitcher, Phillip. 2011. *The Ethical Project*. Cambridge, MA: Harvard University Press.

Kiverstein, Julian. 2015. "Empathy and the Responsiveness to Social Affordances." *Consciousness and Cognition* 36: 532–42.

Kiverstein, Julian, and Erik Rietveld. 2021. "Scaling-up Skilled Intentionality to Linguistic Thought." *Synthese* 198: 175–94.

Kleinman, Arthur. 1980. *Patients and Healers in the Context of Culture*. Berkeley: University of California Press.

Knuuttila, Simo. 2004. *Emotions in Ancient and Medieval Philosophy*. Oxford: Clarendon Press.

Kool, Wouter, Fiery A. Cushman , and Samual J. Gershman. 2016. "When Does Model-Based Control Pay Off?" *PLoS Computational Biology* 12: e1005090.

Koriat, Asher. 2000. "The Feeling of Knowing: Some Metatheoretical Implications for Consciousness and Control." *Consciousness and Cognition* 9: 149–71.

Kostić, Milutin, Anna Munjiza, Danilo Pesic, Amir Peljto, Ivana Novakovic, Valerija Dobricic, Dusica Lecic Tosevski, and Millija Mijajlovic. 2017. "A Pilot Study on Predictors of Brainstem Raphe Abnormality in Patients with Major Depressive Disorder." *Journal of Affective Disorders* 209: 66–70.

Kovach, Bill, and Rom Rosenstiel. 1999. *Warp Speed: America in the Age of Mixed Media*. New York: Century Foundation Press.

Kramer, Peter. 1993. *Listening to Prozac. A Psychiatrist Explores Antidepressant Drugs and the Remaking of the Self*. New York: Viking.

Kreuger, Joel. 2011. "Extended Cognition and the Space of Social Interaction." *Consciousness and Cognition* 20: 647–57.

Kristjánsson, Kristjan. 2018. *Virtuous Emotions*. Oxford: Oxford University Press.

Kruglanski, Arie W. 1990. "Lay Epistemic Theory in Social-Cognitive Psychology." *Psychological Inquiry* 1: 181–97.

Kruglanski, Arie W., et al. 2009. "Three Decades of Lay Epistemics: The Why, How, and Who of Knowledge Formation." *European Review of Social Psychology* 20: 146–91.

Kunda, Ziva. 1990. "The Case for Motivated Reasoning." *Psychological Bulletin* 108 (3): 480.

Kurth, Charlie. 2015. "Moral Anxiety and Moral Agency." In *Oxford Studies in Normative Ethics*, edited by Mark Timmons, 171–95. Oxford: Oxford University Press.

———. 2016. "Anxiety, Normative Uncertainty, and Social Regulation." *Biology and Philosophy* 31: 1–21.

———. 2018. *The Anxious Mind: An Investigation into the Varieties and Virtues of Anxiety*. Cambridge, MA.: MIT Press

. 2018. "Emotion, Deliberation, and the Skill Model of Virtuous Agency." *Mind and Language* 33: 299–317.

———. 2018. "Anxiety: A Case Study in the Value of Negative Emotion." In *Shadows of the Soul: Philosophical Perspectives on Negative Emotions*, edited by Christine Tappolet, Fabrice Teroni, and Anita Ziv Konzelmann, 95–104. New York: Routledge.

———. 2019. "Politicians, Policy, and Anxiety." *Center for the Study of Ethics and Society Papers* 25: 1–19.

———. 2022. "Inappropriate Emotions, Marginalization, and Feeling Better." *Synthese* 200: 155.

Kurth, Charlie, and Panu Pihkala. 2022. "Eco-anxiety: What It Is and Why It Matters." *Frontiers in Psychology* 13:981814.

Kvarven, Amanda, Erik Strømland, Conny Wollbrant, David Andersson, Magnus Johannesson, Gustav Tinghög, Daniel Västfjäll, and Kristian Ove R. Myrseth. 2020. "The Intuitive Cooperation Hypothesis Revisited." *Journal of the Economic Science Association* 6: 26–42.

Lacewing, Michael 2005. "Emotional Self-Awareness and Ethical Deliberation." *Ratio*, 18: 65–81.

Lange, Marc. 2007. "The End of Diseases." *Philosophical Topics* 35: 265–92.

Larsen, Randy J., and Zvjezdana Prizmic. 2008. "Regulation of Emotional Well-Being: Overcoming the Hedonic Treadmill." In *The Science of Subjective Well-Being*, edited by Michael Eid and Randy J. Larsen, 258–89. New York: Guilford Press.

Lauria, Federico. (forthcoming). "Interest and the Affective Springs of Inquiry—The '*Chiaroscuro*' Epistemic Emotion."

Leary, Mark, and Robin Mark Kowalski. 1995. *Social Anxiety*. New York: Guilford Press.

LeDoux, Joseph. 2016. *Anxious: Using the Brain to Understand and Treat Fear and Anxiety*. London: Penguin.

Lee, Jennifer, Daniel Waldeck, Andrew Holliman, Moitree Banerjee, and Ian Tyndall. 2022. "Feeling Socially Anxious at University: An Interpretative Phenomenological Analysis." *The Qualitative Report* 27: 897–919.

Lee, Michael D., and Tarrant D, Cummins. 2004. "Evidence Accumulation in Decision Making: Unifying the 'Take the Best' and the 'Rational' Models. *Psychonomic Bulletin and Review* 11: 343–52.

Leknes, Siri, and Brock Bastian. 2014. "The Benefits of Pain." *Review of Philosophy and Psychology* 5: 57–70.

Liebow, Nabina, and Trip Glazer. 2019. "White Tears: Emotion Regulation and White Fragility." *Inquiry* 66: 122–42.

Liji 禮記. 2011. In *Chinese Text Project*, edited by Donald Sturgeon. https://ctext.org/liji/zh.

Lin, Muyu, Stefan G. Hofmann, Mingyi Qian, Shelley Kind, and Hongyu Yu. 2016. "Attention Allocation in Social Anxiety During a Speech." *Cognition and Emotion* 30: 1122–36.

Liu, JeeLoo. 2011. "The Is-Ought Correlation in Neo-Confucian Qi-Realism: How Normative Facts Exist in Natural States of Qi." *Contemporary Chinese Thought* 42: 60–77.

———. 2014. "Was There Something in Nothingness? The Debate on the Primordial State between Daoism and Neo-Confucianism." In *Nothingness in Asian Philosophy*, edited by JeeLoo Liu and Douglas L. Berger, 181–96, New York: Routledge.

———. 2018. *Neo-Confucianism: Metaphysics, Mind, and Morality*. Malden, MA: Wiley.

Lormand, Eric. 1985. "Toward a Theory of Moods." *Philosophical Studies* 47: 385–407.

Lunyu 論語. 2011. In *Chinese Text Project*, edited by Donald Sturgeon. https://ctext.org/analects/zh.

Lutz, Catherine. 1988. *Unnatural Emotions: Everyday Sentiments on a Micronesian Atoll and Their Challenge to Western Theory*. Chicago: University of Chicago Press.

Lyons, William. 1980. *Emotion*. Cambridge: Cambridge University Press.

MacKuen, Michael, Jennifer Wolak, Luke Keele, and George E. Marcus. 2010. "Civil Engagements: Resolute Partisanship or Reflective Deliberation." *American Journal of Political Science* 54: 440–58.

Maibom, Heidi. 2005. "Moral Unreason: The Case of Psychopathy." *Mind and Language* 20: 237–57.

———. 2022. "Don't Worry, Be Happy?" *Synthese* 200: 67.

Maiese, Michelle. 2021. "Enactivism, the Field of Affordances, and Mental Disorder." *Journal of Mind and Behavior* 42: 175–96.

Mancini, Anthony D., George A. Bonanno, and Andrew E. Clark. 2011. "Stepping Off the Hedonic Treadmill. Individual Differences in Response to Major Life Events." *Journal of Individual Differences* 32: 144–52.

Marcus, George E., Michael MacKuen, and Russell W. Neuman. 2011. "Parsimony and Complexity: Developing and Testing Theories of Affective Intelligence." *Political Psychology* 32: 323–36.

Marcus, George E., Russell W. Neuman, and Michael MacKuen. 2000. *Affective Intelligence and Political Judgment*. Chicago: University of Chicago Press.

Marcus Aurelius. 2013. *Meditations*. Translated by Christopher Gill. Oxford: Oxford University Press.

Margolis, Joseph. 1966. *Psychotherapy and Morality: A Study of Two Concepts*. New York: Random House.

———. 1976. "The Concept of Disease." *Journal of Medicine and Philosophy* 1: 238–55.

Marques, Luana, Donald J. Robinaugh, Nicole J. LeBlanc, and Devon Hinton. 2011. "Cross Cultural Variations in the Prevalence and Presentation of Anxiety Disorders." *Expert Review of Neurotherapeutics* 11: 313–22.

Marguia, Edward, and Kim Díaz. 2015. "The Philosophical Foundations of Cognitive Behavioral Therapy: Stoicism, Buddhism, Taoism, and Existentialism." *Journal of Evidence-Based Psychotherapies* 15: 39–52.

Martínez, Róger Marcelo, Chin-Yau Chen , Cheng Tsai-Tsen Liao , Yawei Cheng, Yang-Ten Fan, Shih Han Chou, and Chenyi Chen. 2020. "The Multifaceted Effects of Serotonin Transporter Polymorphism (5-HTTLPR) on Anxiety, Implicit Moral Attitudes, and Harmful Behaviors." *Frontiers in Psychology* 11: 1521.

Mealey, Linda. 1995. "The Sociobiology of Sociopathy: An Integrated Evolutionary Model." *Behavioral and Brain Sciences* 18: 523–41.

Mendelovici, Angela. 2013. "Intentionalism about Moods." *Thought: A Journal of Philosophy* 2: 126–36.

Mental Health America. 2023. "Policy Agenda: 2023." https://mhanational.org/policy-issues.

Mertz-Weigel, Dorothée. 2005. *Figuring Melancholy: From Jean de Meun to Molière, Via Montaigne, Descartes, Rotrou and Corneille.* Columbus: Ohio State University Press.

Meynen, Gerben. 2011. "Generalized Anxiety Disorder and Online Intelligence: A Phenomenological Account of Why Worrying Is Unhelpful." *Philosophy, Ethics, and Humanities in Medicine* 6: 1–7.

Miceli, Maria, and Cristiano Castelfranchi. 2005. "Anxiety as an 'Epistemic' Emotion: An Uncertainty Theory of Anxiety." *Anxiety, Stress, and Coping* 18: 291–319.

———. 2015. *Expectancy and Emotion*. Oxford: Oxford University Press.

Morris, W. N. 1989. *Mood: The Frame of Mind*. Berlin: Springer.

Morton, Adam. 2010. "Epistemic Emotions." In *The Oxford Handbook of Philosophy of Emotion*, edited by Peter Goldie, 385–400. New York: Oxford University Press.

Moscowitz, Eva. 2001. *In Therapy We Trust: America's Obsession with Self-Fulfillment*. Baltimore: Johns Hopkins University Press.

Moser, Susanne C. 2019. "Not for the Faint of Heart." In *Climate and Culture*, edited by Giuseppe Feola, Hilary Geoghegan, and Alex Arnall, 141–67. Cambridge: Cambridge University Press.

Mulligan, Kevin. 1998. "From Appropriate Emotions to Values." *The Monist* 81: 161–88.

Munch-Jurisic, Ditte Marie. 2020. "The Right to Feel Comfortable." *Ethical Theory and Moral Practice* 23: 237–50.

———. 2022. "Lost for Words: Anxiety, Well-Being, and the Costs of Conceptual Deprivation." *Synthese* 199: 13583–600.

Murphy, Dominic. 2012. *Psychiatry in the Scientific Image*. Cambridge, MA: MIT Press.

Naar, Hichem. 2018. "Sentiments." In *The Ontology of Emotions*, edited by Hichem Naar and Fabrice Teroni, 149–68. Cambridge: Cambridge University Press.

———. Forthcoming. "What Ontology for Emotions?" In *Emotion Theory: The Comprehensive Routledge Guide*, edited by Andrea Scarantino. New York: Routledge.

Nabi, Robin L., Abel Gustafson, and Risa Jensen. 2018. "Framing Climate Change: Exploring the Role of Emotion in Generating Advocacy Behavior." *Science Communication* 4: 442–68.

Nagel, Jennifer. 2010. "Epistemic Anxiety and Adaptive Invariantism." *Philosophical Perspectives* 24: 407–35.

Newell, Ben R. 2005. "Re-visions of Rationality?" *Trends in Cognitive Sciences* 9: 11–15.

Newton, Lillith. 2022. "Epistemic Anxiety and Epistemic Risk." *Synthese* 200: 1–23.

Nickerson, Raymond S. 1998. "Confirmation Bias: A Ubiquitous Phenomenon in Many Guises." *Review of General Psychology* 2.2: 175–220.

Nichols, Shaun. 2004. *Sentimental Rules*. Oxford: Oxford University Press.

Norton, Alice R., and Maree J. Abbott. 2016. "Self-Focused Cognition in Social Anxiety: A Review of the Theoretical and Empirical Literature." *Behavior Change* 33: 44–64.

Oatley, Keith, and P. N. Johnson-Laird. 1990. "Semantic Primitives for Emotions: A Reply to Ortony and Clore." *Cognition and Emotion* 4 (2): 129–43.

Odgerel, Z., A. Talati, S. P. Hamilton, D. F. Levinson, and M. M. Weissman. 2013. "Genotyping Serotonin Transporter Polymorphisms 5-HTTLPR and rs25531 in European- and African-American Subjects from the National Institute of Mental Health's Collaborative Center for Genomic Studies." *Translational Psychiatry* 3(9), e307.

Ojala, Maria. 2012. "Regulating Worry, Promoting Hope." *International Journal of Environmental Science Education* 7: 537–61.

Olatunji, Bunmi O., Jonathan S. Abramowitz, Nathan L. Williams, Kevin M. Connolly, Jeffrey M. Lohr. 2007. "Scrupulosity and Obsessive-Compulsive Symptoms." *Journal of Anxiety Disorders* 21: 771–87.

Oliver, Michael. 1990. *The Politics of Disablement*. London: Palgrave Macmillan.

Owens, Howard, and Jerrold S. Maxmen. 1979. "Mood and Affect: A Semantic Confusion." *The American Journal of Psychiatry* 136 (1): 97–99.

Patriquin, Michelle A., and Sanjay J. Mathew. 2017. "The Neurobiological Mechanisms of Generalized Anxiety Disorder and Chronic Stress." *Chronic Stress* 1: 1–10.

Pearson, Patricia. 2007. *A Brief History of Anxiety (Yours and Mine)*. Toronto: Random House.

Pekrun, Reinhard, and Lisa Linnenbrink-Garcia. 2012. "Academic Emotions and Student Engagement." In *Handbook of Research on Student Engagement*, edited by Sandra L. Christenson, Amy L. Reschly, and Cathy Wylie, 259–82. Boston: Springer.

Pekrun, Reinhard, Elizabeth Vogl, Krista R. Muis, and Gale M. Sinatra. 2017. "Measuring Emotions During Epistemic Activities: the Epistemically-Related Emotion Scales." *Cognition and Emotion* 31: 1268–76.

Penson, William J. 2015. "Unsettling Impairment: Mental Health and the Social Model of Disability." In *Madness, Distress, and the Politics of Disablement*, edited by Helen Spandler, Jill Anderson, and Bob Sapey, 57–66. Bristol, UK.: Bristol University Press.

Pickard, Hannah. 2009. "Mental Illness Is Indeed a Myth." In *Psychiatry as Cognitive Neuroscience*, edited by Matthew R. Broome and Lisa L. Bortolotti, 82–102. Oxford: Oxford University Press.

Pigliucci, Massimo, and Gregory Lopez. 2019. *A Handbook for New Stoics—How to Thrive in a World Out of Your Control. 52 Week-by-Week Lessons.* New York: The Experiment.

Pihkala, Panu. 2021. "Eco-Anxiety." In *Situating Sustainability: A Handbook of Contexts and Concepts*, edited by Parker C. Krieg and R. Toivanen, 119–34. Helsinki: Helsinki University Press.

Pijpers, Jan Robert, Raoul R. D. Oudejans, Frank C. Bakker, and Peter J. Beek. 2006. "The Role of Anxiety in Perceiving and Realizing Affordances." *Ecological Psychology* 18: 131–61.

Price, Carolyn. 2006. "Affect Without Object: Moods and Objectless Emotions." *European Journal of Analytic Philosophy* 2 (1): 49–68.

Prinz, Jesse J. 2004. *Gut Reactions: A Perceptual Theory of the Emotions*. New York: Oxford University Press.

———. 2012. *Beyond Human Nature: How Culture and Experience Shape the Human Mind*. New York: W.W. Norton.

Pritchard, Duncan. 2005. *Epistemic Luck*. Oxford: Clarendon Press.

Proust, Joëlle. 2009. "Is There a Sense of Agency of Thought?" In *Mental Actions and Agency*, edited by Lucy O'Brien and Matthew Soteriou, 253–75. Oxford: Oxford University Press.

Puett, Michael J. 2004. *To Become a God: Cosmology, Sacrifice, and Self-Divinization in Early China*. Cambridge, MA.: Harvard University Press.

Railton, Peter. 1986. "Moral Realism." *Philosophical Review* 95: 163–97.

———. 2009. "Practical Competence and Fluent Agency." In *Reasons for Action*, edited by David Sobel and Steven Wall, 81–115. New York: Cambridge University Press.

Ramstead, Maxwell J. D., Samuel P. L. Veissiere, and Laurence J.Kirmayer, 2016. "Cultural Affordances: Scaffolding Local Worlds Through Shared Intentionality and Regimes of Attention." *Frontiers in Psychology* 7 (1090), 1–21.

Rand, David G. 2019. "Intuition, Deliberation, and Cooperation: Further Meta-Analytic Evidence from 91 Experiments on Pure Cooperation." Available at SSRN 3390018. Retrieved from http://dx.doi.org/10.2139/ssrn.3390018.

Rand, David G., Joshua D. Greene, and Martin A. Nowak. 2012. "Spontaneous Giving and Calculated Greed." *Nature* 489: 427–30.

Ratcliffe, Matthew. 2005. "The Feeling of Being." *Journal of Consciousness Studies* 12: 43–60.

———. 2008. *Feelings of Being: Phenomenology, Psychiatry and the Sense of Reality*. Oxford: Oxford University Press.

———. 2015. "The Interpersonal World of Psychosis." *World Psychiatry* 14(2): 176.

———. 2017. *Real Hallucinations: Psychiatric Illness, Intentionality, and the Interpersonal World*. Cambridge, MA: MIT Press.

Ratcliffe, Matthew, Mark Ruddell, and Benedict Smith. 2014. "What Is a 'Sense of Foreshortened Future?' A Phenomenological Study of Trauma, Trust, and Time." *Frontiers in Psychology*: 1026.

Rebughini, Paola. 2021. "A Sociology of Anxiety: Western Modern Legacy and the Covid-19 Outbreak." *International Sociology* 36: 554–68.

Rickett, W. Allyn (trans). 1998. *Guanzi: Political, Economic, and Philosophical Essays from Early China*. Vol. 2. Princeton: Princeton University Press.

Rietveld, Erik. 2012. "Bodily Intentionality and Social Affordances in Context." In *Consciousness in Interaction: The Role of the Natural and Social Context in Shaping Consciousness*, edited by Fabio Paglieri, 207–26. Amsterdam: John Benjamins Publishing.

Rietveld, Erik, and Julian Kiverstein. 2014. "A Rich Landscape of Affordances." *Ecological Psychology* 26: 325–52.
Rietveld, Erik, Damiaan Denys, and Maarten van Westen. 2018. "Ecological-Enactive Cognition as Engaging with a Field of Relevant Affordances: The Skilled Intentionality Framework (SIF)." In *The Oxford Handbook of 4e Cognition*, edited by Albert Newen, Leon de Bruin, and Shaun Gallagher, 41–70. Oxford: Oxford University Press.
Rietveld, Erik, Ronald Rietveld, and Janno Martens. 2019. "Trusted Strangers: Social Affordances for Social Cohesion." *Phenomenology and the Cognitive Sciences* 18: 299–316.
Roberts, Robert C. 2003. *Emotions: An Essay in Aid of Moral Psychology*. Cambridge: Cambridge University Press.
Roberts, Robert C., and Jay W. Wood. 2007. *Intellectual Virtues: An Essay in Regulative Epistemology*. Oxford: Clarendon Press.
Roberts, Tom, and Lucy Osler. 2023. "Social Doubt." *Journal of the American Philosophical Association*, 1–18.
Robertson, Donald. 2019. *The Philosophy of Cognitive-Behavioral Therapy (CBT): Stoic Philosophy as Rational and Cognitive Psychotherapy*. New York: Routledge.
Robinson, Andrew. 2011. *Genius: A Very Short Introduction*. Oxford: Oxford University Press.
Rodriguez, Benjamin F., Risa B. Weisberg, Maria E. Pagano, Steven E. Bruce, Michael A. Spencer, Larry Culpepper, and Martin B. Keller. 2006. "Characteristics and Predictors of Full and Partial Recovery from Generalized Anxiety Disorder in Primary Care Patients." *Journal of Nervous and Mental Disease* 194: 91–97.
Roets, Arne, Arie W. Kruglanski, Malgorzata Kossowska, Antonio Pierro, and Ying-Yi Hong. 2015. "The Motivated Gatekeeper of Our Minds: New Directions in Need for Closure Theory and Research." In *Advances in Experimental Social Psychology* 52, 221–283. Cambridge, MA: Academic Press.
Roskies, Adina. 2003. "Are Ethical Judgments Intrinsically Motivational? Lessons from 'Acquired sociopathy.'" *Philosophical Psychology* 16: 51–66.
Rossi, Mauro. 2021. "A Perceptual Theory of Moods." *Synthese* 198(8): 7119–47.
———. Forthcoming a. "An Evaluativist Theory of Sensory Pleasures."
———. Forthcoming b. "What is Loneliness? Towards a Receptive Account."
Roth, Harold D. 1999. *Original Tao*. New York: Columbia University Press.
Ruscio, Ayelet Meron, Lauren Hallion, Carmen C. Lim, et al. 2017. "Cross-Sectional Comparison of the Epidemiology of *DSM-5* Generalized Anxiety Disorder Across the Globe." *JAMA Psychiatry* 74: 465–75.
Ruscio, Ayelet Meron, Timothy A. Brown, Wai Tat Chiu, Jitender Sareen, Murray B. Stein, and Ronald C. Kessler. 2008. "Social Fears and Social Phobia in the USA: Results from the National Comorbidity Survey Replication." *Psychological Medicine* 38: 15–28.
Rutherford, Donald. 2004. "On the Happy Life: Descartes vis-à-vis Seneca." *In Stoicism: Traditions and Transformations*, edited by Steven K. Strange and Jack Zupko, 177–97. Cambridge: Cambridge University Press.

———. 2014. "Reading Descartes as a Stoic: Appropriate Actions, Virtue, and the Passions." *Philosophie Antique* 14: 129–55.

Salerno, Steve. 2005. *SHAM: How the Self-Help Movement Made America Helpless*. New York: Crown Publishers.

Samuelson, Peter L., and Ian M. Church. 2015. "When Cognition Turns Vicious: Heuristics and Biases in Light of Virtue Epistemology." *Philosophical Psychology* 28: 1095–1113.

Sander, David. 2013. "Models of Emotion: The Affective Neuroscience Approach." In *The Cambridge Handbook of Human Affective Neuroscience*, edited by Jorge Armony and Patrik Vuilleumier, 5–53. Cambridge: Cambridge University Press.

Scarantino, Andrea, and Ronald de Sousa. 2018. "Emotion." In *Stanford Encyclopedia of Philosophy*, edited by Edward N. Zalta. https://plato.stanford.edu/entries/emotion/.

Schmitter, Amy. 2002. "Descartes and the Primacy of Practice: The Role of the Passions in the Search for Truth." *Philosophical Studies* 46: 99–108.

Schneck, Ariane Căcilie. 2019. "Elisabeth of Bohemia's Neo-Peripatetic Account of the Emotions." *British Journal for the History of Philosophy* 27: 753–70.

Schwartz, Bennet, and Janet Metcalfe. 2014. "Tip-of-the-Tongue (TOT) States: Mechanisms and Metacognitive Control." In *Tip-of-the-Tongue States and Related Phenomena*, edited by Bennet L. Schwartz, and Alan S. Brown, 15–31. Cambridge: Cambridge University Press.

Scott, Erin L., Winnie Eng, and Richard G. Heimberg. 2002. "Ethnic Differences in Worry in a Nonclinical Population." *Depression and Anxiety* 15: 79–82.

Self, John. 2022. "The Rise and Fall of Sad, White Men." *The Critic* (July 2022). https://thecritic.co.uk/issues/july-2022/the-rise-and-fall-of-sad-white-men/.

Seneca, Lucius Annaeus. 2014. *Hardship and Happiness*. Translated and edited by Gareth D. Williams. Chicago: University of Chicago Press.

———. 2015. *Letters on Ethics: To Lucilius*. Translated and edited by Margaret Graver and A. A. Long. Chicago: University of Chicago Press.

Shapiro, Lisa. 1999. "Princess Elizabeth and Descartes: The Union of Soul and Body and the Practice of Philosophy." *British Journal for the History of Philosophy* 7: 503–20.

———. 2014. "Je ne Regrette Rien: Élisabeth, Descartes et la Psychologie Morale du Regret." In *Élisabeth de Bohême face à Descartes: Deux philosophes?*, edited by Delphine Kolesnik-Antoine and Marie-Frédérique Pellegrin, 155–69. Paris: J. Vrin.

———. (ed. and trans.) 2007. *The Correspondence Between Princess Elisabeth of Bohemia and René Descartes*. Chicago: University of Chicago Press.

Shepherd, Joshua. 2019. "*The Anxious Mind: An Investigation into the Varieties and Virtues of Anxiety*, by Charlie Kurth." *Mind* 128: 1337–44.

Shorter, Edward. 1994. *From the Mind into the Body: The Cultural Origins of Psychosomatic Symptoms*. New York: Free Press.

Siemer, M. 2009. "Mood Experience: Implications of a Dispositional Theory of Moods." *Emotion Review* 1 (3): 256–63.

Silvia, Paul J. 2010. "Confusion and Interest: The Role of Knowledge Emotions in Aesthetic Experience." *Psychology of Aesthetics, Creativity, and the Arts* 4: 75–80.

Simeon, Daphne, and Jeffrey Abugel. 2006. *Feeling Unreal: Depersonalization Disorder and the Loss of the Self.* New York: Oxford University Press.

Sims, Laura, Rhéa Rocque, and Marie-Élaine Desmarais. 2020. "Enabling Students to Face the Environmental Crisis and Climate Change with Resilience." *International Journal of Sustainability in Higher Education* 3: 112–31.

Sizer, Laura. 2000. "Towards a computational theory of mood." *British Journal for the Philosophy of Science* (4): 743–70.

Slaby, Jan. 2012. "Affective Self-Construal and the Sense of Ability." *Emotion Review* 4: 151–56.

Slaby, Jan, Asena Paskaleva, and Achim Stephan. 2013. "Enactive Emotion and Impaired Agency in Depression." *Journal of Consciousness Studies* 20: 33–55.

Sloman, Steven A. 2002. "Two Systems of Reasoning." In *Heuristics and Biases: The Psychology of Intuitive Judgment*, edited by Thomas Gilovich, Dale Griffin, and Daniel Kahneman, 379–96. Cambridge: Cambridge University Press.

Solomon, Robert C. 1976/1993. *The Passions: Emotions and the Meaning of Life.* Indianapolis: Hackett Publishing Company.

Sommers, Christina Hoff, and Sally Satel. 2005. *One Nation Under Therapy: How the Helping Culture Is Eroding Self-Reliance*. New York: St. Martin's Press.

Songhorian, Sarah. 2022. "Adam Smith's Relevance for Contemporary Moral Cognition." *Philosophical Psychology* 35: 662–83.

Sosa, Ernest. 1999. "How to Defeat Opposition to Moore." *Philosophical Perspectives* 13: 141–53.

———. 2007. *A Virtue Epistemology: Apt Belief and Reflective Knowledge*, volume I. Oxford: Clarendon Press.

Stanghellini, Giovanni. 2004. *Disembodied Spirits and Deanimated Bodies: The Psychopathology of Common Sense*. Oxford: Oxford University Press.

Stanley, Jason. 2005. *Knowledge and Practical Interests*. Oxford: Clarendon Press.

Stanovich, Keith E., and Richard F. West. 1997. "Reasoning Independently of Prior Belief and Individual Differences in Actively Open-Minded Thinking." *Journal of Educational Psychology* 89: 342–57.

———. 2000. "Individual Differences in Reasoning: Implications for the Rationality Debate." *Behavioral and Brain Sciences* 23: 645–65.

Stosny, Steven. 2021. "How Social Media Differences Can Warp Relationships." *Psychology Today* (23 June 2021).

Stossel, Scott. 2013. *My Age of Anxiety: Fear, Hope, Dread, and the Search for Peace of Mind.* New York: Vintage Books.

Sweeny, Kate, and Michael D. Dooley. 2017. "The Surprising Upsides of Worry." *Social and Personality Psychology Compass* 11:e12311.

Szasz, Thomas. 1960. "The Myth of Mental Illness." *American Psychologist* 15: 113–18.

———. 1974. *The Myth of Mental Illness: Foundations of a Theory of Personal Conduct* (Revised edition). New York: Harper & Row.

Tappolet, Christine. 2015. "Value and Emotions." In *The Oxford Handbook of Value Theory*, edited by Iwao Hirose and Jonas Olson, 80–95. Oxford: Oxford University Press.

———. 2016. *Emotions, Values, and Agency*. Oxford: Oxford University Press.

———. 2018. "The Metaphysics of Moods." In *The Ontology of Emotions*, edited by Hichem Naar and Fabrice Teroni, 169–86. Cambridge: Cambridge University Press.

———. 2022. *Philosophy of Emotion: A Contemporary Introduction*. New York: Routledge.

Thomas, Carol. 1999. *Female Forms: Experiencing and Understanding Disability*. London: Open University Press.

Thomson, Valerie. 2008. "Dual-Process Theories: a Metacognitive Perspective." In *In Two Minds: Dual Processes and Beyond*, edited by Jonathan Evans and Keith Frankish, 171–95. Oxford: Oxford University Press.

Tiberius, Valerie. 2008. *The Reflective Life: Living Wisely Within Our Limits*. New York: Oxford University Press.

Todd, Peter M., and Gerd Gigerenzer. 2000. "Précis of Simple Heuristics That Make Us Smart." *Behavioral and Brain Sciences* 23: 727–41.

Tone, Andrea. 2009. *The Age of Anxiety: America's Turbulent Affair with Tranquilizers*. New York: Basic Books.

Tremain, Shelley. 2001. "On the Government of Disability." *Social Theory and Practice* 27: 617–36.

———. 2017. *Foucault and Feminist Philosophy of Disability*. Ann Arbor: University of Michigan Press.

Tversky, Amos, and Daniel Kahneman, Daniel. 1973. "Availability: A Heuristic for Judging Frequency and Probability." *Cognitive Psychology* 5: 207–32.

Twenge, Jean M. 2017. "Have Smartphones Destroyed a Generation?" *The Atlantic* (September 2017).

University of Rhode Island. 2021. "Researchers find Pandemic Exacerbates Anxiety, Depression, Impulsivity and Lack of Mindfulness among Faculty." *Rhody Today* (29 January 2021). https://www.uri.edu/news/2021/01/researchers-find-pandemic-exacerbates-anxiety-depression-impulsivity-and-lack-of-mindfulness-among-faculty/.

Valentino, Nicholas, Vincent Hutchings, Antoine Banks, and Anne Davis. 2008. "Is a Worried Citizen a Good Citizen?" *Political Psychology* 29: 247–73.

Van Dijk, Ludger, and Erik Rietveld. 2017. "Foregrounding Sociomaterial Practice in Our Understanding of Affordances: The Skilled Intentionality Framework." *Frontiers in Psychology* 7.

Van Norden, Bryan W., trans. 2001. "Mengzi (Mencius)." In *Readings in Classical Chinese Philosophy*, edited by Philip J. Ivanhoe and Bryan W. Van Norden, 115–59. Indianapolis: Hackett.

Vargas, Manuel, and John Doris. 2022. "Introduction." In *The Oxford Handbook of Moral Psychology,* edited by Manuel Vargas and John Doris, 1–5. Oxford: Oxford University Press.

Vazard, Juliette. 2021. "(Un)reasonable Doubt as Affective Experience: Obsessive-Compulsive Disorder, Epistemic Anxiety and the Feeling of Uncertainty." *Synthese* 198: 6917–34.

———. 2022. "Everyday Anxious Doubt." *Synthese* 200 (3): 1–19.

Vazard, Juliette, and Catherine Audrin. 2022. "The Noetic Feeling of Confusion." *Philosophical Psychology* 35: 757–70.
Vazard, Juliette, and Charlie Kurth. 2022. "Apprehending Anxiety: An Introduction to the Topical Collection on Worry and Wellbeing." *Synthese* 200 (4): 1–17.
Vesga-López, Oriana, Franklin R. Schneier, SAmuel Wang, Richard G. Heimberg, Shang Min Liu, Deborah S. Hasin, and Carlos Blanco. 2008. "Gender Differences in Generalized Anxiety Disorder: Results From the National Epidemiologic Survey on Alcohol and Related Conditions (NESARC)." *The Journal of Clinical Psychiatry* 69: 1606–16.
Wakefield, J. C. 1992. "The Concept of Mental Disorder: On the Boundary Between Biological Facts and Social Values." *American Psychologist* 47: 373–88.
———. 2021. "Must Social Values Play a Role in the Harm Component of the Harmful Dysfunction Analysis? Reply to Rachel Cooper." In *Defining Mental Disorder: Jerome Wakefield and His Critics*, edited by Luc Faucher and Denis Forest, 553–76. Cambridge, MA.: The MIT Press.
Watson, Lani. 2018. "Curiosity and Inquisitiveness." In *The Routledge Handbook of Virtue Epistemology*, edited by Heather Batally, 155–66. New York: Routledge.
Wheeler, Michael. 2005. *Reconstructing the Cognitive World: The Next Step*. Cambridge, MA.: The MIT Press.
Whitcomb, Dennis. 2010. "Curiosity Was Framed." *Philosophy and Phenomenological Research* 81: 664–87.
Wierzbicka, Anna. 1992. *Semantics, Culture, and Cognition: Universal Human Concepts in Culture-Specific Configurations*. New York: Oxford University Press.
Williams, Bernard. 1981. "Persons, Character, and Morality." In *Moral Luck*. New York: Cambridge University Press.
Williamson, Timothy. 2002. *Knowledge and Its Limits*. Oxford: Oxford University Press.
Wilson, Robert C., Andra Geana, John M. White, Elliot A. Ludvig, and Jonathan D.Cohen. 2014. "Humans Use Directed and Random Exploration to Solve the Explore-Exploit Dilemma." *Journal of Experimental Psychology, General*. 143: 2074–81.
Wittchen, H., and E. Beloch. 1996. "The Impact of Social Phobia on Quality of Life." *International Clinical Psychopharmacology* 11(Suppl. 3): 15–23.
Witte, Kim, and Mike Allen. 2000. "A Meta-Analysis of Fear Appeals." *Health Education and Behavior* 27: 591–615.
Wolf, Susan. 1992. "Moral Saints." *Journal of Philosophy* 79: 419–39.
Wordsman, Scott. 2021. "Trump, AOC, and the Triumph of Trauma Politics." *Tablet* (11 March 2021). https://www.tabletmag.com/sections/news/articles/triumph-of-trauma-politics.
Wunderlich, Klaus, Peter Smittenaar, and Raymond Dolan. 2012. "Dopamine Enhances Model-Based over Model-Free Choice Behavior." *Neuron* 75: 418–24.
Xie, Dong. 2020. "Cultural Perspectives in Understanding, Treating, and Studying: Worry and Generalized Anxiety Disorder (GAD)." In *Generalized Anxiety Disorder and Worrying: A Comprehensive Handbook for Clinicians and*

Researchers, edited by A. L. Gerlach and A. T. Gloster, 173–201. London: Wiley Blackwell.

Yang, Janet Z., and LeeAnn Kahlor. 2013. "What, Me Worry?: The Role of Affect in Information Seeking and Avoidance." *Science Communication* 35: 189–212.

Yoon, K. Lira, and Richard E. Zinbarg. 2007. "Generalized Anxiety Disorder and Entry into Marriage or a Marriage-like Relationship." *Journal of Anxiety Disorders* 21: 955–65.

Zagzebski, Linda Trinkaus. 1996. *Virtues of the Mind: An Inquiry into the Nature of Virtue and the Ethical Foundations of Knowledge*. New York: Cambridge University Press.

———. 2017. *Exemplarist Moral Theory*. New York: Oxford University Press.

Zeldin, Theodore. 1981. *France, 1848–1945: Anxiety and Hypocrisy*. New York: Oxford University Press.

Index

About the Contributors

Michael S. Brady is professor of philosophy and head of the school of Humanities at the University of Glasgow. His research centers on the philosophy of emotion, and its links with moral philosophy and epistemology. He is the author of three books: *Emotional Insight* (Oxford University Press, 2013); *Suffering and Virtue* (Oxford University Press, 2018); and *Emotion: The Basics* (Routledge, 2018), and the editor of six volumes. He was Director of the British Philosophical Association, having previously served as Secretary of the Scots Philosophical Association. Outside of academia, he is philosopher-in-residence with the Manchester-based theater and performance company Quarantine.

Deborah J. Brown is professor of philosophy and director of the University of Queensland Critical Thinking Project. She is a specialist in early modern philosophy, author of *Descartes and The Passionate Mind* (Cambridge University Press, 2006) and coauthor with Calvin Normore of *Descartes and the Ontology of Everyday Life* (Oxford University Press, 2019). She lives in Brisbane, Australia, near a sandy, anxiety-free beach.

Samir Chopra is philosophical counselor and professor emeritus of philosophy at Brooklyn College and the Graduate Center of the City University of New York.

Ian Dowbiggin is professor of history at the University of Prince Edward Island, Canada. The author of eight books on the history of medicine, he is also a Fellow of the Royal Society of Canada.

Leah Kalmanson is associate professor and the Bhagwan Adinath Professor of Jain Studies in the Department of Philosophy and Religion at the University of North Texas. She is the author of *Cross-Cultural Existentialism: On the Meaning of Life in Asian and Western Thought* (Bloomsbury 2020) and coauthor with Monika Kirloskar-Steinbach of *A Practical Guide to World Philosophies* (Bloomsbury 2021). Her articles have appeared in *Comparative and Continental Philosophy*, *Continental Philosophy Review, Frontiers of Philosophy in China, Hypatia, Journal of World Philosophies*, *Philosophy East & West*, *Pragmatism Today*, *Shofar*, and *Studies in Chinese Religions*, as well as the online magazine *Aeon*.

Charlie Kurth is professor of philosophy at Western Michigan University and a Core Fellow at the Helsinki Collegium for Advanced Studies. His research focuses on issues in ethics, emotion theory, and moral psychology. He has published on these topics in venues like *Ethics, Philosophy of Science, Emotion Review, Oxford Studies in Normative Ethics, Philosophical Studies,* and *Mind & Language*. He is the author of *The Anxious Mind: An Investigation into the Varieties and Virtues of Anxiety* (MIT Press, 2018) and *Emotion* (Routledge, 2022).

Michelle Maiese is professor of philosophy at Emmanuel College in Boston. Her research addresses issues in philosophy of mind, philosophy of psychiatry, and emotion theory. She has authored or coauthored five books: *Embodied Minds in Action* (coauthored with R. Hanna, Oxford University Press, 2009), *Embodiment, Emotion, and Cognition* (Palgrave Macmillan, 2011), *Embodied Selves and Divided Minds* (Oxford University Press, 2015), *The Mind-Body Politic* (coauthored with R. Hanna, Palgrave Macmillan, 2019), and *Autonomy, Enactivism, and Mental Disorder* (Routledge, 2022).

Massimo Pigliucci is the K. D. Irani Professor of Philosophy at the City College of New York. His academic work is in evolutionary biology, philosophy of science, the nature of pseudoscience, and the practical philosophy of Stoicism. His books include *How to Be a Stoic: Using Ancient Philosophy to Live a Modern Life* (Basic Books) and *Nonsense on Stilts: How to Tell Science from Bunk* (University of Chicago Press). His most recent book is *A Field Guide to a Happy Life: 53 Brief Lessons for Living* (Basic Books).

Jesse Prinz is distinguished professor of philosophy and the director of the Committee for Interdisciplinary Science Studies at the Graduate Center of the City University of New York. He works primarily in the philosophy of psychology and ethics, and has authored many books, and over one hundred articles, addressing such topics as emotion, moral psychology, aesthetics, and consciousness.

David Rondel is associate professor in the department of philosophy at the University of Nevada. He is the author of *Pragmatist Egalitarianism*

(Oxford University Press, 2018), and *A Danger which We Do Not Know: A Philosophical Journey into Anxiety* (forthcoming with Oxford University Press). He is also editor or coeditor of three books: *Pessimism of the Intellect, Optimism of the Will: The Political Philosophy of Kai Nielsen* (University of Calgary Press, 2012), *Pragmatism and Justice* (Oxford University Press, 2017) and *The Cambridge Companion to Rorty* (Cambridge University Press, 2021).

Mauro Rossi is full professor in the Department of Philosophy at the Université du Québec à Montréal. His main research interests are in value theory, prudential psychology, and emotion theory. He is currently working (with Christine Tappolet) on a monograph on the relation between well-being and psychological happiness.

Christine Tappolet is full professor in the philosophy department at the Université de Montréal. Her research interests lie mainly in metaethics, moral psychology, and emotion theory. She has edited a number of volumes, including, with Sarah Stroud, *Weakness of Will and Practical Irrationality* (Oxford University Press, 2003) and, with Fabrice Teroni and Anita Konzelman Ziv, *Shadows of the Soul. Perspective on Negative Emotions* (Routledge, 2018). In addition to close to a hundred articles and chapters, she has published several books, including *Emotions, Values, and Agency* (Oxford University Press, 2016) and *Philosophy of Emotions: A Contemporary Introduction* (Routledge, 2022).

Juliette Vazard is postdoctoral fellow at the City University of New York (Graduate Center) and at the University of Toronto (Department of Philosophy). She works at the intersection of philosophy of mind, epistemology, and cognitive science. She has written on emotions such as anxiety, guilt, and hope, and how these relate to future thinking, doubt, and affective disorders such as obsessive-compulsive disorder and depression. Her work has appeared in *Mind & Language, Erkenntnis, Synthese, Philosophical Psychology, Philosophical Explorations,* and *Philosophy, Psychiatry, & Psychology*. She completed her PhD jointly at the Jean Nicod Institute in Paris and the Swiss Center for Affective Sciences in Geneva.

www.ingramcontent.com/pod-product-compliance
Ingram Content Group UK Ltd.
Pitfield, Milton Keynes, MK11 3LW, UK
UKHW041835031026
15587UKWH00002B/793

9 781666 928402